MySpace for Musicians

Fran Vincent

THOMSON

COURSE TECHNOLOGY

Professional ■ Technical ■ Reference

ISBN-10: 1-59863-359-7

ISBN-13: 978-1-59863-359-7

Library of Congress Catalog Card Number: 2006909694

Printed in the United States of America

07 08 09 10 11 TW 10 9 8 7 6 5 4 3 2 1

Publisher and General Manager, Thomson Course Technology PTR:
Stacy L. Hiquet

Associate Director of Marketing:
Sarah O'Donnell

Manager of Editorial Services:
Heather Talbot

Marketing Manager:
Mark Hughes

Acquisitions Editor:
Orren Merton

Marketing Assistant:
Adena Flitt

Project Editor/Copy Editor:
Cathleen D. Snyder

Technical Reviewer:
Joe Kostecki

PTR Editorial Services Coordinator:
Erin Johnson

Interior Layout:
Shawn Morningstar

Cover Designer:
Mike Tanamachi

Indexer:
Katherine Stimson

Proofreader:
Sara Gullion

THOMSON

COURSE TECHNOLOGY ™

Professional ■ Technical ■ Reference

Thomson Course Technology PTR, a division of Thomson Learning Inc.
25 Thomson Place ■ Boston, MA 02210 ■ http://www.courseptr.com

To my parents, John and Priscilla, who always cheer me on and remind me to be grateful for every one of life's opportunities and blessings.

And to my brother, John, who is the best MySpace marketer and natural promoter I know.

I love you! Thank you.

Acknowledgments

First, I'd like to thank God for blessing me with so many wonderful people and opportunities. Thank you to my editor, Orren Merton, for giving me the chance to write this book and for his encouragement and impromptu pep talks. I also want to thank my project editor, Cathleen Snyder, for her persistence and wonderful attention to detail. Special thanks are due to editors Mike Levine and Steve Oppenheimer of *Electronic Musician* magazine for printing my first MySpace marketing article, which led to this book.

I am grateful to my parents, family, and friends for their love, support, and belief in me. My parents, John and Priscilla, especially deserve special recognition and gratitude. They worked so hard to help me with home renovations, from assembling cabinets, to tearing out the kitchen, shopping for supplies, and even delivering food, all throughout the writing of this book. Without them, I never would have stayed sane through this process!

Throughout the years I've been able to work with a number of professionals who have taught me about this industry. Thank you especially to Jim Progris, chair of the University of Miami's Music Media and Industry department and director of the Music Business and Entertainment Industries program. I am fortunate to count you as a mentor and advisor. And also to the late Maurice Oberstein... I never got to thank you for all you taught me about the business. I'm lucky to have had you as a teacher.

My sincere appreciation goes out to all of the friends and colleagues who shared with me their wisdom and advice on MySpace, marketing, and the music industry at large. Thank you also to my good friends who let me use their words and faces as examples throughout the book.

This project wouldn't have been possible without the positive vibes and support of everyone mentioned here. My gratitude goes out to each and every one of you.

About the Author

Fran Vincent is the founder and president of Retro Island Productions, Inc., a public relations, marketing communications, and music services consulting company. Before starting her own company, Fran spent six years as the marketing and public relations specialist for Warner Bros. Publications, a division of Warner Music Group.

Fran has previously worked at some of America's most prestigious companies, including AOL Time Warner, General Motors, Campbell-Ewald Advertising (Chevrolet's agency of record for almost 100 years), and Independent Newspapers, and is a former journalist and editor herself. She holds a master's degree in music business (a hybrid music and business degree) from the University of Miami and a bachelor's degree in journalism from Oakland University. Fran is also an accomplished musician, performer, and college instructor, and she taught music licensing, marketing, public relations, and management courses at the University of Miami.

She has also authored articles for *Electronic Musician* and *In Tune* magazines. Fran now resides in the Detroit area and continues to work with marketing and PR clients around the world.

Contents

Chapter 5
Identifying Your Target Market   57

Chapter 6
Getting Started   79

Chapter 7
Signing Up and MySpace Profile Basics — 101

Chapter 8
Customizing Your Page — 119

Chapter 16
Protecting Your Virtual and Physical Security   299

Chapter 17
Managing MySpace   309

Chapter 18
MySpace and Marketing   325

Chapter 19
Last Words   329

Appendix A
Marketing and Merchandise Resources   331

Appendix B
MySpace Resources   341

Appendix C
Music Business Resources   347

Index   351

Introduction

There's hardly a person who hasn't heard of MySpace. Stories of the website's marketing possibilities, the millions it fetched when sold, and the unfortunate tales of predators' exploits flow through print and broadcast media almost constantly. It seems MySpace is firmly entrenched in today's popular culture as an icon of Web 2.0, the next generation of the Internet.

It's no wonder that so many people, especially those ages 16 to 34, can attest to the "magic" of MySpace. Everyone seems to know someone from MySpace. Maybe a local cutie they met on the service or a business associate who found their profile through another MySpacer. And in a world where people say they are feeling increasingly socially isolated, they somehow manage to build lists of cyber friends numbering in the hundreds or thousands, some of which they are able to parlay into real-life friendships.

But MySpace is not just a giant marketing machine. For some it is an essential part of their social lives, the primary way they keep in touch with friends and customers, and their main method of meeting new people in their real lives.

And then there are those who see it as a way to reach out to others, to communicate beyond their home, town, or even country—to say to both friends and strangers, "I am here. I am looking, and I want to be found."

What You'll Find in This Book

The flurry of activity on MySpace, with its millions of pages of user-generated content, seems to be unprecedented. The scope of it is overwhelming. There are almost 200 million profiles as of this day. It has outpaced every other social networking site before or after. That's not to say it will always be on top, but for now it is. That makes it a powerful marketing force, and one worth learning about.

MySpace for Musicians will introduce you to MySpace and what you will find on the site, how you can manipulate it, and how to use the service to your promotional advantage as an artist and entertainer.

While the book attempts to be comprehensive, it cannot cover every possible aspect of the MySpace experience. The technology, the site, and its offerings are changing almost daily. Even as programmers the world over quickly catch up and develop more tweaks and new ways of manipulating the site, it changes yet again. The code recommendations and site links offered here worked at the time the book was written, but there's no guarantee they will work forever. MySpace develops code blocks and filters all the time, and third-party "tweak" and "layout" sites come and go. Therefore, this book is only a snapshot in time.

Despite the unpredictable nature of the site and its usage, this book will introduce you to what's possible, with the hope that you will continue to keep abreast of new developments on your own.

MySpace for Musicians will walk you through the maze of grassroots marketing using the MySpace site. You'll become a proficient MySpacer and hopefully an adept marketer.

One other note... MySpace is heavily laden with advertisements, banners, and sponsored links, so you'll notice that parts of some of the artwork featured in this publication are blurred out to obscure the advertisements.

Who This Book Is For

MySpace for Musicians is for every band, soloist, side musician, record label, publisher, music manager, and entertainment industry–affiliated company who wants to use MySpace to its fullest potential. It's for all those who are not sure what they should be doing with MySpace. Maybe you've heard of it, but you think it's only for teenagers or you are too intimidated to get started. Perhaps all of your friends and colleagues are on it, and they're always asking you, "Are you on MySpace?" But you haven't made that first step. Anyone who is starting out on MySpace and is overwhelmed by the task at hand now has a guide to walk them through the process. You don't have to spend countless hours figuring it out on your own.

This book is also for those who have signed up, but don't really know what to do with their profile now. You may be new to marketing or unsure about how to maximize your experience on MySpace.

For every artist who wants to hop on the MySpace bandwagon, but doesn't think he or she is web-savvy enough to do it, this book is for you.

How This Book Is Organized

MySpace for Musicians is organized logically, from an introduction to MySpace and social marketing, to determining what kind of account to open, all the way through to customizing your profile, adding friends, leaving comments, crafting bulletins and blogs, and then on to learning the basics of email marketing, protecting your security, and even managing your experience. This book takes you on a step-by-step journey through the service in a way that makes sense for most people who have thought of joining the community, but haven't jumped in yet.

Each chapter will first introduce the content, giving you the basics of the topic, and then further break down the information so you learn how to accomplish each task yourself. The best way to learn is by doing, so you can follow along and try the pointers in the book right in your own MySpace account.

Throughout the book, you'll find references to other resources outside of MySpace, such as image hosting sites, code generators, and more. The appendixes at the end of this book offer even more resources, organized by category, such as music industry, music downloading, mobile marketing, and more. You won't have to hunt for this info by spending what would normally be an exorbitant amount of time web-searching to find the best sites. Most of what you'll need has been sourced and listed in the appendixes for you.

Are you ready? Fire up the computer. Make sure you're connected to the Internet, and let's get you turned on to MySpace!

1 Intro to MySpace and Social Networking

You've no doubt heard about the viral marketing phenomenon that is MySpace. Even the least media-savvy among us have no doubt caught snippets of the hoopla surrounding it—the numbers of business and friendship connections being made daily; the new music being discovered by consumers and labels alike; and unfortunately, like virtually all interactive sites, the sex predators and weirdos who plague every corner of both the real and virtual worlds.

Though it's one of many similar sites, MySpace slides into the forefront of new media marketing. It's a free site comprised of user-created profiles where the community views and shares content in a variety of interactive media (music, video, blogs) and links with others to form "friend" groups, all with powerful results (see Figure 1.1).

As of this writing, almost 200 million people call MySpace home, a virtual hangout comprised of teenagers, urban hipsters, stay-at-home moms, yuppies, bands, businesses, and entertainers of every stripe (see Figure 1.2). Imagine the force of marketing, advertising, and promotional possibilities that exist in a community of that size and with such a varied demographic. Media giant News Corp., owners of Fox Broadcasting, Fox News, 20th Century Fox studios, and a cadre of media outlets, saw the potential and in 2005 purchased MySpace's parent company, Intermix Media, for $580 million. At that time, MySpace had about 20 million members, a tenth of what it is at this moment. In just a few short years, it already rivals Internet heavyweights Google, AOL, Yahoo, MSN, Amazon, and even eBay (see Figure 1.3).

Figure 1.1
MySpace.com's home page

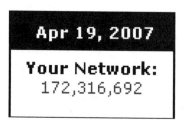

Figure 1.2
Your MySpace account home page shows the community's tally.

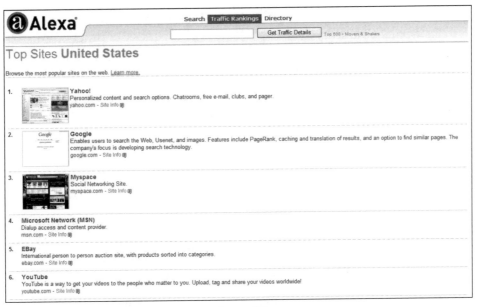

Figure 1.3
Alexa Internet ranks websites globally and by language, country, and other parameters.
These results in March 2007 show the top six at the time (www.alexa.com).

What was just an idea a few years ago has become a marvel of marketing, advertising, big business, and social networking. But what is social networking? One of the latest Internet and marketing buzz terms isn't a new term at all. It was invented in the 1950s by J. A. Barnes to describe a chart of the relationships between people and how they are connected to one another. In today's marketing-driven world, social networking denotes part word-of-mouth marketing and part Six Degrees of Kevin Bacon. It's turning others on to what you like and getting them in the groove with your friends. Whether online or in the real world, social networking has been an important part of building ties in the community, in business, and sometimes even in the dating scene. After all, many a match has been made when a friend of a friend's single cousin was introduced to the neighbor's daughter's accountant!

And so it is with MySpace and its contemporaries. People connect in virtual spaces, making friends, dates, and business contacts and turning each other on to favorite bands. They post blogs and videos, music, poetry, and photo journals of their vacations. They find old classmates and discover new friends, adding these "friends" to their profiles.

Notable Social Networking Sites

MySpace gets a lot of media attention, but it's not the only player in the world of online social networking. Following are just a few of the dozens of related sites making waves on the Internet.

- **Bebo.com.** Launched in 2005, Bebo's offerings are similar to many other social networking sites. It has become one of the most popular social networking sites in Ireland.

- **Facebook.com.** Particularly popular with the college crowd, Facebook connects students and alumni around the world.

- **Friendster.com.** An early comer in the social networking scene, and the most popular until MySpace overtook it around 2004. Friendster is still huge in some non-U.S. markets.

- **MEETin.org.** A free grassroots site that connects people in various cities. Members plan events with the aim of building real-life friendships in their local metropolis.

- **Meetup.com.** Want to form clubs and groups in the real world? Meetup.com assists users in finding local people with similar interests. (This site is unrelated to MEETin.org.)

- **Multiply.com.** A fairly new addition to the social networking scene, it operates in much the same fashion as MySpace and Friendster.

- **Orkut.com.** Google's answer to social networking, Orkut has been a fairly quiet endeavor in the U.S., but it still has tens of millions of members and is growing.

- **SecondLife.com.** This Sims-esque 3D virtual world by Linden Labs allows users to create avatars and the environment around them, and even hold virtual concerts and events.

- **TagWorld.com.** A newer site launched to compete with MySpace. It allows users to upload up to 1 GB of music and other media.

- **Tribe.net.** Organized by geographic area, Tribe encourages discussion and interaction amongst members who share tips on job leads, their favorite websites and activities, and more.

- **Windows Live Spaces (spaces.live.com).** Microsoft's version of a social portal, Live Spaces users post profiles, blogs, and more.

- **Xanga.com.** Another popular networking and blog site, Xanga has tens of millions of members. It began in the late '90s as a portal for people to share book and music reviews.

- **Yahoo! 360° (360.yahoo.com).** Yahoo members now have a social networking portal that integrates other Yahoo features, such as groups and forums.

Unlike most other sites in the social networking category, MySpace's unprecedented growth can be attributed to its reputation as a must-stop for indie music. Once upon a time, you went into your local record store and chatted up the sales associates to find out what was new and groundbreaking. Their recommendations were gold, and you took them seriously and even based your purchases on the shoppie's list of must-haves. I'm sure some of you reading this remember those good ol' days. Unfortunately, the local record shop is largely gone now. With radio stations mostly playing the same 10 songs day in and day out, where is a person supposed to look for new music? The tradition of interfacing with the local music guru may be defunct, but the idea lives on in MySpace. Here, people recommend bands to each other and feature song clips and videos of their favorites on their profiles. If you like to browse and discover for yourself, the MySpace Music section is a directory of more than a million bands and solo artists in every genre imaginable, as well as a few that defy classification (see Figure 1.4).

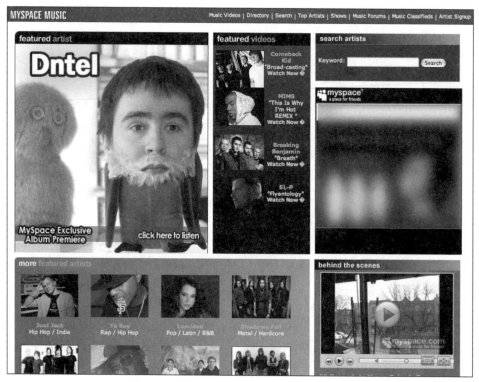

Figure 1.4
The main page of MySpace Music, the home of the community's musical artists.

Unsigned and signed, major and indie—bands flock to MySpace to hock their wares in snapshot form. And by all accounts, they do so with quite a bit of success. There's no guarantee that you'll end up with a record deal, but you will have gained more exposure than the day before you signed up with MySpace. At the end of the day, that's really the purpose—getting your music out there to the masses who are waiting to discover you. This direct-to-consumer model has changed the face of music industry sales and promotion forever.

For all its hype, MySpace is not a perfect environment. It has got its share of problems. Although it's a design-it-yourself community in many ways, the basic layout fields can be restrictive. Anyone who has been a member for more than a week will tell you that there are times it slows to a crawl and often a dead stop. The overwhelming amount of traffic, especially after work hours, is taxing on the servers. Errors and bugs pop up enough to try the patience of even the most low-key of Type B personalities (see Figure 1.5). And browsers crash when presented with profiles by overzealous MySpacers who are sure everyone wants to wait for 50 pictures and 10 videos to load.

MySpace Announcement

Latest Update:

12:36PM PST, Thu, Oct 05

Tom

hey folks, your pic comments are still there. just click on your pics. we are rolling out a fix to correct comment count. sit tight. :)

Figure 1.5
MySpace's tech team regularly posts info about bugs and twitches that are in the process of being resolved.

That's just from a functional perspective. You're not competing with tens or hundreds of bands anymore. Now you're competing with millions, all living in the same place. That's a lot of promotional noise to sift through, a task not lost on users and musicians alike. MySpacers are inundated with requests from bands to listen to their songs. Never before has there been this level of musician/consumer interaction. Bands put themselves out there, and not just passively. They're vying for attention on a one-on-one level.

At this point you may be wondering, if there's so much competition, why bother? You really could say that about anything in life, but should that stop you from getting in the game? It *is* possible to differentiate yourself and break through the noise. But it takes consistency, patience, and a willingness to devote your time and energy to it. You shouldn't neglect your music, of course, but if anyone's going to buy it, they have to be aware of it first. You want people to listen, talk, and recommend. And that's where MySpace can help.

In Chapter 2, we'll explore the impact that MySpace has had on the music and entertainment industry.

2 The Impact of MySpace on Music and Entertainment

Music industry insiders and watchers have definitely taken notice of MySpace's impact on music and entertainment. The old models of the music industry—record deal, mass radio play, major distribution—have been turned on their ears a bit. That's not to say that the standard business model is irrelevant. It's still vital in achieving mass-market penetration. But now there's a change in how musicians can get their songs heard. They're no longer solely reliant on radio as a means of reaching consumer ears, nor are they dependent on a record label for selling music. Instead, artists can market themselves directly to consumers, who in turn pass the word on to their friends. The web in general has made a direct-to-consumer approach possible for a long time now, but not until the proliferation of MySpace users who love music was there a ready-made community just sitting there waiting to hear the next big music star.

In this chapter we'll take a brief look at how MySpace has affected the landscape of the entertainment industry.

In the Beginning...

The generally accepted story of MySpace's founding is that two guys from California, Tom Anderson and Chris DeWolfe, created the site in 2003 along with a small group of programmers. It may have started as a new way to keep people in the know about local Los Angeles bands and club gigs, but it grew into a place to meet new friends and keep in touch with old. Artists of all stripes, including poets and filmmakers and especially bands, flocked to the site, and it got a reputation as an indie music portal. There are some who dispute this story and the founders' accounts, including Brad Greenspan, former head of parent company Intermix, who claims to be the real founder of MySpace on his website: www.freemyspace.com.

Nevertheless, it's hard to believe that a few short years ago, MySpace was just a fledgling creation. In 2005, only two years after its founding, Rupert Murdoch's News Corporation bought Intermix for a whopping $580 million. More than $300 million of that is said to be for the MySpace properties alone, which easily draw in the coveted 16 to 34 demographic.

The Evolution

Today, nearly 200 million users later, MySpace can brag about its desirability. Every time you visit the home page MySpace.com, you'll see another major label, movie studio, or TV network advertising its latest project or launching its newest product (see Figure 2.1). And we're not just talking banner ads, either (although MySpace has no shortage of those). Entertainment heavyweights look to MySpace to showcase fabulous customized profiles that fit the label, studio, or network's branding like a well-programmed glove (see Figure 2.2).

Those of you who aren't on MySpace yet may wonder why the industry sees it as an essential marketing venue. Why not just use a regular website, as people have been doing for years? It's not enough anymore. With MySpace, your audience is built in. Millions of people are going to the homepage to log in and check their email and peruse their friends' profiles anyway. Each and every one of them will see a homepage promotion, and they'll click and find more than just some static advertisement. They may find select video clips, contests, posts from artists and actors themselves, music, giveaways, free videos, and downloads. They're interacting with the product in a quicker way than by visiting a website. Not only will you see a movie's or an artist's official website address on a trailer, ad, or CD, but more and more lately you'll see the MySpace address too.

Matt Crossey, creative director for Working Class Records in the UK, sums up the beauty of a MySpace profile like this: "People's attention spans are so minute. [MySpace] is bite-sized—a brief summary for most people is all they need."

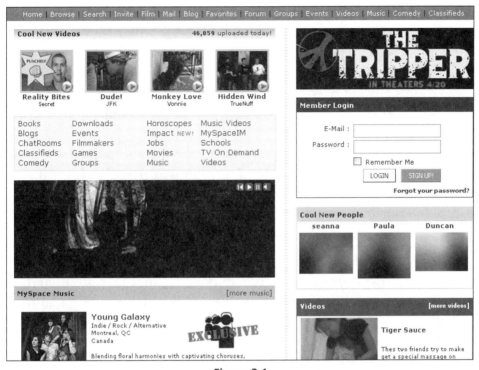

Figure 2.1
This portion of the MySpace homepage shows links to movie websites and
featured band profiles.

Figure 2.2
This MySpace profile for the movie *Transformers* is a great
snapshot of the movie and its brand.

You may not be promoting your music on the homepage like major record labels and movie studios do, but you are still a MySpacer with music to market. The same mentality about it applies. I, too, find myself seeking out artists' MySpace pages more than their websites now. I eventually get over to the website, but sometimes I find the profile much nicer to deal with. It all loads on one page, including music clips, and that's that. If I want a few extras, I hop over to the official website, and once in a while I sign up for the official mailing list. But when I want to check quickly for tour dates or news, I click on the artist's profile. You'll find this is true of many MySpacers. Do a web search on your favorite artists, and you're likely to see their MySpace page pop up pretty close to the top of the search results.

Don't think you don't need an official website, your own dot-com. You *do*. The key is to marry the two and realize that they are used differently. Remember that old saying about putting all your eggs in one basket? MySpace is hot now, but who's to say it will stay that way forever? What if they start charging for access? What if another site usurps its popularity and users jump ship? If all you've got is a MySpace profile and nothing else, you're in trouble. Use MySpace to build your own marketing list by getting people over to your website too. You're not just building a profile or a site—you're building relationships with your customers and fans.

How to Be Successful

The number of artists who were discovered through MySpace is growing all the time. From the Hollywood Undead (see Figure 2.3)—a bunch of teenagers who a couple of years ago recorded some songs on their computer, posted them on their profile, and ended up with a massive following and a record deal with Interscope—to the tale of the Arctic Monkeys (see Figure 2.4)—a UK band promoted by fans on MySpace and beloved by the underground way before they were ever offered a record deal—the list goes on, and there isn't enough room to recount all their stories.

Hollywood Undead
Hip Hop / Alternative / Screamo

"Its hard to choose between religion & gangsterism"

LOS ANGELES, United States

Profile Views: 7918892

Last Login: 4/8/2007

View My: **Pics | Videos**

Figure 2.3
A few short years ago, the Hollywood Undead were just kids
in masks with a MySpace profile.

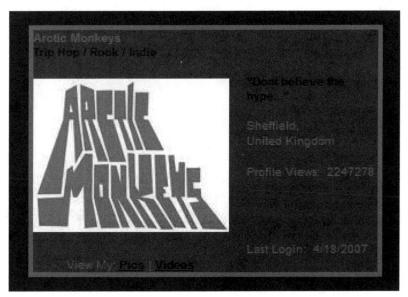

Figure 2.4
The Arctic Monkeys' profile headline ironically declares, "Don't believe the hype…"

It's true that people are finding their own way more and more, circumventing the initial need for label support, developing their own images, recording and manufacturing their own albums, and even selling them to customers without a distributor. But let's be honest with ourselves. Stories like that of the Hollywood Undead, the Arctic Monkeys, and others like them are not going to happen for everyone. MySpace, for all its positive attributes, is not a panacea for artists. You should, however, take note of how important and required it has become in the normal course of industry marketing. "If someone didn't have a MySpace page, I'd think they weren't very cleaned up," states Crossey. "The novelty is past. Now it's part of the standard marketing portfolio."

Internet aficionados and recording execs alike do indeed see MySpace as a standard marketing element now. Even consumers are surprised if their favorite major label artists don't have profiles. Unless it's part of your anti-marketing plan, sort of thumbing your nose to all things commercial, Crossey noted, you have to have one if you want to be taken seriously.

Marketing companies are popping up all over the web, swearing that they can inflate the number of hits your profile receives, making you more desirable to labels. One even claims that a record label won't look at you unless you've got at least 75,000 hits on your profile, meaning that many people have visited your page. But is that true? Does the number of hits, friends, or music plays you have determine your appeal to a label? "No. If it's a low number of people [who have accessed your profile], then that's brilliant. I would be excited because I'd think I'd discovered you early," says Crossey. "Record labels are competing over the same artists once they get big."

Crossey also doesn't take notice of the number of music plays because the player usually starts automatically when you visit an artist page. Therefore, it's not a true indicator of the song's popularity. As for friends, the numbers are not that important unless you have 50,000 friends or more, which is an intriguing amount.

It may surprise you that Crossey looks for the kind of traffic you get on your main artist website, not on your MySpace profile. This is where your analytics come in: How many hits is your website getting daily and monthly? How many visitors lingered there, and for how long? And how many migrated from your website over to your MySpace profile and vice versa? These factors, along with the quality of your music, the professionalism of your demo, and your photos (are they artsy and "glossy" looking?), are what labels look at more and more. Very few record companies want to spend much time or invest much money developing an artist nowadays.

Over the past couple of years, MySpace has not only been a music portal, but it has become a record label itself (www.myspace.com/myspacerecords) (see Figure 2.5). Culling talent from among its members, MySpace Records' distribution is through Universal Music Group's Fontana Distribution and its marketing is through Universal's Interscope Records. MySpace also now offers all of the community's artists a built-in record store to sell downloads through a partnership with SNOCAP, a digital licensing and copyright services company.

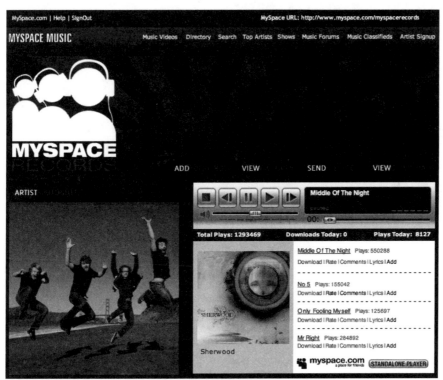

Figure 2.5
MySpace Records finds talent among the MySpace ranks.

No matter where you are headed in your career, MySpace is really useful for getting exposure and creating hype. Your profile is like a little online press kit. It's much easier for people to take in who you are and what you're about by visiting that one page. You want to sell records and get people to shows, of course, but you have to get into their consciousness first, which is why you bought this book in the first place.

Crossey continues, "Before MySpace, people would always have a mailing list. But now, if a band has buzz, with MySpace the buzz can get around much faster."

In addition to connecting you with fans, MySpace is bringing artists and businesspeople together as well. Many find it essential for networking with other musicians, booking agents, and the like.

It's time to get started. First, let's decide what type of MySpace account is for you. Chapter 3 will take you through the kinds of accounts and who should use them.

3 Which MySpace Is for Me?

When you first hop onto the MySpace.com homepage, the natural inclination of an enthusiastic music marketer is to click on that enticing bright orange SIGN UP! button. But wait! MySpace offers several types of user accounts, and before you jump in feet first, you should know what they are so you can make the right decision (see Figure 3.1).

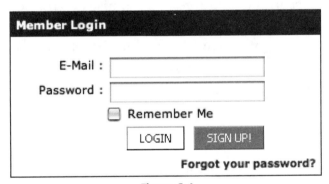

Figure 3.1
The SIGN UP! button beckons would-be MySpacers, but consider other types of MySpace accounts first!

That SIGN UP! button on the homepage will help you create a regular MySpace account only. Musicians will want to steer away from a regular account because it won't allow you to upload and market your music—which of course won't do a musician any good. In Chapter 7, we'll cover exactly how to open up an artist (musician) account.

For now, we will cover all the types of accounts offered by MySpace and which ones might be appropriate for the various categories of potential users.

I'll Just Have the Regular

The regular MySpace account is the bread and butter of the biz, so to speak. It's what most MySpacers use and it is ideal for the non-entertainer. This type of account has all the bells and whistles the average netizen would want. Your basic profile (see Figure 3.2) allows you to:

- Create a customizable profile with distinctive URL
- Fill out information fields for: Basic Info (Gender, Birthdate, Occupation, Location, Ethnicity); About Me; Who I'd Like to Meet; Interests (General, Music, Movies, Television, Books, Heroes); Background and Lifestyle Details (Relationship Status, Reason for Being on MySpace, Sexual Orientation, Religion, Children, Hometown, Body Type, Drink/Smoke, Zodiac Sign, Education, Occupation, Income); Schools Attended; Companies; and Networking
- Enter a profile headline
- Send and answer email-type messages
- Upload photos and write captions
- Upload videos
- Add and deny friends
- Arrange Top Friends
- Search for users
- Write comments for, and accept comments from, friends
- Create a blog
- Chat using the IM feature
- Generate an address book

- Manage a public calendar
- Add songs and videos to your profile
- Invite people to join MySpace
- Implement privacy and mobile settings
- Block users
- Save favorite profiles
- Post bulletins and event invitations
- Start and join groups
- Access classifieds
- Participate in forums

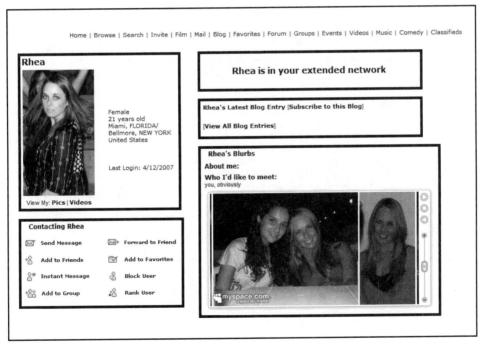

Figure 3.2
A basic profile created by signing up for a regular MySpace account.

All MySpace accounts, whether regular, artist (musician), comedian, or filmmaker, offer at least these basic features, with the exception of the information fields. Those for a regular account are much more personal than fields you would find in an artist, comedian, or film-maker signup, such as relationship status, sexual orientation, body type, occupation, income, and so on (see Figure 3.3). All of these are optional, and you don't have to fill in any field with which you are uncomfortable.

Chris's Details	
Status:	Single
Orientation:	Straight
Hometown:	Hendersonville, NC
Zodiac Sign:	Aries
Smoke / Drink:	No / Yes
Children:	Someday
Education:	Grad / professional school

Figure 3.3
A sample of the personal information fields of a basic profile.

The regular account is probably for you if:

- You are joining MySpace to promote a business or organization that does *not* require you to upload sound, video, or appearance dates.

- You are *not* a musician, artist manager, record company, pro-ducer, music publisher, radio station, DJ, filmmaker, comedian, voiceover artist, or motivational speaker.

- You are only joining MySpace to keep in touch with your friends and maybe make some new ones.

The types of industries that may benefit from use of a regular account include:

- **Acting.** Embed your headshots and video reel clips; mention recent theatre, TV, commercial, or film appearances and positive reviews; link to your acting resume; and list your agent contact, union affiliations, and upcoming performances.

- **Modeling.** Post your modeling card and create a portfolio slideshow; or post agency info, as well as most recent bookings/clients.

- **Real estate.** Put together a slideshow of virtual tours; list properties for sale plus recent successes; and offer home buying/selling tips and info about your expertise.

- **Law.** Tout your education and legal know-how, and offer helpful blogs for your target audience.

- **Sports.** Whether you're a professional, amateur, or local team/league, build continued fan loyalty with player bios and blogs, exclusive photos, video clips, and updated stats.

- **Book and magazine publishing.** Showcase your latest publishing projects and issues; reveal centerfolds and photo essays; and post calls for submissions as well as subscription and order information.

- **Beauty and fashion.** Makeup artists, hairstylists, and fashion designers can boast about their newest clients, looks, styles, and more. Show off a portfolio; throw in beauty and fashion suggestions; and post where/how you can be booked.

- **Event and party planners.** From bridal bashes to corporate functions, event and party planners can brag about their triumphs in taming bridezillas, offer a guide on how to throw small (but fantastic) soirees, and entice new clients with photos of successful gatherings.

- **Printing and graphics.** Post your latest discounts for "friends"; dazzle with retouching before-and-afters and graphic design projects; and include some helpful print promotion ideas.

- **Photography and videography.** With permission from your clients, use your profile to show the breadth of your work, such as head-shots, modeling photos, wedding and engagement photography and videography, lifestyle work, and magazine or product work. Team up with a makeup artist and a fashion stylist to give would-be customers tips for making the most of their shoot.

You may also want to use a regular account if you are in an entertainment industry–affiliated business, but you don't rely on sound samples to sell your product or service. Examples include:

- **Public relations, marketing, and advertising agencies.** Tell the world about how you've helped clients boost sales and product awareness; showcase your best work by posting ad campaign graphics, press releases, and video clips; and offer promotional tips and articles.

- **Booking.** Your profile is an excellent place to show visitors what your booking company does and how artists can be on your roster of acts. Be sure to list booking needs and any specialty genres.

- **Entertainment and sports law.** Focus on what you can do for entertainment or sports clients, and keep "friends" up to date on the latest in licensing and industry trends. You may even have an introductory rate for new clients.

- **Licensing.** The world of music licensing and publishing changes quickly, with new court rulings altering the way the game is played. Consultants and clearing houses may offer licensing services, list fees, and even a primer in music copyright and the types of licenses artists may encounter.

- **Club promoter.** Build a list of savvy club-going friends, issue VIP invites, promote special events and guests artists, and even offer specials on bottles and cover charges.

- **Concert promoter.** Advertise shows, opening and feature acts, and ticket sales.

- **Talent agent.** Build a strong list of actors in your area and send out calls for castings as they come in, or list new calls on your profile. Show off your clients and where they are booking.

- **Music writer, columnist, or photographer.** Your profile is the perfect place to link to your published stories, books, columns, and photos. Use it as a portfolio where you can send prospective publishers to view your work.

- **Graphic designer, animator, or illustrator.** All specialties, including CD packaging, band merchandise/poster design, and video animation, have a place to brag about their work, linking to client's websites and profiles.

- **Stylist or fashion designer.** Many musical artists of all genres want help with their imaging. Stylists and designers can offer their consulting services for overall artist imaging and styling, as well as video and photo-shoot styling.

- **Choreographer.** It isn't only dancers who need choreographers. Singers, rappers, and many other types of stage performers benefit from learning how to use the space around them. Promote new client packages, embed video of your performance work, and offer free consultations.

- **Venue.** No matter what kind of venue you have—nightclub, bar, theatre, or stadium—a profile will help you promote open mics, artist appearances, and drink specials.

- **Show producer or designer.** For the musical act that is taking it big time, a show producer or designer is a must. Someone has to plan out the sets, lighting, and more. Use your profile to brag about what you've done and what you can do to make big shows and festivals spectacular.

- **Educators and trainers.** This broad category encompasses musical and studio instruction, industry training, seminars and panels, and even university programs. Attract new students and keep current ones with a profile that gives all the details on upcoming events, cutting-edge curriculum, and free guides on making the most of a music career.

- **Music organizations.** What better way to grab the attention of new members than with a profile filled with useful information about the organization, benefits, membership costs, and other perks?

The Artist Signup

The artist account, also referred to as an *artist profile, band profile*, or *musician account* (see Figure 3.4), differs from the regular account in a few main areas, including the information fields that can be displayed on a profile and the crucial ability to upload music. Some of the ways an artist account is more tailored to the music community include the ability to:

- Upload up to five songs and accompanying photos to your profile. Users can stream the songs, download them (optional), and add them to play on their profiles.

- Upload music videos, which are searchable by artist name, song title, and genre.

- Fill out Artist Information fields: Basic Info (Band Name, Region), Genres, Bio, Members, Influences, Sounds Like, Website, Record Label, and Label Type.

- Advertise upcoming shows and appearances, which are also searchable by zip code.

- Make your profile available in the MySpace music directory.

- Contend for the Top Artists list.

- Sell downloads through your own MySpace/SNOCAP Music Store.

The artist account also includes the same features as the regular account plus the previous exceptions.

You should consider opening an artist account if:

- You are a music maker who wants to keep in touch with your current fans with MySpace accounts, and/or you want to expand your global audience.

- You are not yourself a music maker, but your desired clients are.

- You are not a music maker, but you are in another business in which sound clips are important, such as keynote speaking.

Figure 3.4
Note that the artist/musician account allows you to offer streaming music samples.

Artist profiles are useful for many types of musicians and music-related companies. The following lists explore the different uses.

The artist profile is made for you to gather an audience, build some marketing momentum, sell records, gain attention for a record or publishing deal, and get people to your shows. It is the ideal place to post music clips, bios, and appearance dates if you are in the following categories:

- Bands, musicians, and vocalists of all types and genres
- Spoken-word artists
- Performing songwriters

The profile is especially useful for networking; telling others what you do; finding collaborators, music jobs, and clients; disclosing union affiliations; and more. If you are in the following categories, post music clips, tidbits on whom you've worked with, and your specialties:

- Session players, background singers, and accompanists
- Non-performing songwriters and arrangers
- Producers and engineers
- Film and video game music composers and music supervisors
- Sound effects, sampling, and audio loops creators
- Event/mobile DJs
- Voiceover artists

Trendsetters, such as those in the club scene, will also love a music profile to bring bodies into the venue or to the station, to hype new artists, and to tout their DJ-ing ability. If you are in the following categories, just remember to only post music and spoken banter to which you have the rights:

- Club DJs
- Record pools
- Turntablists
- Remixers
- Radio stations and radio DJs

Companies and music-business types also use profiles to gain exposure for their artists, plug songs, and sell their music or artist services. These categories include:

- Record companies of all sizes
- Music publishers
- Artist and tour managers
- Recording studios

- Music-specific promotion and PR houses
- Mobile content and ringtone providers

Coaches and instructors who help artists can post audio tips and mini-lessons to help build their clientele. Examples include:

- Speech therapists and accent-reduction coaches
- Vocal coaches and singing teachers
- Recording studio consultants who teach you how to use or set up gear

Even non-musicians who rely on sound as their bread and butter will find music profiles to be helpful in letting their audience hear what they have to offer. They can also couple this with other products and services, such as books, manuals, seminars, and maybe even votes. Examples of such categories include:

- Motivational speakers
- Audio book publishers
- Political and activist speechmakers

Comedian and Filmmaker Accounts

Like the artist accounts, comedian and filmmaker profiles (see Figures 3.5 and 3.6) have largely the same features offered by regular accounts, with a few modifications (noted in the following sections). However, unlike artist profiles, comedians and filmmakers can also include the same personal information as regular account holders.

For the Funny Girls and Boys

Comedian accounts allow one to:

- Upload comedy video clips
- Fill in Comedian Information fields: Career Details (Bio, Members, Influences, TV Appearances, Film Appearances, Albums, Website); Basic Info (same as a regular account); Listing Info (type of comedy performed)

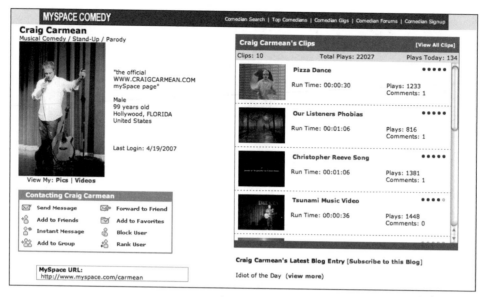

Figure 3.5
Florida comedian and radio personality Craig Carmean loads up his
video clips onto his comedian profile.

Figure 3.6
Young filmmaker David Lehre's short films appear in a scrolling box on his profile.

- Advertise upcoming shows and appearances, which are also searchable by zip code

- Be searchable in the MySpace comedian directory

- Compete for the Top Comedians list

Comedian accounts are ideal not only for comedians of all types, but also for comedy venues who want to showcase upcoming performers, include show times and directions, offer drink specials, and provide links for people to buy tickets.

It's Time for Your Close-Up

Filmmaker accounts allow you to:

- Upload video clips

- Customize Filmmaker Information fields: Filmmaker Details (Roles, Status, Website, Influences, Directors, Awards, Festivals, Professional Affiliations) and Basic Info (same as Regular Accounts)

- Advertise upcoming screenings, which are also searchable by zip code

- Include a profile in the filmmaker directory

- Be a contender for the Top Filmmakers list

Filmmaker accounts allow you to specify your field (options are included in the following list) and are also ideal for:

- **Directors, producers, screenwriters, and documentarians.** Your film clips, whether professional, amateur, or student, are the main draw for this kind of profile. Also, you can offer info on project help you are seeking, casting calls, as well as notes on upcoming release dates.

- **Cinematographers, lighting experts, and editors.** Examples of your work can be posted, but remember also to give plenty of information on what you can do for a filmmaker. You can also include testimonials from previous clients and notice of any unions to which you belong.

- **Animators and special effects gurus.** Post shorts and B-roll video clips touting your expertise and the kind of work you've done for other clients.

- **Costumers and makeup artists.** Sketches, B-roll footage, actual film clips and photos of your work, plus any specialties you offer are all excellent fodder for a profile.

- **Set designers and location companies.** Feature photo slideshows showing off your design and location work, plus a list of films on which you've personally assisted, along with testimonials.

- **Archivists, historians, preservationists, and restoration experts.** Discuss your collections, any publications you've authored, and the importance of preservation. Offer before and after photos and video clips of films you've restored.

You can also specify whether you are a student, amateur, or professional filmmaker.

Have you narrowed down which type of account is for you? If so, it's time to become one of almost 200 million MySpacers!

4 Membership and Community Features

MySpace is known for helping members network with others and keep in touch with friends. MySpace has many other features that make the community experience enjoyable and more interactive, including an ever-expanding photo album, video uploads, and much more. Lesser-discussed aspects designed to amuse and entertain the community are also a fun part of the experience. While additional features are being added all the time, this chapter will take a look at the better known—as well as the often overlooked but worthwhile—offerings of the MySpace community.

MySpace Is Your Place

The most media-touted element of MySpace is the Profile. Signing up for a free account automatically generates a profile for you, the body of which you populate by filling in fields about yourself, from your entertainment interests, to a bio, to descriptions of who you'd like to meet, and more. Those who are more web-savvy (or at least like a good adventure) can learn to add customized code to their profiles to change the look, layout, background and text colors, fonts, and so on. Learn how to embed photos, slideshows, videos, and other third-party bells and whistles. MySpace as a social networking vehicle encourages you to reach out to others, find old friends, and add them to your friends list. This alone makes it a titan of user-generated content.

MySpace manages to get almost 200 million people to their servers to hang out and interact with one another. But it aims to be more than a virtual community of people who are seeking and those hoping to be found. It is also a place that merges myriad interests with corporate cross-promotions, bringing layer upon layer of entertaining and help-ful modules to the masses that congregate there. It's more than banner ads and sponsored links, however. Even bookworms and job seekers can get in on the action.

Because most of this book already focuses on the profile, pics, videos, and other means of promoting yourself, let's begin with some other offerings that make MySpace a pretty entertaining place for you and your potential audience to hang your hat.

The Little Grey Box

It's true, there's something for almost everyone on MySpace. If you can't find the entertainment you seek on someone's profile, you should try looking at the multitude of links and menus offered on the site. There's a little grey box of goodies on the MySpace.com homepage (see Figure 4.1) that could keep a netizen busy for a long while—or at least for a lunch hour. This is our first stop in the MySpace Member Features Tour.

Books	Downloads	Horoscopes	Music Videos
Blogs	Events	Impact NEW!	MySpaceIM
ChatRooms	Filmmakers	Jobs	Schools
Classifieds	Games	Movies	TV On Demand
Comedy	Groups	Music	Videos

Figure 4.1
A menu of entertaining and helpful links appears on the MySpace.com home page. It changes now and again, so remember to inspect it once in a while to see what's new!

Bet You Didn't Know There Was a Book Club

Yes, there is even a place on this trendy website for devotees of the written word. Click on Books, and you'll find a spot where some of the most intellectual of MySpacers gather. This virtual book club highlights:

- A featured blog where selected members postulate on plots and characters

- Book discussion groups for myriad genres, such as classic literature, sci-fi, and teen, as well as groups for celebrated authors and unknown writers alike

- Featured book reviews and archives where members evaluate their favorite books and others can comment, assign a rating, and add a thumbs up or down

- A list of top books on MySpace with convenient links to Amazon.com for purchase

- A reader search to locate others in the community with the same literary interests as yours (see Figure 4.2)

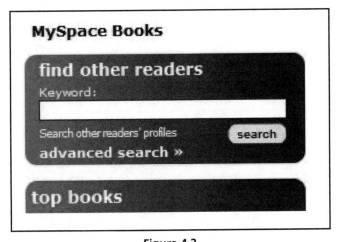

Figure 4.2
The MySpace Books section lets you search for other readers
with like interests, offers a list of top books, and more.

MySpacers Love to Write

Looking at the millions of profiles, it should be obvious that MySpacers are a gregarious bunch. But beyond that, there is an outlet for the most verbose among us. Every user gets space for a *blog*, an online journal of sorts where they can post musings on any topic. (See Chapter 13, "Blogging in the MySpace World," for more about blogs.)

Millions of blog posts can be pretty difficult to sort through, unless you click on the Blog link. Here you'll find the Most Popular Blog Posts on MySpace page (see Figure 4.3), which is updated daily, a blog search tool, plus a cacophony of blog categories about everything from photography, to sports, to movies, and to the art of blogging itself (see Figure 4.4).

Most Popular Blog Posts - Updated Daily
Total Blogs: 122,947,646
Blog Today: 725,147

Figure 4.3
The Blogs section tracks the most popular MySpace blog entries.

Blog Categories
All Categories
Art and Photography
Automotive
Blogging
Dreams and the
Supernatural
Fashion, Style, Shopping
Food and Restaurants
Friends
Games
Goals, Plans, Hopes
Jobs, Work, Careers
Life
Movies, TV, Celebrities
Music
MySpace
News and Politics
Parties and Nightlife
Pets and Animals
Podcast
Quiz/Survey
Religion and Philosophy
Romance and Relationships
School, College, Greek
Sports
Travel and Places
Web, HTML, Tech
Writing and Poetry

Figure 4.4
Each category lists the most popular blogs of the day.

Chat Me Up

What Internet portal would be complete without chat rooms? They are the staple of the Internet experience and might even be considered a classic by now. MySpace has many chat rooms for all age groups. The ChatRooms link will take you to an area where you can find rooms to join by age group (see Figure 4.5), interest (see Figure 4.6), as well as geographic location. There is no special software to install—the chat interface appears as a pop-up and is easy to use and navigate, as shown in Figure 4.7.

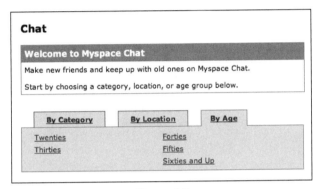

Figure 4.5
Find a chat room by age group. Note that there is no room for teenagers or children.

Chat

Welcome to Myspace Chat

Make new friends and keep up with old ones on Myspace Chat.

Start by choosing a category, location, or age group below.

By Category	By Location	By Age

Automotive	Music
Business & Money	MySpace
Computers & Technology	News & Politics
Culture, Arts & Literature	Religion & Philosophy
Food & Drink	Schools and Education
Games	Science
Health & Fitness	Sports
Hobbies & Crafts	Television
Love & Relationships	Travel & Vacations
Movies	Video Games

Figure 4.6
The chat room category list is diverse. These top list categories
lead to subcategories (such as Sports>Basketball).

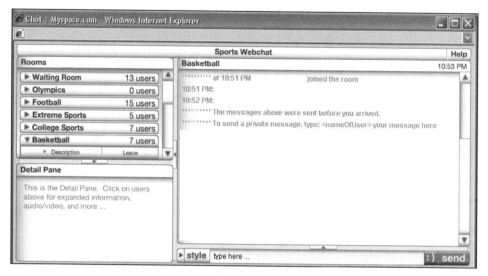

Figure 4.7
The actual chat room interface is similar to other Internet chat
rooms and works within your browser.

Put It in the Want Ads

Internet classified ad sites, such as Craigslist.org and Backpage.com, have become a great way to find jobs, connect with other musicians, locate rentals, and more. MySpace offers its own Classifieds section, too, exclusively for members. It's populated with many of the same categories you'll find on other classifieds sites, such as jobs, personals, and housing, but it also has a few categories that appeal to the many MySpace artsy types. Sections including Casting Calls, Musician Xchange, and Filmmakers are helpful for finding entertainment-industry gigs, partners, band members, lessons, and more. Figure 4.8 shows some of the dozens of possible categories.

It is free to place a classified ad on MySpace; however, there are rules about what you cannot post—namely "adult" services and Internet moneymaking schemes, the latter of which will get you booted from the community. Ads are compartmentalized by city, as shown in Figure 4.9. You can also search by keyword within your city, making it easier to find only the ads about "jazz hip-hop fusion" or some other needle in a haystack.

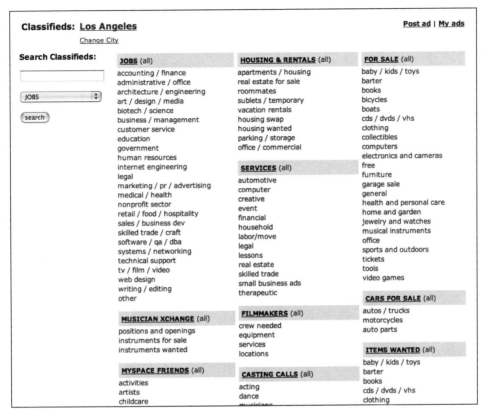

Figure 4.8
MySpace classified ads are not unlike traditional newspaper ads,
except they're free and much easier to navigate.

Posting an ad is very simple and entails only filling out some text fields and attaching an image if needed. See Figure 4.10 for a look at the interface and the rules of posting.

Classifieds - Change City

US	Jacksonville	San Antonio	Ireland	Singapore
Albany	Kansas City	San Diego	Dublin	Taiwan
Albuquerque	Las Vegas	Santa Barbara		Tokyo
Anchorage	Los Angeles	Seattle	UK	
Atlanta	Louisville	SF Bay	Edinburgh	Americas
Austin	Memphis	Spokane	Glasgow	Buenos Aires
Bakersfield	Miami	St. Louis	London	Mexico City
Baltimore	Milwaukee	Stockton	Manchester	Sao Paulo
Boise	Minneapolis	Syracuse		
Boston	Monterey	Tampa Bay	AU	
Buffalo	Nashville	Tucson	Adelaide	
Burlington	New Orleans	Tulsa	Auckland	
Charlotte	New York	Washington DC	Brisbane	
Chicago	Norfolk	Wichita	Melbourne	
Cincinnati	Oklahoma City		Perth	
Cleveland	Omaha	Canada	Sydney	
Columbia	Orange County	Calgary		
Columbus	Orlando	Edmonton	Europe	
Dallas	Philadelphia	Montreal	Amsterdam	
Denver	Phoenix	Ottawa	Berlin	
Desmoines	Pittsburgh	Toronto	Brussels	
Detroit	Portland	Vancouver	Paris	
El Paso	Providence	Winnipeg	Rome	
Eugene	Raleigh			
Fresno	Reno	UK	Asia	
Hartford	Richmond	Belfast	Bangalore	
Honolulu	Riverside County	Birmingham	China	
Houston	Rochester	Cardiff	Malaysia	
Indianapolis	Sacramento		Manila	
Inland Empire	Salt Lake		Seoul	

Figure 4.9
Classifieds are grouped by city, both in the U.S. and in other select countries.

Comedians, Filmmakers, and Musicians, Oh My!

In Chapter 3 we discussed the different types of MySpace accounts and what they have to offer. The three entertainment-related accounts include Comedy, Filmmaker, and Music/Artist, and each category has its own section where MySpacers can browse through the thousands of comedian, filmmaker, and musical artist profiles, respectively. Find and watch videos, read bios, learn about gigs and appearances, peruse special promotions and corporate-sponsored profiles, and even rank your favorite entertainers. You'll also find featured entertainers in each of the sections, genre directories, search fields to find your faves, and forums to discuss the latest stars.

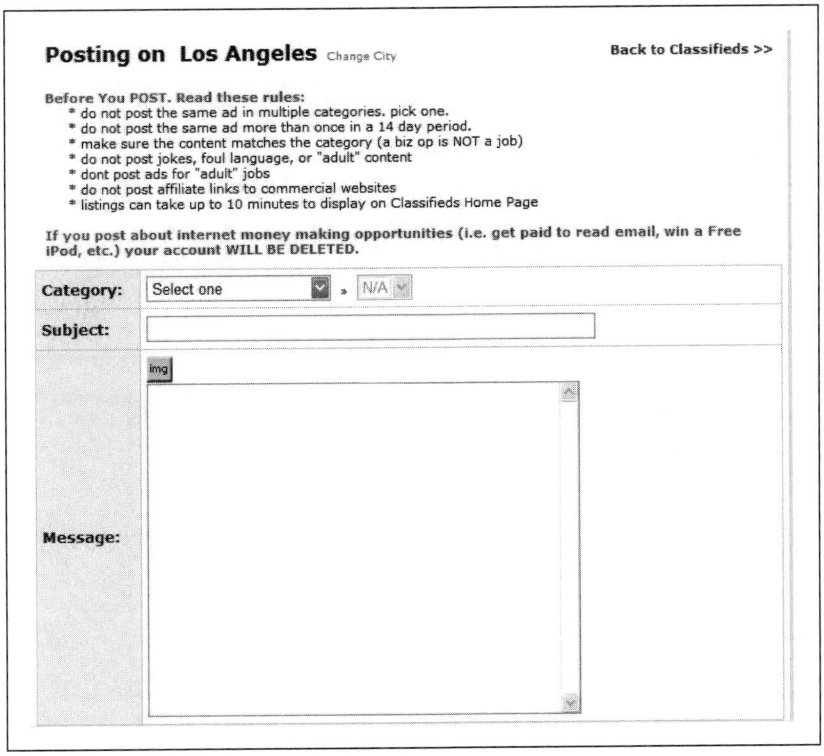

Posting on Los Angeles Change City   Back to Classifieds >>

Before You POST. Read these rules:
* do not post the same ad in multiple categories. pick one.
* do not post the same ad more than once in a 14 day period.
* make sure the content matches the category (a biz op is NOT a job)
* do not post jokes, foul language, or "adult" content
* dont post ads for "adult" jobs
* do not post affiliate links to commercial websites
* listings can take up to 10 minutes to display on Classifieds Home Page

If you post about internet money making opportunities (i.e. get paid to read email, win a Free iPod, etc.) your account WILL BE DELETED.

Category: Select one ▼ » N/A ▼

Subject:

img

Message:

Figure 4.10
Pay special attention to the rules of posting, in bold.

The Music Videos link takes you to a section within the Music area that is focused only on music vids. Always a popular item with MySpacers, music videos are categorized by artist name and genre, with featured top picks highlighted on the main Music Videos page.

(Mostly) Free Downloads

The Downloads section of MySpace may not be for music, but it does have lots of excellent free and demo software. Cleanly arranged by usage type, MySpace downloads offers a nice selection to help you in your online adventures (see Figure 4.11). Especially handy for those new to MySpace or the Internet in general are the Spyware, Audio & Video, and Design & Photo sections. Here you can find programs to keep your computer free of troublesome malware, and you can get some goodies for resizing and tweaking photos or listening to music.

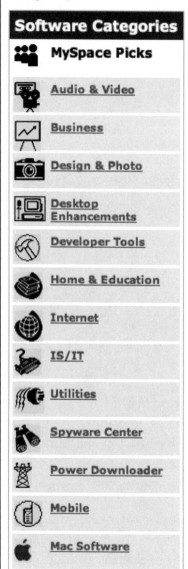

myspacedownloads

Software Categories

MySpace Picks

- Audio & Video
- Business
- Design & Photo
- Desktop Enhancements
- Developer Tools
- Home & Education
- Internet
- IS/IT
- Utilities
- Spyware Center
- Power Downloader
- Mobile
- Mac Software

MySpace Picks

1. Internet Explorer
Browse the Web with tabs, improved RSS support, and robust security features.
↓ **Download**

2. MySpace IM
IM your MySpace friends any time.
↓ **Download**

3. Mozilla FireFox
The award-winning Web browser is now faster, more secure, and fully customizable to your online life.
↓ **Download**

4. iTunes
Buy music, movies, TV shows, and audiobooks, or download free podcasts from the iTunes Store 24 hours a day, 7 days a week.
↓ **Download**

5. QuickTime
Beautiful video from mobile phone to widescreen HD.
↓ **Download**

6. Adobe Flash Player
Adobe Flash Player is the high-performance, lightweight, highly expressive client runtime that delivers powerful and consistent user experiences across major operating systems, browsers, mobile phones, and devices.
↓ **Download**

Figure 4.11
MySpace Downloads offers a bunch of free and shareware programs to boost your online experience.

It's All Fun and Games

The Games section of MySpace is chock full of third-party games for all ages and in several genres, such as action games, arcade games, and puzzles (see Figure 4.12). Many are downloadable demo programs that give you 30 to 60 minutes of free playing time before you must purchase the full version. However, there are quite a few that are free to play and enjoy. This section has featured games, the most popular ones, new arrivals, as well as staff favorites. On any given night there may be several thousands of players logged into the site.

Figure 4.12
The Games navigation panel shows the various game categories and number of users playing.

Your Future Is in the Stars

MySpace knows how to set up a good partnership. Why recreate the wheel when somebody else already does it better? The Horoscope section (see Figure 4.13), with its decidedly New Age aura, gives MySpacers all the karmic tools they could want. This area is powered by promotional partner Tarot.com and boasts horoscopes, compatibility summaries (are Taurus and Aquarius a good match?), tarot readings, numerology, planet alignments, and other cosmic tools. Much of the content is free, although the tidbits often act as teasers to get you to purchase that complete compatibility profile or astrology reading.

Figure 4.13
The Horoscopes banner on the MySpace homepage beckons
users to click and discover their divine selves.

Making an Impact

The MySpace Impact page features people who are making waves in
their communities and in the national media. The section's tagline, "a
place to make a difference," really sums it up. Here you can find out
about scene-makers in politics, philanthropy, business, the environment,
medicine, and more.

You Better Get Yourself a Job

In addition to the Classified job postings, MySpace also has a swanky
jobs section powered by SimplyHired.com, a job search engine that
not only scans the biggest job sites with one query, but also helps you
post your resume to multiple career sites at once. The Jobs area has a
special section that seemingly caters to the inexperienced, offering
links to internships, back-to-school, and part-time jobs nationwide
(see Figure 4.14).

An unexpected but hilarious touch is the link to the SimplyFired.com
blog, which irreverently gossips about the nation's firings, from the
ridiculous to the unlawful in both the public and private sectors.

Figure 4.14
MySpace Jobs gives users a simple way to search for their dream career.

Movies for MySpacers

The MySpace Movies section (see Figure 4.15) rivals other movie websites by providing everything one needs to be in the know about contemporary cinema. Get current and upcoming movie summaries, watch trailers, find show times, and even purchase tickets. RottenTomatoes.com provides links to the latest movie news articles, and MovieTickets.com powers the ordering system for purchasing tix. The section also showcases featured movies and keeps tabs on top box office flicks.

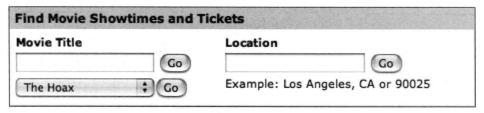

Figure 4.15
The movie search helps you find films in your area.

MySpaceIM

MySpaceIM is an instant Internet messaging program that works a lot like AOL, MSN, and Yahoo's Internet messaging programs. However, you can chat with fellow MySpacers, whether or not they are friends. While every MySpacer has an Instant Message link on his or her profile, MySpaceIM makes chatting one on one with your favorite MySpace buddies a lot easier. Click on the MySpaceIM link to go to the IM download section (see Figure 4.16). The program will be installed on your computer, and from there setup is easy (see Figure 4.17). You can add your current MySpace friends to your IM list simply by picking them from a list (see Figure 4.18). Or you can add other MySpacers even if they're not on your friends list. The program will show you who on your list is online, and from there a quick click will put you in contact with that person so you can chat in real time. The MySpaceIM program also opens a secondary window to allow you to easily access your profile (see Figure 4.19).

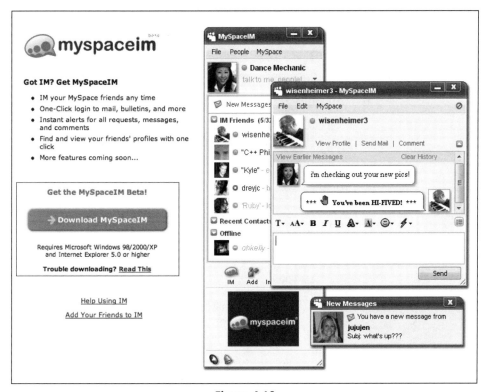

Figure 4.16
The MySpaceIM page is the place to go if you like to chat with MySpace pals.

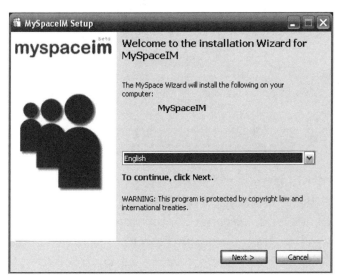

Figure 4.17
MySpaceIM installs as a stand-alone application.

Figure 4.18
You can easily add your friends to your IM list.

Figure 4.19
The open MySpaceIM program shows which of your friends are online, as well as a control panel for easy clicking on your MySpace Inbox and other account features.

Connect with Classmates

The link to schools is a quick way to access your high school or college. Find old friends and classmates, and see the top-rated schools on MySpace based on the number of current classmates and alums from each school. The initial Schools page (see Figure 4.20) offers a basic search for your school, but once you've found it you can search by age range, graduation year, fraternity/sorority, and more.

Find Your School		Top Colleges		
			School	**Members**
School Name		1	**Arizona State University–Main Campus**	74199
Country ⇕		2	**University Of Florida**	65533
State/Province/Territory ⇕		3	**University Of California–Los Angeles**	65511
(Find)		4	**Florida State University**	65197
		5	**University Of Central Florida**	64514
Welcome to Myspace Schools		6	**The University Of Texas At Austin**	60277
Find old classmates, keep in touch with your friends, and participate in your school's message boards.		7	**San Diego State University**	57762
		8	**Ohio State University–Main Campus**	52905
Start by adding a school now. Select the country, state, and city of your school using the menus above.		9	**University Of South Florida**	51537
		10	**Pennsylvania State University–Main Campus**	51457

Figure 4.20
The Schools page helps you find old classmates.

TV On Demand

TV On Demand gives you access to some of your favorite Fox shows, such as *Family Guy* and *Prison Break*. Both owned by News Corp., Fox and MySpace's collaboration to offer streaming TV came on the heels of ABC and NBC's foray into Web TV. Viewers can watch previously aired episodes of select Fox shows, which is especially helpful if you've missed your favorite because you've been out gigging! TV On Demand can also be accessed from the Videos page (see Figure 4.21).

Figure 4.21
A featured link to Fox's TV On Demand gives MySpacers access to previously aired programs.

Viewing Videos

The Videos section (see Figure 4.22) acts as a catch-all area for MySpace videos in every category, from music, comedy, and filmmaker videos, to vids about sports, cars, and travel (see Figure 4.23). From this page, you can access your own videos, upload new vids, and browse through everyone else's. The search function will try to pin down your choices by keywords. The first navigation tab is MySpace's pics for featured clips, but if you click on the Videos tab, you can check out the picks that have gotten the most comments and plays, those that have been the most favorably rated, and even the newest to be uploaded (see Figure 4.24). TV On Demand is also featured in the Videos section.

Figure 4.22
The Videos page is an easy way to search and access
all the clips on MySpace, even your own.

Figure 4.23
The directory helps you find videos easily.

> User Videos - Today's Top Plays
> **Top Plays | Just Added | Most Comments | Top Rated** Now Browsing:
>   All Categories
> Show for: **Today | Week | Month | All**

Figure 4.24
The Videos tab within the Videos page breaks down the top plays.

Other Goodies

There's more than the "little grey box" when it comes to amusing content. Here are a few other nuggets you'll find in the community.

Selling through SNOCAP

The MySpace/SNOCAP Music Store allows you to sell your music online for a fee of $0.39 per track (as of this writing). For MySpacers with artist (music) accounts only, the custom music store appears below your profile's music player. Because it's non-exclusive, you can sign up with other download services outside of MySpace as well. And, they don't try to gobble up your rights. You keep your copyrights to all your music. Access this feature by clicking on the link in your artist account home control panel (see Figure 4.25). For more options in music downloading, consult Appendix A.

Figure 4.25
Artists can create their own MySpace/SNOCAP Music Store any time by clicking this link.

Photo Opps

MySpace gives users tools to create slideshows and albums of photos they have uploaded to their profiles. You used to have to do this by using a third-party photo website, but now it can all be done from within the service. In your Add/Edit Photos section of your account, click on the link to create a slideshow (see Figure 4.26). You will be given code to embed into your profile (see Figure 4.27). See Chapter 8 for information on how to do this. Photo albums allow you to arrange your photos within groups by theme or however you wish to categorize them.

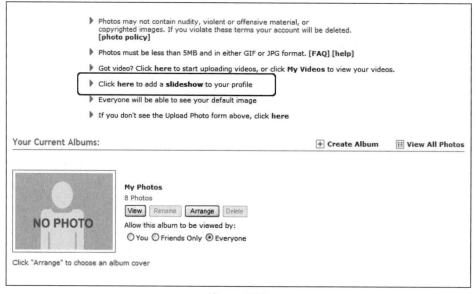

Figure 4.26
Create a slideshow or photo album of your uploaded photos.

Rate Your Professor

Within your own account control panel, you'll see a link to Professor Grading in the area where your schools are linked (see Figure 4.28). Students really do use this feature to boast and bellow about their profs, as well as check out teachers on their schedules for the next semester. After you've found a school, browse by teacher last name or department. Or, you can add a new professor to be graded.

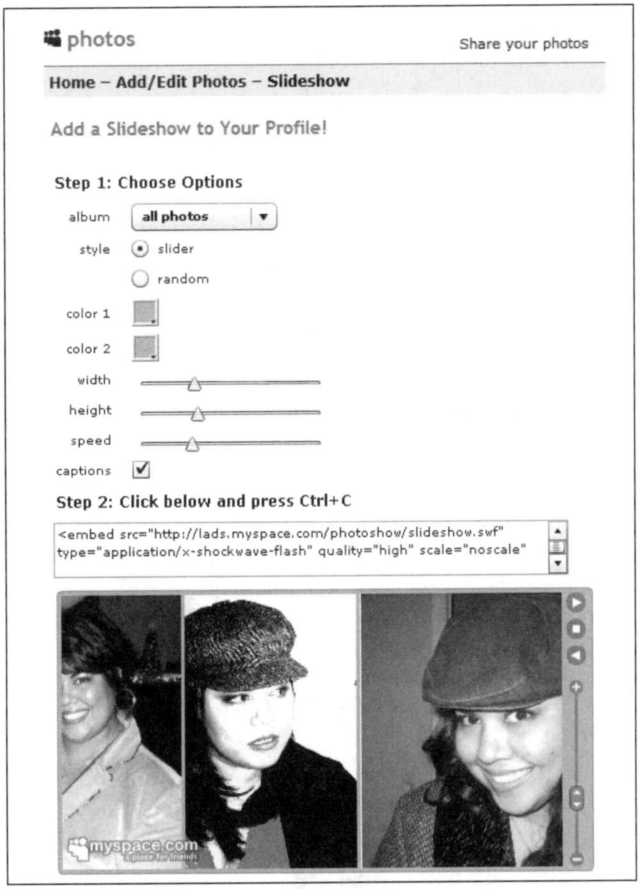

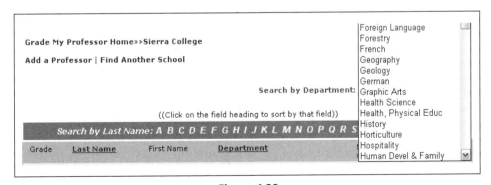

Figure 4.27
Take the provided code and pop it into your profile
wherever you want the slideshow to appear.

Figure 4.28
Students grade their professors and make comments in Professor Grading.

Social Surfing the Events

Why mope at home when you can get out there and mingle? The Events area will help you do just that. Events can be accessed in the medium-blue navigation bar near the top of your profile control panel, and MySpace community pages (such as the homepage and other common areas). Set your zip code to search, and MySpace pulls up all the events in your area, as in Figure 4.29. You'll see club promotions, birthday parties, live music, arts/crafts, and CD release parties. Click on the event of your choice and RSVP or leave a comment. Events will come in handy when it's your turn to promote your performances. (See Chapter 12, "Bulletins and Event Invitations.")

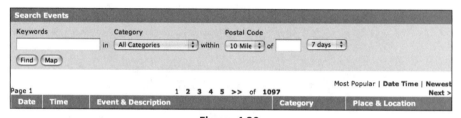

Figure 4.29
The Events area is the perfect place to find social gatherings,
live music, and more... or to post your own!

You'll Have to Get on My Calendar

Also found in your account control panel, your Calendar keeps you organized and can even alert friends to where you'll be any day of the week by appearing on your profile. A similar function appears in artists accounts, but there it is focused on gigs as opposed to personal appointments.

Click on Manage Calendar in your account (the link appears next to your profile pic). Add your appointments (as simple as Studying at the Library) with or without locations, as in Figure 4.30. Then set your Options to remind you of your appointments through MySpace or to send an alert email to your regular email address (see Figure 4.31). You can make your calendar public to everyone, private for friends, or for your eyes only. However, unless you are using your personal calendar to let people know which business conventions or other non-public-accessible events you'll be attending, it's not a good idea to post your comings and goings for every would-be stalker to see.

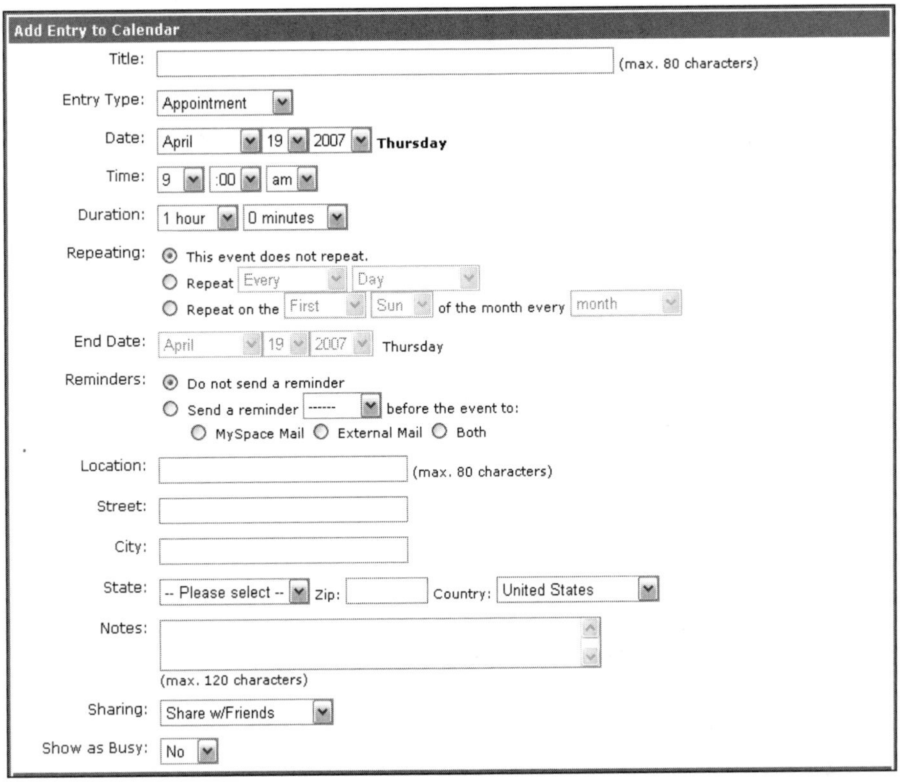

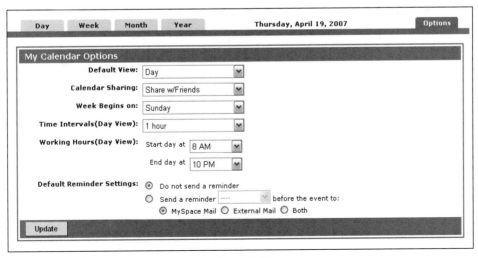

Figure 4.30
Enter your schedule into the Calendar to help remind you where you need to be.

Figure 4.31
Set Calendar options to remind you of events by sending you an email.

Gathering Groups

Click on Groups in the medium-blue nav bar and be awed by the number of discussion areas, from pets and politics, to sororities and science. Each group is categorized and searchable by keyword. Or browse through the category of your choice (see Figure 4.32). The sheer number of groups is staggering, so this is no easy task. At this time, music alone has 250,000 groups! When you find the one you want, you may need to join the group in order to view it. In some cases, you can only join a private group if you are invited by the moderator to do so. But once you're in, you may find some great resources and interesting rapport.

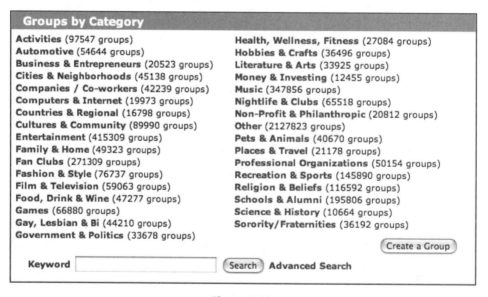

Groups by Category

Activities (97547 groups)	**Health, Wellness, Fitness** (27084 groups)
Automotive (54644 groups)	**Hobbies & Crafts** (36496 groups)
Business & Entrepreneurs (20523 groups)	**Literature & Arts** (33925 groups)
Cities & Neighborhoods (45138 groups)	**Money & Investing** (12455 groups)
Companies / Co-workers (42239 groups)	**Music** (347856 groups)
Computers & Internet (19973 groups)	**Nightlife & Clubs** (65518 groups)
Countries & Regional (16798 groups)	**Non-Profit & Philanthropic** (20812 groups)
Cultures & Community (89990 groups)	**Other** (2127823 groups)
Entertainment (415309 groups)	**Pets & Animals** (40670 groups)
Family & Home (49323 groups)	**Places & Travel** (21178 groups)
Fan Clubs (271309 groups)	**Professional Organizations** (50154 groups)
Fashion & Style (76737 groups)	**Recreation & Sports** (145890 groups)
Film & Television (59063 groups)	**Religion & Beliefs** (116592 groups)
Food, Drink & Wine (47277 groups)	**Schools & Alumni** (195806 groups)
Games (66880 groups)	**Science & History** (10664 groups)
Gay, Lesbian & Bi (44210 groups)	**Sorority/Fraternities** (36192 groups)
Government & Politics (33678 groups)	

(Create a Group)

Keyword [   ] (Search) Advanced Search

Figure 4.32
The number of MySpace groups in each category is overwhelming.
Together there are a million-plus discussion groups in this community alone.

Sponsored Profiles

Sponsored profiles and corporate promotions are peppered throughout MySpace, usually featured on the homepage or on the Music, Comedy, and Filmmaker landing pages. It's becoming more and more commonplace for big-budget movie studios to promote their flicks to the MySpace world (see Figure 4.33), and you will even notice MySpace URLs on movie trailers. TV shows, record labels, politicians, cell phone carriers, and even non-profit charity groups all promote their wares on MySpace, hoping to build a brand relationship with the coveted MySpace demographic, primarily ages 16 to 34. The promos come and go quickly, so enjoy the ones of interest while they're there.

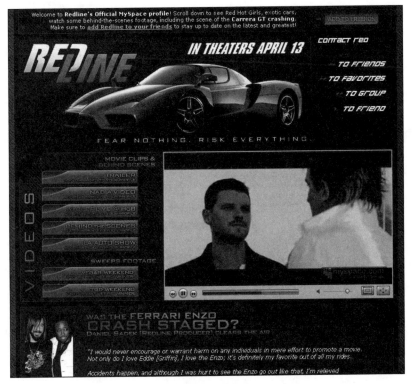

Figure 4.33
The movie *Redline* from Chicago Pictures has its official profile on MySpace. Visitors can watch trailers, listen to the movie's music, check out the hot cars, chat in the official Redline forum, and enter the sweepstakes.

Favorites

You can keep track of profiles of interest by adding them to your Favorites list (see Figure 4.34). Then, review your list by either clicking Favorites in the medium-blue navigation bar or by going into your account's home control panel and accessing your favorites from there.

You may not want to add everyone you encounter to your friends list, but perhaps someone has something amusing or memorable on her profile that you'd like to go back to later. That's what the Favorites list is for. To add a profile to your list, click on the Add to Favorites link on the person's profile. The link is in the person's contact table, where you'll also find links to Send a Message and Add to Friends.

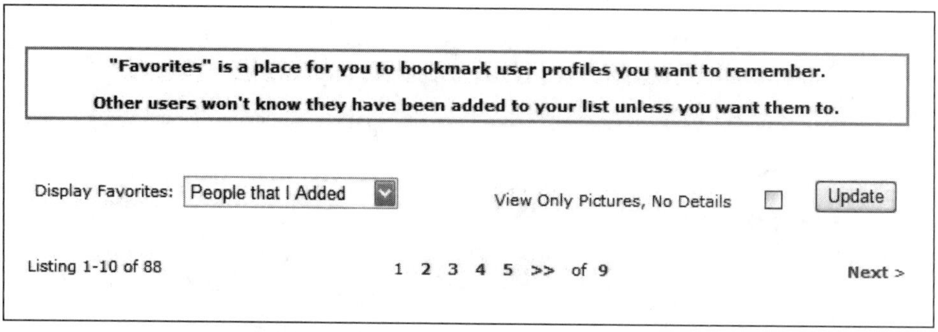

Figure 4.34
Keep track of interesting profiles in your Favorites list.

MySpace Mobile

For those on the go who must have their MySpace everywhere, there is MySpace Mobile for AT&T (plus the former Cingular) and Helio users. Access your profile from your cell phone. MySpacers on different cell phone networks can get text-message alerts sent to their phones when they have new friend requests, comments, invites, and email messages.

You may have already known about all the different treats described in this chapter, but you'd be surprised by how many people don't have any idea that much of this exists. They go straight to their profile, check emails, maybe leave a few comments for friends, and that's it. It's advantageous for MySpace to offer you many other options, however. The longer they can keep you within the community, the more time they have to expose you to their advertisers. So enjoy the fun features, but just remember you're here to market yourself and your art, too! Let's learn how to get started....

5 Identifying Your Target Market

All marketers must find out who their target audience is before they can hope to reach them. This is true whether you are a self-marketing artist or a record company executive. You may already have a preliminary idea of who your audience is based on the people who come to your shows and sign up for your mailing lists. But for those of you who are just starting out and who don't yet have a following, determining who will listen to your music, buy your records, and come to your shows can be a daunting task. In this chapter, I'll show you some tips for figuring out who your audience is and how to reach them. You'll find this useful not just for creating and marketing your MySpace presence, but for planning all your marketing, promotion, and publicity endeavors as well.

Who Are You?

Instead of wading through marketing theory and principles, let's take a homegrown approach to defining your product (you and your music) and learning about your target market. This is not a mental exercise; you must write down everything. The goal is to wrap up your brand and who your fans are in a concise paragraph or two.

If you've ever watched *American Idol*, you know that image and song choice are key to progressing in the contest. Randy, Paula, and Simon say it over and over again to singers who don't shine in their performance: "That just wasn't the right song for you." Singing the wrong song for your voice and ability, trying to emote lyrics inappropriate for your age group, or not jiving your image with your music is the kiss of death on *Idol*. The same is true for the regular Joe and Jane Musician.

First you must figure out, in a nutshell, who you are. Your MySpace profile, CD art, posters, emails, website, and more will be a reflection of you the artist. The "brand" you present must match up with your music and image.

The following questions will help you pin down what you have to offer. New artists struggling to find their niche will find this helpful in their quest for identity. Seasoned artists will likely find the answers flowing more easily. The exercise is important for both.

- How do I describe my music?

- How do friends, fans, or business associates describe my music?

- If I had to put my music into categories, what would they be?

- Are there deficiencies in my music? (Be honest). If so, what are they? (Examples include songwriting, lyrics, guitar skills, vocal range, production, and so on.)

- What kinds of people come to my show? What do they wear? How do they behave? How old are they?

- What kinds of places do I gig? What venues are appropriate for me?

- Who buys my music and where do they buy it?

- What kind of lyrics do I write (or prefer to sing)?

- Is there a common message, theme, or tone in my music?

- How do I see myself in terms of physical image? Is this compatible with my music and what people are hearing?

- What kind of image do I want to portray?

- Whom do I hope to reach with my music?

- What, musically, am I passionate about?

- What do I prefer to sing/play?

- What kind of voice do I have? What is its range and color?

- What kind of songs really let my talent shine through? What do I absolutely love to play/sing?

- Who are my contemporaries? What other artists (signed or unsigned) are in similar categories to mine, and how would I describe them?

As in *Idol*, self-awareness can make or break a performance and a following. This means knowing what you're good at, what people want to see you play, and how you affect others. Gather the information you've just generated and roll it into an Artist Summary paragraph of about 150 to 250 words. Be concise and direct. Write in detached third-person, as if you are writing about someone else.

This is a snapshot of who you are as a musical talent—what kind of music you make, what you excel at, and what your image and musical message are. You don't have to plug in the answers to all the questions. Instead, take what you've learned about yourself and wrap up the highlights into your summary.

You may have holes in some of your answers. Perhaps the image you portray as an artist does not gel with what you envision or isn't compatible with your music in general. You may be aware of things you need to fix in your music, such as getting a great co-writer or producer. Make a note of what you have to change and work on. It is your roadmap for improvement. Write your summary wrap-up as if you have already fixed all these things. When you have a clear, written understanding of who you are *and* what you want to be, you will aspire to fulfill it.

Here is a sample of an Artist Summary written by the artist herself:

> Jane Vocalist is an award-winning singer/songwriter from Portland, Oregon. Her crystalline soprano voice radiates warmth into her songs and is coupled with ethereal and emotive piano playing. Her lyrics are sometimes considered impressionistic, with interpretations varying depending on the listener. Yet she admits her themes are often about relationships, including those between family members, and even her relationship with God. While Jane writes most of her songs, she often indulges in creating new arrangements of favorite cover songs, mostly in the pop genres of the '60s and '70s, as well as jazz standards. This acoustic pop piano artist appears throughout the Portland area. Jane's fans describe her live shows as captivating and enveloping. She peppers

her performances with poetry of favorite writers between songs. Jane is an urban songstress who is both sophisticated and down to earth in her music, style, and interaction with fans. She believes in the truth of the human being, both beautiful and sometimes ugly. And her music attempts to unveil the human spirit as optimistic and enduring, despite its downfalls.

As you can see, it reads a bit like a bio. It can certainly be the beginnings of your bio. You can make it longer and more encompassing. The more experience you have, the more you will have to say. Your Artist Summary, however, should be no more than one page long, no less than 150 words.

Take a look at the MySpace profile snapshots in Figures 5.1 through 5.3. How would you describe these artists, and do their profiles seem to be reflective of their music and image?

Figure 5.1
Sugarcult tailors their MySpace profile to match their official website and convey their brooding yet sometimes glossy brand of punk rock (www.myspace.com/sugarcult).

Figure 5.2
Former *American Idol* contestant rocker Chris Daughtry's band shows off an
organic, rough-around-the-edges profile (www.myspace.com/daughtry).

Figure 5.3
Pop artist Nelly Furtado's profile mirrors her new image and
album artwork (www.myspace.com/nellyfurtado).

Your task is to clearly define who you are and what kind of music you offer. Believe it or not, that's the easy part. Read on to discover how to pin down your audience and craft your Target Market Summary.

How and Where to Research

The next stage of identifying your target market entails researching who your would-be fans are. There are a lot of questions to answer, so before you get that deer-in-the-headlights look, I want you to be fortified with a guide for how to find all this information.

- **Pay attention.** The first thing you need to do is tune in to what's happening in music, media, print, technology, business, popular culture, and consumer promotions. The best way to get a real sense of what your potential audience is experiencing is to look around. Get in the habit of knowing what's going on in the careers of other artists, in the lives of consumers in your country, and in sports and entertainment—and especially technology. If you saw this book and said, "Hmmm... what's a MySpace?" then you've been tuned out for too long.

- **Listen and watch.** As a musician, you probably already have a voracious appetite for music. But you can always listen *more*. It's easy to get into our little comfort zones and surround ourselves with only a certain type of music. You're not doing yourself any good. Listen to music that you never thought you would. Hate country music? Can't stand punk? Don't understand world music? Then go online and partake of the many free radio stations and streaming music video sites. You'll find them by using Rhapsody.com's player (see Figure 5.4), visiting VH1.com (see Figure 5.5), or music.Yahoo.com (see Figure 5.6). And that is just the tip of the iceberg. There are so many music freebies out there that it'll make your head spin. Consume as much as you can until you think you've listened to darn near everything ever created. This is what musical greats do. They are inspired by others.

And they know what kind of music is out there, what new and exciting things people are doing musically today, and what the legends have done in the past. They start to get in tune with the audiences of various types of music. They absorb the vibe and get a better understanding of what music consumers want across the board.

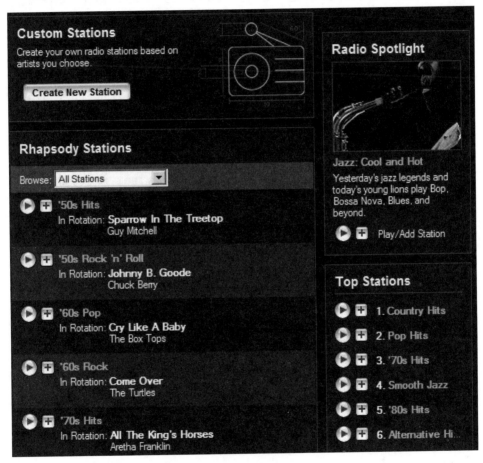

Figure 5.4
RealNetwork's Rhapsody player offers dozens of radio stations, or you can customize your own.

Figure 5.5
VH1.com's glitzy Radio page offers tons of stations in myriad genres.

Figure 5.6
Music.Yahoo.com showcases videos from top artists, as well as video premieres.

- **The tube is your friend.** It's very hip to say you don't watch TV. "Nah, I never touch the stuff," you balk. It makes you seem intellectual and mysterious. Seriously, you need to turn on the TV once in a while and absorb a little pop culture. Bands and records are being broken on commercials all the time. WhatsThatCalled.com lets users search to find out which artist and song were featured on a particular commercial (see Figure 5.7). Adtunes.com tracks the top ad music (see Figure 5.8). Little-known artists are finding followings when their music is played on TV shows. Music is everywhere, not just on the radio or online—it's in movies, too. TuneFind.com (see Figure 5.9) breaks down the music featured in films and on TV and lists the most popular artists. Hearing all this music on the tube or in the theatre should be giving you ideas. That artist who has a similar vibe as you is getting play on a teeny-bopper drama or maybe a prime-time suspense series. What does that say about who your audience might be? They're using your genre of music to sell cars. And who buys these kinds of cars? Yep, you're seeing the connection now....

Figure 5.7
WhatsThatCalled.com helps you figure out what song you
keep hearing on your favorite ad.

10. Fast and Furious
The group N.E.R.D. (with the help of remixer Jason Nevins) created a popular song for fast cuts/edits in movie trailers. Their track "Rock Star (Jason Nevins Remix Edit)" was most recently in the *The Fast and the Furious: Tokyo Drift* trailer. The remix has also been in spots for the movie *Taxi*, *Shanghai Knights* and on the *Blue Crush* film soundtrack.

9. Mad World War
One thing we learned in 2006: Not many Xbox 360 owners saw the movie Donnie Darko. The Gary Jules "Mad World" (iTunes) / Tears for Fears cover moved from the Darko movie soundtrack to the very popular Gears of War commercial (with a few other appearances along the way). The song has become a game trailer remix fan favorite.

8. A Real Spektor
Singer-songwriter Regina Spektor lent her brand of indie folk-rock (the kids like to call it "anti-folk") goodness to a XM Satellite Radio commercial with her song Better" (iTunes). This capped a year that saw Spektor's music appearing in many outlets, including TV shows like *CSI:NY*, *Verionica Mars*, *Weeds*, and *Grey's Anatomy*. Some are even (mistakenly) convinced she's been subbing for Cat Power.

7. Golden Age
For the second time, the *Overseer Overexposed Award* goes to the band Goldfrapp. Alison Goldfrapp and her electronica backed vocals were everywhere in 2006. The band's music has been in ads for Verizon, Alltel, Motorola, L'Oreal, Diet Coke, ABC, F/X, Target and countless others. EMI Music Marketing Senior VP Cynthia Sexton on licensing Goldfrapp: "With some pitching and pushing, all of the songs on 'Supernature' have what it takes." Overexposed runner-up goes to "Somewhere Over the Rainbow / What a Wonderful World" (iTunes) by Israel "IZ" Kamakawiwo'ole being used *again*, this time to sell Rice Krispies.

Figure 5.8
Adtunes.com is a compendium of ad music news and info,
as well as the top-ranked advertising songs.

Figure 5.9
TuneFind.com is a comprehensive guide to TV and film songs, complete with top artist and song charts.

■ **Read, read, read.** Pull out a print magazine or a newspaper, and you'll see features, CD reviews, profiles, and more about musical artists of every stripe. Visit your local bookstore or library once a month and flip through pubs you might not normally read. Yes, guys, you can look at women's magazines. Absorb who gets coverage in which magazines. What audience does each magazine reach? What kind of music is appropriate for that publication? Artists in *Source* might not be in *Ladies' Home Journal*. Then again, maybe they are. Can you see how an artist might be appropriate for both? This is how you get familiar with the media and who fits in where, and why. It's not just editorial, however. Look at the advertisements and observe which artists are endorsing or promoting which products. That says a lot about who their audience is. Beyoncé may be modeling hair color, but she's probably not endorsing athletic shoes. Also, get familiar with industry trade magazines, including *Billboard, Hollywood Reporter, Variety,* and *Rolling Stone,* as well as genre-specific titles, such as *Source, Vibe, Downbeat, Country Weekly, Christian Musician, Remix,* and *Alternative Press.*

- **Get out of the house.** Want to see what's out there? Go to live shows, both large and small—especially those of your contemporaries. Check out who's on tour and the reviews from layman and critic alike. What companies are sponsoring these tours? Pollstar.com keeps the pulse of the concert industry (see Figure 5.10). Take note of who goes to these shows and what they say. Chat with people. Find out what they do and don't like. Why are they there? Where do they buy their music? What other bands do they listen to? If you are also gigging around town, invite people you chat with to your show. Be casual and nonchalant. Attract, don't attack.

Figure 5.10
Pollstar.com is the concert industry bible and features the latest touring news.

- **Network like you mean it.** Going to shows was the first step; now you have to branch out. Attend some music business, film music, or songwriter seminars or panels. Go to a convention or two. Visit record stores (if there are any left in your area). Talk to people. But listen more. Ask people what they think of the industry, of your favorite musical artists, of the state of *[fill in the blank with your favorite genre]*, and so on. You may find out that coalitions of club DJs (record pools), popular in Atlanta, New York City, Los Angeles, and a few other urban areas, are breaking hip-hop unknowns and helping send them to the top of the charts. Someone may slip you the tip that an indie music supervisor he or she knows is looking for unsigned talent for a new project. Bring business cards and demos or even press kits. You never know who you'll meet. Take these people's cards and follow up with them.

- **Be a joiner.** So you're going to shows and seminars. While you're at it, get even further connected with your artistic community by joining some organizations. Not only do they provide opportunities for meet-and-greets, they may also offer resources, membership directories, discounts to conventions and seminars, and more. The National Academy of the Recording Arts and Sciences (the Grammy people) is a great place to start. If you're a songwriter, you should belong to a performing rights organization, such as ASCAP or BMI. Also, look for artist coalitions and songwriter groups in your area. Billboard sponsors events all over the country. Check out BillboardEvents.com for a complete calendar (see Figure 5.11).

- **Crawl the web.** It probably goes without saying, but I'll say it anyway. Web research is a must in this day and age. Run web searches on musical genres, contemporaries, and even yourself to see what comes up. Look for press coverage of similar artists. Visit artist websites and check out how they are marketed. Comb through music sites, such as AllMusic.com, Billboard.com, VH1.com, music.AOL.com, music and tech blogs (DigitalMusicNews.com, AOLMusicNewsBlog.com, and Billboard's Jaded Insider blog at Billboard.blogs.com are three favorites), and even the media search tool LexisNexis.com. Many local and state libraries also now offer magazines online.

Figure 5.11
BillboardEvents.com is the place to go to find out about all the
many Billboard-sponsored events throughout the year.

Of course, you'll want to pour through MySpace music profiles to get a feel for what's out there. Remember to visit the profiles of your favorite band's friends as well to see what kind of audience the band attracts.

- **Look for "intelligent" feedback.** Search for similar artists on sites and services such as Amazon.com, Rhapsody's Player at rhapsody.com (see Figures 5.12 and 5.13), and Last.fm (see Figure 5.14), and these sites will kick back additional artists you might like. This will help you understand who shares a similar fan base. For instance, do you like Fergie? Last.fm also suggests you might enjoy Beyoncé, Justin Timberlake, and Nelly Furtado as well. A fan of Nickelback? Amazon says customers who like Nickelback also bought music by Evanescence, Staind, and The Fray. So start typing in your contemporaries and you'll begin to get a better idea of who their audience is.

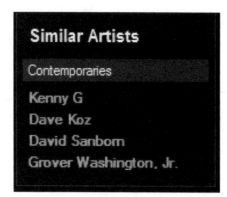

Figure 5.12
Rhapsody's Player has a search feature that suggests similar artists. In this case, the searched artist was smooth jazz saxophonist Marion Meadows.

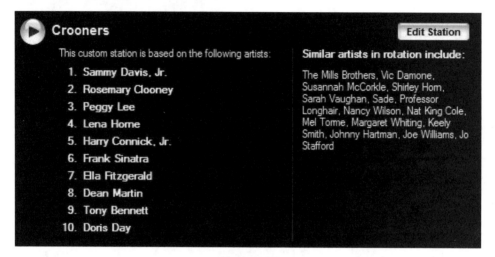

Figure 5.13
Also in Rhapsody, when you create a custom radio station, the system suggests other artists similar to those you listed.

- **Get it from the horse's mouth.** You needn't rely solely on third-party research. You can ask your fans directly. Implement a mailing list form on your website and MySpace page that asks a few questions about your fans' interests and buying habits. You can even offer a freebie for their time, such as a coupon good toward music or merchandise, a free download, or an entry into a drawing for something small but cool (such as said download or merchandise). Cultivate a good list, and you'll have people to come back to for future feedback.

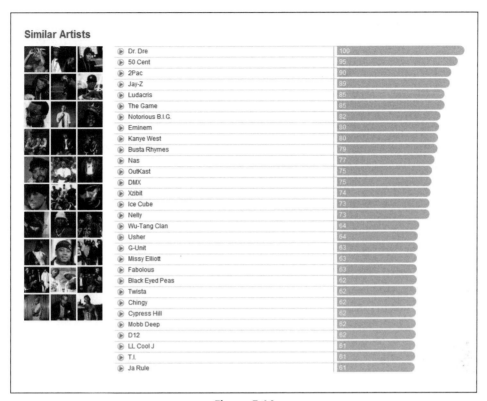

Figure 5.14
Last.fm has the ability to offer up comparable artists and even ranks them in terms of how alike they are. This gives the marketer a better look at what other artists in similar genres a fan might be interested in. The searched artist here was Snoop Dogg.

Asking the Right Questions

Now that you know where to look for answers, it's time to ask the questions. Just as you had to ask yourself a litany of queries to get to the core of what you have to offer, you will do the same of your target audience. Some of the answers will be based on concrete research. Some will be anecdotal evidence and supposition. It's not all hard science. To find out more about your current and potential consumers and fans, try to answer these questions:

- How would I describe my first impression of my target audience?

- Where does my target market shop?

- What are their ages?
- Where do they come from?
- What kinds of clothing do they buy and wear?
- Do they have any particular characteristics as a group?
- What magazines do they read?
- What radio stations do they listen to?
- Where do they live?
- What is their lifestyle?
- What are their views on life?
- What kind of education do they have?
- What is their income?
- What type of expendable income do they possess?
- What kinds of entertainment do they enjoy and purchase?
- What is the ideal way to reach these consumers?
- How do they prefer to be contacted?
- What kinds of products, in various categories, do they buy?
- What do they drive?
- What kind of movies and television shows do they enjoy?
- What websites do they frequent?
- Where/how do they purchase their music?
- With what consumer brands do they identify?
- What other types of music, besides mine, do they listen to?
- What is their comfort level with technology? Explain...

You may think of other questions that are relevant. Our example artist, Jane Vocalist, answered a few based on her experience, online research, and a mailing list survey through her website:

Q: How would I describe my first impression of my target audience?

A: Mostly women in their late teens through early 40s. They seem to identify less with the saccharin pop female icons of the day and more with contemporary male and female singer/songwriters. Some dress in a sophisticated manner; others are more free-spirited types. All seem to be interested in personal empowerment, musical quality, and intellectual pursuits. My listeners are both single and married. They are mostly college educated.

Q: What magazines do they read?

A: *Rolling Stone; Harp; Performing Songwriter; Yoga Journal; O, the Oprah Magazine.*

Q: Where/how do they purchase their music?

A: The younger end of the target audience tends to be very web savvy and will likely download much of their music. The older spectrum (late 30s+) tends toward purchasing music at well-known retail outlets, such as Target and Best Buy, but they are not above learning how to download music. The older group especially tends to listen to music at work on their computers.

The quest doesn't end there. Looking at what others are doing and to whom they appeal is essential.

Researching Contemporaries and Competitors

One of the best ways to answer questions about your potential audience is to research how similar artists in the same or a similar category to you reach *their* consumers.

List your contemporaries and find out:

- What magazines are they featured in?

- What products do they endorse?

- With which other artists do they collaborate and how?

- What TV shows and movies feature their music?
- How does their record company position and market them?
- Where is their music sold?
- Who attends their shows?
- What are their website and MySpace profile like?
- What does their CD packaging look like?
- What kinds of publicity do they receive?
- Where do they play (what kinds of venues and in what parts of the country/world)?
- What is their image like?
- What kinds of clothes do they wear?
- Who do they appeal to?
- What can you extrapolate about this artist's fans from this information?
- How might this info apply to you?

Now that you are up to your eyeballs in info, you are ready to trim it down into a usable paragraph or two, called your Target Market Summary.

Like your Artist Summary, you won't need to throw in every answer to every question. You're gleaning overall impressions and demographic information and rolling this into a concise blurb.

Jane Vocalist's sample Target Market Summary reads like this:

> Jane Vocalist's audience, although primarily female, is diverse in age and socioeconomic background. The group that will have the greatest interest in Jane is the 20- to 40-something age range. They are drawn to her unique, almost performance-artist style of acoustic pop alternative, with lyrics that touch upon their own life experiences. She tends to appeal to positive-minded, deep-thinking women who have an appetite for new and non-homogenous music,

are opinionated on politics and world events, and read publications such as Rolling Stone, Alternative Press, the New Yorker, and even O, the Oprah Magazine. Her fans are both married and single and tend to be college educated. Retailers apt to carry Jane's music are local and some regional record store chains, as well as online merchant eMusic. Appropriate radio stations include those in the alternative, top 40, and adult contemporary genres. Her audience is very web focused and download savvy, so particular attention will be paid to reaching out to a non-local fan base through sites such as GarageBand.com and Live365.com.

As Jane learns more about her audience and herself, she will be able to flesh out her Target Market Summary even further and narrow it down more.

Realize that your two summaries—one about you as an artist and the other explaining your target market—are dynamic in nature. They may change over time. You will need to tweak it as you grow and learn. This kind of focus is essential to your success. It keeps you from taking the "spaghetti on the wall" approach. (You know, throwing everything and anything out there and hoping something sticks.) Instead, your summaries will keep you on track. They are like your mission statements, guiding your activities toward the goal of reaching that coveted target audience. When opportunities come by that don't fit into your goal, you'll know they aren't right for you.

You too will be able to identify your target market in a concise paragraph. Doing this initial research and planning will help keep your message and marketing activities, both online and off, focused and on track.

Now that you've laid the foundation for your marketing efforts, it's time to get started on your profile.

6 Getting Started

By this time you've already read about the pros and cons of MySpace, social networking in general, its impact on entertainment, what types of accounts are available, the features of the community, and how to pinpoint who your audience is. But before you jump in and sign up, let's come up with a game plan. This chapter will help you round up all the information and materials you should have in your arsenal to create a basic profile. Many of these details will come right off the top of your head, but others will be harder to come up with on the fly. Gathering the items you need will save you time. And while you can always go back later and populate your profile with info, giving thought first to how and what you want to do will keep you focused on your marketing message.

What You Need to Be on MySpace

Following are the basic items you should have on hand to create a MySpace account. Use this as your checklist. We'll go into greater detail later in this chapter about what you'll do with these things.

- An email account separate from your usual email account

- A main photo or graphic

- Other band photos

- Some basic thoughts about what you want your profile to look like, what backgrounds (if any) would be appropriate, and what color schemes you like

- A unique URL (web address) for your MySpace page

- A biography or short "about" writeup

- A list of band members and notable collaborators (such as producers, songwriters, vocalists, and other featured musicians)

- A compelling profile headline

- A selection of up to four songs for streaming with a different accompanying graphic for each one

- Lyrics for songs

- Touring and gig dates and info

- Your main website URL

- Record label and management info

- A list of who you sound like

- A list of musical influences

- A list of genres that fit your musical style

- A list of keywords that Internet and MySpace searchers might use to find you

Picking an Email Account

On MySpace, your email address is your login name. The advantage of using your current personal email to sign up with MySpace is that friends who know that email will be able to search for you more easily. This is helpful for personal friends and family members who may have lost touch over time.

Some people, however, prefer to use a separate email account for their MySpace and other social networking activities. This is advantageous in a number of ways. You are very easy to locate if anyone can search for your commonly known email address. Using an unadvertised email makes you a bit harder to find by employers, students, military officers, and others you may not want to be privy to your MySpace activities. Using a separate email address also compartmentalizes everything so that MySpace marketing activities don't mingle with personal and business mail. Of course, never use an employer-provided email address to access MySpace or any other social site. For more details on using a unique email to protect your security, see Chapter 16, "Protecting Your Virtual and Physical Security."

Free email accounts can be obtained from a number of providers, including AOL, Yahoo, Hotmail, and others. If you have your own domain name, you can also create a special address just for social networking activities. Remember not to list your email address on your profile. It's better for fans to email you through the MySpace system.

Your Photos

The very first thing anyone on MySpace notices about you is your profile pic. This thumbnail pops up in searches, shows itself when you leave a comment, and peeks out from friends lists (as in Figure 6.1). The kind of photo or graphic you choose to be your main profile pic is very important and should be considered carefully. It is your first impression with your audience, and it often determines whether someone will take a chance and click on your profile.

Music » Search Results

Page   1 of 1

Nazia
Genre: Pop / Classical - Opera and Vocal / Jazz
Location: Dallas, TEXAS
Last Update: Mar 19, 2007

Plays: 5,567
Views: 4,222
Fans: 526

Figure 6.1
This artist has a compelling photo that entices searchers to click on her profile.

Here are some guidelines when choosing photos or graphics for your profile:

- *Never* forego your main photo/graphic. Not having a photo is a marketing kiss of death (see Figure 6.2).

Figure 6.2
If this is the image you're presenting to the world,
you're in trouble. Always have a picture to represent you.

- Always be sure your pic is of good quality and clarity. Retouch as necessary to diminish dark shadows that obscure the photo or your face, sharpen blurriness, correct odd coloring (a person who looks unnaturally pink or yellow, for example).

- Do not use blinking, flashing graphics or animated GIF images. They are annoying fan repellents that scream "amateur."

- Steer clear of cutesy pics that have nothing to do with your band. No thumbnails of your favorite cartoon character or some other jokey graphic.

- The best main photo is one that is compelling and ties into who you are as an artist. Ask yourself, would you click on this photo if you were seeing it for the first time?

- For solo artists, photos in which you can see your face are ideal. It doesn't have to be a happy-go-lucky pic; it can be edgy, moody, smirky, glam, or anything else you want that conveys the essence of you.

- Nothing says "click me" like a great photo of your gorgeous face, so don't hide it, especially if you're a female artist.

- Sexy photos are okay as long as they aren't outright porn. For more on the kinds of content and photos that are acceptable on MySpace, see the Terms of Use, consult Chapter 17, "Managing MySpace," or view a snapshot of MySpace's photo rules in Figure 6.3.

- For music-related companies, a logo that is interesting works best. Just be sure that it's more than a bunch of teeny, tiny unreadable text.

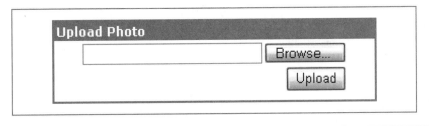

Figure 6.3
The upload page for pics gives you a brief rundown of what
you can and cannot use for pics.

- Do some music searches in your favorite genres and see what compels you to click. Make note of the boring and the repellent. This will give you an idea of what to use and what to stay away from.

In addition to the main photo that will represent you in the MySpace world, gather other pics of your band (or yourself if you're a soloist). You'll also have room to add short captions, as shown in Figure 6.4. Your MySpace account will hold up to 300 photos as of this writing, so you've got plenty of room. Think of various band and soloist possibilities, live performance pics, photos of you in the studio, and of course publicity stills.

The Evolution V: Mr. India East
Coast 2006 oh yeah!!

» Post A Comment
» E-Mail to a Friend
» Report This Image

1 Comment(s)

Figure 6.4
This artist/model noted his latest
accomplishment in his photo caption.

Those of you who are starting out may not have any usable photos to speak of. Look for a photographer in your area by browsing through Internet classifieds such as Craigslist.org or MySpace's classifieds sections, posting your own call for photographers, or contacting media arts programs at your local colleges. You may even be able to barter for photos—you get pics, and they get samples for their portfolio.

Some of you may want to go with a more established photo studio. Search on the Internet or in the yellow pages for photography studios in your area. Even franchise studios such as Glamour Shots work with lots of actors, musicians, and models. Ask around at local talent and modeling agencies and acting schools and find out whom they recommend. Beware of the agency who tries to get you to sign up with them and use their photographers. A reputable place won't take a cut; they will only give you a name or two of photographers whose work they like. Check references and ask to see samples of work.

Most photographers will retain their rights to their photographs, negatives, and digital files. Therefore, always ask for a copyright release and the image on disk. Make sure the copyright release implicitly states that you own the photos, negatives, and/or files and you have the exclusive right to reproduce them, put them on the web, and use them in any capacity you want. You may have to pay extra to buy the rights from the photographer, but the photos will be yours, and you won't be breaking any laws or taking away your photographer's ability to make a living.

Your Profile URL and Website Address

You'll want to specify a unique address for your MySpace profile. It will be http://www.myspace.com/*insert one-of-a-kind name here*. Assuming you've already come up with a band name, you could simply insert that at the end. If you're a soloist, you could use your first and last name. A popular tactic to differentiate personal profiles from music profiles is to use the word "music" at the end. For example, Joe Performer's music MySpace page could be http://www.myspace.com/joeperformermusic. Here are a few more ways to craft a URL:

- Add the word "online" or "official" after your name to differentiate you from fake and fan profiles.

- Mirror your official website URL. For example, artist Pink's website is www.pinkspage.com, and her MySpace page is www.myspace.com/pinkspage.

- Should you find yourself competing with unofficial profiles for your band, you could also use "thereal" before your name.

Remember that the MySpace address you pick is yours forever and can't be changed, so make sure you can live with it before you commit.

When you sign up, you will also have an opportunity to add your main website address (www.yourdomainname.com) as a link within your profile. If you don't have a main website, don't worry. You can always plop that into your profile later when you get one.

Upcoming Shows and Appearances

Artists have a special place to add their touring and gig details (see Figure 6.5). Gather this info before you sign up so it will be a snap to add it all in. At the minimum, you'll need to list the show date and time, the name of the venue, the city/state, and the description (such as "CD release party"). It's not imperative, but if you've got more details, such as cost and a full address, so much the better.

Upcoming Shows			(view all)
Jul 6 2007	8:00P	**Stucky's Bar and Grill**	Braverman
Aug 15 2007	9:00P	**MacInerney's**	Clermont, Delaware

Figure 6.5
Your gig list will look like this on a default music profile.

Band Members and Collaborators

You'll want to list the names of all your band members. A list of notable collaborators also is a great idea, especially for soloists. But you can list them if you're in a band too. Is there a Bernie Taupin to your Elton John? Give props to those who help make your music what it is. This includes producers, songwriters, arrangers, DJs, side musicians, other vocalists, lyricists, and choreographers.

Pay special attention to names of note. Gather those names in a text file so you can just plug them in below your band members' names. There isn't a special field for collaborators, so you'll just have to put in a couple of paragraph returns after your list of band members, and then note the title "Collaborators," as shown in Figure 6.6. See Chapter 8, "Customizing Your Page," for more information on customizing your profile using basic HTML.

Band Members	Emeline Jones (vocals), Erving Jones (Piano), Jonnie Williams (bass) Collaborators: Sly Winkert (charts) April Tu (string arrangements) Chad Millar (producer)

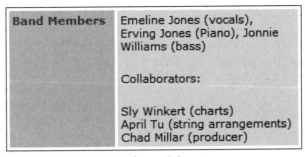

Figure 6.6
Be sure to note your band members and collaborators.

Your Posse

Your profile will also have room to note whether you're signed to a record label and the label name. You can say "unsigned" if you are. You may have a manager, a distributor, a publicist, a booking agent, or another member of your team who assists you in your career. List those who are relevant below your bio, especially the aforementioned ones. Your manager may prefer that all business queries be directed to her, and she may want you to note her email address just for that purpose (see Figure 6.7).

> Please direct all booking and publicity queries to Vincent Management at 555-555-0000, or email VincentManagement@anyemail05.com

Figure 6.7
Listing your manager's phone number and email address is a suitable way to redirect business queries.

Profile Headline

Your headline is the short snippet or quote that appears next to your main photo on your profile. Many acts don't utilize this field, but they're missing out on another opportunity to market themselves. You don't have to quote Shakespeare or anything, but use that little slice of real estate to say something about yourself. Here are some headline ideas:

- A phrase you're known for.

- A quote from a positive review ("Angelic vocals and powerful songs—Littleton Ledger").

- A snippet from your lyrics.

- A mention of an award ("Voted Best New Jazz Artist by the *Sun Times*").

- "*[Album title]* now available on iTunes!"

- "*[Album title]* in stores 2-5-08" or "… in stores now."

- "CD release party in Miami May 1st!"

- "Touring Summer 2008."

- "The Official *[Your Name]* MySpace Profile."

- A boiled-down mission statement for your organization and company: "Supporting independent artist tours nationwide."

Just say no to desperate pleas for friend adds and album sales (as shown in Figure 6.8). No one likes someone who tries too hard.

Figure 6.8
A headline like this screams, "Lame!" Tout your new album release, gig, or lyrics, or plug in a personal quip instead.

Genres, Influences, and Who You Sound Like

It's frustrating as an artist to feel as if you have to fit into a box. But this is marketing, and if you want electronic dance music fiends, classical music aficionados, or jazz hipsters to be able to find you, you'll have to figure out which categories you belong in.

You can choose up to three genres to help users locate your music. MySpace offers dozens of options, but it's always possible that you are so unique you won't find your particular niche. If that happens, you'll just have to think like a music consumer and determine which genres make the most sense. And you do have three options, so you can cross-reference.

Let's say you are a classical crossover vocalist who also sings jazz standards. This would be along the lines of Josh Groban, Linda Eder, Sarah Brightman, or Il Divo, all considered adult contemporary artists as well. There isn't a category for that or for classical crossover, so you might choose "Classical-Opera and Vocal, Pop, and Jazz" as your three categories instead. Or if you're heavily into musical theatre favorites, perhaps "Classical-Opera and Vocal/Pop/Showtunes" would be more up your alley. Users search by categories when they're looking for new music in their favorite genres, and you want them to find you.

Before you sign up, brainstorm the types of genres that might fit you. To preview the list of available MySpace genres, go to MySpace.com, click on Music, then choose Search in the MySpace Music navigation bar. Here you'll find a drop-down list of genres from which to choose, and you can even narrow your search by local proximity (see Figure 6.9).

Figure 6.9
Get a preview of genres by looking under Advanced Search in the Music section.

Likening Yourself to Others

Using the Influences and Sounds Like fields tends to generate a bit of debate among the MySpace music community (see Figures 6.10 and 6.11). Some people love listing their influences because they know it help builds an instant rapport with someone who loves the same artists they do. Those of you who dig Stevie Wonder and Al Green will instantly bond with an artist who is influenced by the same artists. You automatically have that in common and you can see where the artist is coming from.

Influences	Diana Krall, Ella Fitzgerald, Dean Martin, Frank Sinatra, Raul Midon, Eva Cassidy, Julie London, Keely Smith

Figure 6.10
A list of influences in the default profile.

Influences	John Coltrane, Joni Mitchell, Mercedes Sosa, Hermeto Pascual, James Taylor, Donny Hathaway, George Benson, Paco De Lucia, Pete Minger, Stevie Wonder, Steely Dan, Willie Nelson, India.Arie, D'Angelo, Miles Davis, Frank Zappa... tbc
Sounds Like	I like Eclectic Soul...
Record Label	Manhattan Records
Type of Label	Major

Figure 6.11
Artist Raul Midón presents a comprehensive list of his influences.

There are artists who, for whatever reason, think telling people about their influences pigeonholes them. But remember that your influences don't necessarily sound anything like you. Alanis Morissette grew up idolizing Olivia Newton-John, and some sources say she credits ONJ for inspiring her to become a singer. However, Alanis doesn't sound anything like Olivia, and being influenced by her didn't make her a carbon copy. Fans understand this and see that your influences begin to paint a picture of what you like and whose talent is inspiring to you.

To list or not to list whom you sound like can be a contentious topic indeed. Many artists will indignantly declare, "I sound like myself!" (See Figure 6.12.) The very idea of someone likening them to anyone else is insulting. Well, maybe you don't sound like anyone else, and that's fine. But perhaps you are in a similar genre as other favorites who are better known than yourself (see Figures 6.13 and 6.14). It's okay to put that you sound like "a bluesier Sarah McLachlan" or "Michael Bublé with a country twist." Make it more creative if you're similar but you bring your own attributes to the mix.

Figure 6.12
Artist Jay-Z scoffs at the idea that he sounds like anyone but himself.

Sounds Like	Kristen Chenoweth, Linda Eder, Renee Fleming, Maria Callas

Figure 6.13
One would guess from this Sounds Like list that this artist is a classical or musical theatre–type vocalist. If you love these types of artists, you may be more apt to give this person a listen.

Paul Oakenfold: General Info

Member Since	9/9/2005
Band Website	pauloakenfold.com
Band Members	Paul Oakenfold w/various guest artists on vocals
Influences	
Sounds Like	Fatboy Slim, The Crystal Method, Paul Van Dyk, Pete Tong, DJ Dan, John Digweed, Tiesto, The Prodigy, Delerium
Record Label	Maverick
Type of Label	Major

Figure 6.14
Electronica guru Paul Oakenfold lists his contemporaries as artists who make similar music to his. If you like electronica but have never heard Paul's music, you still get an idea of his sensibilities.

When you explore profiles of major-label artists and unsigned artists alike, you'll notice that some ignore the Influences and Sounds Like fields, while others gamely fill them in. There's no set rule. You'll have to decide for yourself.

If you're hesitant to list anything in the Influences or Sounds Like field, you can still use the fields for other information, as shown in Figure 6.15.

| Sounds Like | Text PANIC to ▮▮▮▮ for official ringtones and to ▮▮▮▮ to join the mobile list.

Works with most handsets on participating carriers. Standard text messaging rates may apply. See your contract for details.

Click ▮▮▮▮ to check out our UK Myspace Profile. |

Figure 6.15
Panic! At the Disco opted to list mobile marketing info in their Influences field instead.

Search Keywords

You may be asking why you would want to list influences and similar artists. The answer is to help Internet search engines better categorize you through the use of keywords, which are words one is likely to use to search for your type of music or product.

Once you determine your "influences" and "sounds like" artists, you'll want to list them elsewhere in your profile (such as in your bio), as well as in their designated fields. Internet search engines crawl through MySpace too, categorizing artists' and musicians' profiles like they do any other type of webpage. They notice repetition of phrases and words, and this helps increase your rankings in search results. This is true for webpages, profiles, and even online press releases. For instance, if you mention Pantera in your Influences and Sounds Like fields and once again in your bio, when users search for "Pantera" in their favorite search engine, you hopefully will be among the search results. By affiliating yourself with artists in a similar vein, you will be more likely to attract new fans who are searching by that keyword (in this case, "Pantera").

Keywords do not only have to be other artists' names. Think carefully about words you might use to describe your music. In addition to influences and sounds like, think about genres and buzzwords for your music. What words might a searcher use to find you on the web? Are you into electronic dance music, or "EDM?" Are you following in the footsteps of techno founder "Derrick Mays"? Perhaps "screamo," "trip hop," or "booty music" is your thing. Are you collaborating with someone well known in his or her field?

Let's say you're a music organization or company. What keywords might someone type into a search engine to find companies like yours? Examples might be "booking agency," "tour support," "promote independent music," "music licensing consultant," or "entertainment law."

Think of what the key search phrases are that others might use to find an artist or company like yours, and pepper your profile with them. A good rule of thumb is three to four phrases, used two to three times.

natural use; otherwise, your profile's copy will feel stilted
d. The Influences, Sounds Like, Bio, and Band Members
logical places for keyword mentions.

and "About Me" Blurb

've covered a bit about keywords, let's move on to what
is usually the biggest block of text in an artist profile... the bio.

Some bios are magazine-style, such as that of former *American Idol*
finalist Chris Daughtry (www.daughtryofficial.com), and read like they
were lifted out of the pages of *Rolling Stone*. Most artists' bios are
more straightforward and to the point, like Fergie's (www.myspace.com/
fergie). Still other artists don't have bios at all—they're so popular they
don't need an introduction.

Writing about oneself (and doing it well) can seem like an impossible
task. But you don't need to be a professional writer to say honestly
who you are and what you're about. There's no one way to write a bio,
no matter what all the websites on the topic say. There are professional
writers who will do the job for you, usually for a fee of $150 or less.
But if you're going it alone, take heed of these tips to build a better bio:

- Write about yourself in the third person. So instead of "I've just
  finished touring with the punk rock band Jonesy," use your name
  or the appropriate pronoun, such as "Betty Bassist recently finished
  touring with the punk rock band Jonesy." Treat it as if you were
  writing about someone else.

- The easiest way to start a bio is with where you're from and, if it
  has influenced your artistry, your ethnic heritage. If you're stuck,
  start this way.

- Steer clear of hyperbole such as "the best artist ever," "the greatest
  jazz trumpeter of the twenty-first century," and "a better guitarist
  than Jimi Hendrix." All that hype is quite a load to back up, and
  few, if any, can do it.

- Clichés such as "a diamond in the rough," "a musical force of
  nature," and other similar contrivances are meaningless as well.

- Include quotes from yourself or band members about your music, your influences, how you came up, your struggle, and so on. This personalizes the bio.

- If you've won a lot of awards and recognition, resist the temptation to list them all. Pick four or five biggies and mention those.

- Talk about what makes you...well, you. What artists and life experiences influence your artistry?

- Discuss what kind of music you make, what themes you prefer to explore, and what your aesthetic sensibilities are.

- Keep your political preferences out of the bio. Remember that half your audience may well belong to the other party.

- Refrain from badmouthing other artists and rivals. It only makes you look petty.

- It's not necessary to list every place you ever went to school and every place you played. It *is* okay to note if you went to a prestigious high school or performing arts program, and where you went to college. Only mention venues and places you've played that carry weight. Saying you've sung at the Met is a big deal.

- Namedrop carefully. Your bio is not the place to thank everyone you've ever worked with. But it is a place to recognize those influential collaborators who have contributed greatly to your sound, your career, and your latest album.

- Do discuss your latest project, album, tour, award, or achievement. Tell your audience about what you're up to.

- Don't just use your word processor's spell check feature! *Read* your bio many times for spelling and grammar errors (and have others do the same). There's no excuse for sloppy errors.

- Have friends and relatives with fresh eyes read and critique your bio. Pick only those who aren't afraid to be honest with you.

- Always remember that your bio tells a brief story of you—what makes you the artist that you are, how your band came together, and where you're headed. Three to seven paragraphs should be plenty to bring readers into your world.

The more bios you read, the better you will be at writing yours. So start surfing MySpace and your favorite artists' official websites for inspiration.

Streaming Songs and Your Built-In Music Player

The most wonderful thing about MySpace artist profiles is that your visitors can listen to your music without having to download a bunch of external applications. Before you sign up, decide which of your songs you want to stream (up to five), plus which graphics/pictures should accompany each. When a song plays, a photo/graphic appears in the player next to it. Ideally, each song should have a different photo, preferably of you or your band (as shown in Figure 6.16). The photo should be compelling, in focus, and interesting to look at, and it should help the listener identify with your song. See the "Your Photos" section earlier in this chapter for more tips on photos. Another option for those short on suitable photos or graphics is to use your album cover for all songs. You can even mock up an album cover just for this purpose.

After you've picked your songs, make sure they are converted to MP3 format. Do this with any CD ripper or other similar audio program. You probably already have a free program on your computer. Apple's iTunes player and RealNetworks' Rhapsody (see Figure 6.17) or Real Player will convert CDs to MP3s.

The best songs are those that are excellent not only in songwriting and musicianship, but also in sound and production quality. Choose clips that have been mixed and mastered, are free of audio anomalies such as clicks and hisses, and have overall excellent sound quality. Avoid clips with muffled vocals. Also rethink putting extended songs that play automatically on your profile's streamer. Many listeners may find a 15-minute song or live cut that starts automatically and drones on and on to be a bit overbearing, and the download time can crash a browser. You can always cut it down to a more manageable size and encourage visitors to download it for a fee elsewhere on your page (explored in Chapter 8). Also, stay away from super-short snippets.

Figure 6.16
The music player at www.myspace.com/naziamusic
showcases a unique photo for each song.

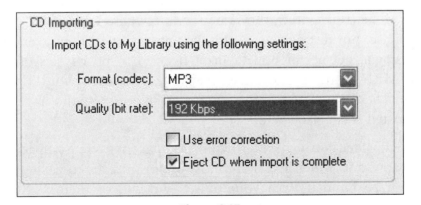

Figure 6.17
RealNetworks' RhapsodyPlayer 3.1 preferences. Choose MP3 as your file
type for importing and converting CDs.

That 20-second clip is not going to do it for most listeners—it's just not enough material. Instead, aim for standard song lengths, usually between two and five minutes.

You have the option of having the first song in the player load automatically, or the player can rotate through songs, loading a different one each time. Artists promoting a particular single, or those with a song they feel is a great "hook" to bring in repeat listeners, may prefer to designate the first song as the "opener."

You're not bound to these four songs and settings forever. You can change your initial song/graphics selections and settings at any time.

Remember that unless you have secured an on-demand streaming license (for listening only) or a digital download license (for downloading to desktop) from a music publisher or through the Harry Fox Agency, you may not upload cover songs. Doing so without proper compensation circumvents songwriters' and publishers' income stream and cheats them out of the right to make money from their works. Visit www.harryfox.com and look at digital licenses for information on how to secure the proper permissions to use another writer's songs.

Lyrics

Along with streaming audio, you can post lyrics for listeners to read. This is done from within the same module where you would upload your music. But just as you must have permission to use cover songs, so must you get permission (a print license) to post lyrics of cover songs. My best advice is to leave cover song lyrics off of your MySpace profile. There are plenty of infringers on the Internet who have probably posted them elsewhere.

But do consider putting lyrics to your original songs on MySpace. This is a situation in which lyrics are most important, because the listener may not be familiar with your music, writing, or themes. Reading lyrics often ties the listener to you in an emotional way and makes for a more profound experience.

To properly post lyrics, you must also include songwriter, copyright, and performing rights organization (PRO) information. An example of how this might be structured is:

[Song Title]

Written by [Songwriter(s) Names]

Copyright [year written] / [Publishing Company Name] / [PRO]

So it would look like this:

Happy Times

Written by Jenny Williams and Stan Fielding

Copyright 2007 / Williams-Fielding Music / ASCAP

This lets everyone know who owns the song, when it was written, and whom they can contact should they wish to perform the song publicly.

Your Style Scheme

You might think that coming up with a style scheme should be done first in one's plan. I like to put it at the end of the process because by now you will have already thought a lot about all the things you want to populate your profile, who your audience is, and what they will respond to. The look of your profile, the design and backgrounds, the colors you employ, the photos and music you post, and the bio you write must all be congruent with who you are as an artist. Here are some fantastic examples of profiles that jive with the artist and complement the marketing message of that singer or band:

- Unearth: www.myspace.com/unearth. Dark, hard-driving metal.

- Colbie Caillat: www.myspace.com/colbiecaillat. Fresh, laidback, acoustic singer-songwriter.

- Cary Brothers: www.myspace.com/carybrothers. Sincere, melodic alternative rock.

- Crossbreed: www.myspace.com/crossbreed. Grinding, screaming, industrial.

- Kari Jobe: www.myspace.com/karijobemusic. Inspirational, contemporary Christian.

These are just a few examples of profiles that fit perfectly with the artist and their target audience. Take a look at the friends each artist has accumulated. You'll notice that by and large even the friends fit in with the theme of the profile. People don't want to be friends with artists whose music they find off-putting or uninteresting. At the time of this writing, the artists mentioned have tailored the look and tone of their profile perfectly to their music *and* the people they want to listen to it.

Your profile should also be tied in with your latest album, and you can take color cues and visuals from the album artwork. However, unless you totally change the kind of music you're making, the profile will still clearly convey who you are no matter which album you're promoting. Think of the other artists to whom your target market likely listens. How do those artists present themselves? Are their profiles dark and brooding? Fierce and scary-looking? Urban and edgy? Pink and flowery?

In Chapter 5 we explored how to identify your potential audience. Now is the time to look back at those conclusions and ask yourself what your music says and to whom it speaks. Think about which colors are suited to your music. What would be completely inappropriate for your profile? Start to have some general ideas of what you like and don't like. Again, the more profiles you look at, the more familiar you will become with the possibilities that exist.

Well, it's time to dive in! Next, we will sign up for our MySpace account....

7 Signing Up and MySpace Profile Basics

Once you've got all your information in order and ready to go, signing up and uploading to the basic profile is a pretty easy affair. Should you get stuck, here is a nuts-and-bolts guide to walk you through it. You'll have your very own profile up and running in no time!

Let's get started on your artist account, also known as a band profile. Mosey on over to MySpace.com, and near the top of the page you'll see the medium-blue navigation bar (Home | Browse | Search | ... and so on). Within this navigation bar is a link to Music, which will transport you to the area where all the musical artists on MySpace live. The MySpace Music section has another submenu in dark red, and the last link is Artist Signup. Click on this link to begin the process of creating your music profile (see Figure 7.1).

Figure 7.1
Be sure to choose Artist Signup in the Music section to create your artist profile.

It's very important that you use only the Artist Signup link, because regular registration using the Sign Up! button on the homepage will not create a music profile for you. Instead, you'll get a regular profile with no music options. And as a musical artist, you definitely will not want that to happen.

Step 1: Sign Up

The first page in the artist signup, shown in Figure 7.2, is similar to the regular, comedian, and filmmaker signup pages. Here you will enter info into a few initial fields, such as which email address you'll use for your profile, a password, your band name (or your stage name if you're a soloist), your first choice of genre, and your location. You will also be asked to agree to the Privacy Policy and Terms of Use. I recommend that everyone read and understand these agreements before signing up. For additional information on these, see Chapter 17, "Managing MySpace."

Figure 7.2
The first part of the sign-up process asks for a few initial account details.

Step 2: Provide Basic Info

The next page will ask you to specify your MySpace URL of choice and a few other details (see Figure 7.3). This MySpace URL is the web address you can give out to people so they can visit your MySpace page.

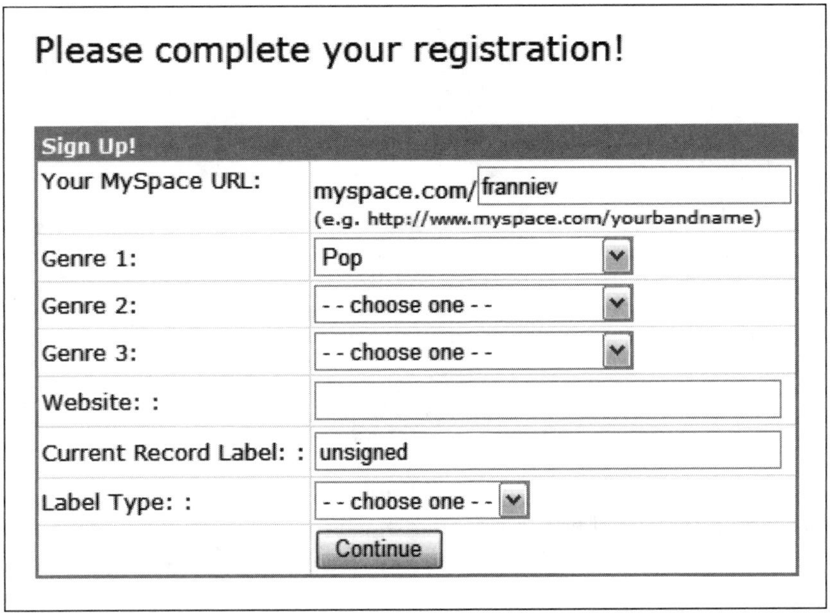

Figure 7.3
Fill out your basic info to help classify you in the MySpace system, and fill in some initial text fields.

Now you'll pick up to two more genres to classify your music. You'll also enter the address of your main artist website (if you have one). The last two fields relate to your record label. If you are signed, list the name of the company. If not, simply put None. Under Label Type, you can choose Major, Indie, or Unsigned. There's no shame in putting Unsigned. It lets labels know you are available (see Figure 7.4).

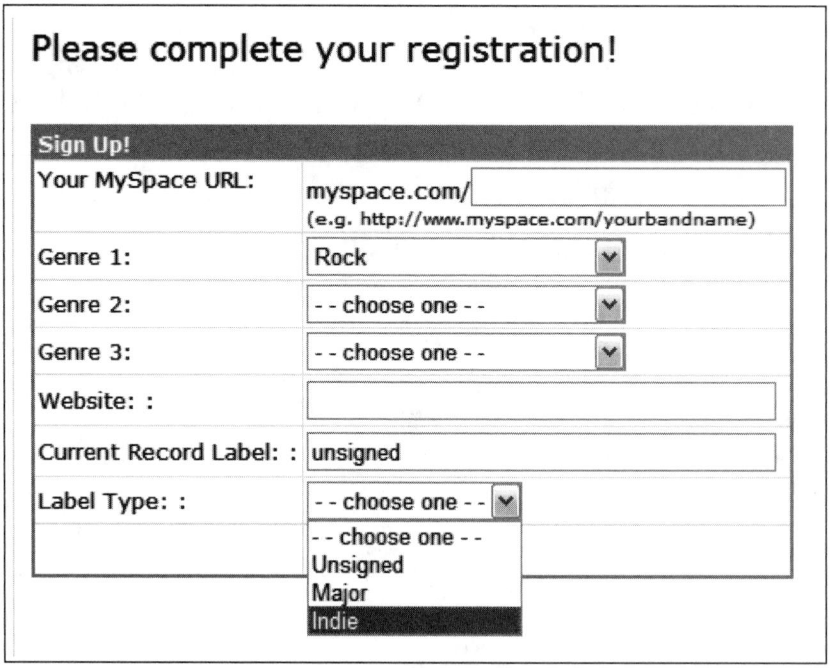

Figure 7.4
Artists choose their label type, such as Indie, which lets visitors know their status.
Should you be without a record label, choose Unsigned.

Step 3: Add Profile Photos

Now it's time to upload those photos you've prepared, as shown in Figure 7.5. Make sure your photos are in GIF or JPG format and are no more than 600K each. Don't worry too much about the physical dimensions of the photos because they'll be resized to fit properly into a standard web browser anyway.

See the Browse button? Click here to find your first photo on your hard drive. Choose it and submit it for uploading. Continue this process one by one until you have chosen all the photos you want to upload at this time. You can always go back later and add more or delete some. You should upload at least one photo. Once your photos are uploaded, make sure you have chosen the one you want to be your default picture. This is the photo or graphic that appears to the outside world on your profile and in search results. It's that first impression, so choose wisely.

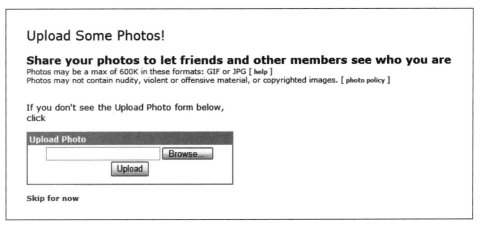

Figure 7.5
Upload your photos by choosing them from your hard drive.

Additionally, you can create captions for each photo by filling in the caption field. It's not necessary, but it's a nice, personal touch.

Step 4: Round Up Your Friends

The next stage gives you the option to paste in the email addresses of your real-life friends (or your band's mailing list), plus a short note to invite them to check out your profile (as shown in Figure 7.6). I recommended skipping this step for now. It's better if you invite people once your profile looks the way you want it to; at this stage, you still have a ways to go before you get all the information in there, get the layout customized, and so on. Once your profile is ready to reveal to the world, you can go back to your home control panel and invite people to view it.

Invite Friends to Your Space!

Now start **adding your friends** to your space
by inviting them to join a great way to meet interesting new people!

Invite Your Friends!	
Use this email form to invite your friends **Just enter each friend's email, separated by commas:**	
Subject:	Crazee Pug invites you to MySpace
From:	
To:	
	(separate multiple emails with a comma)
Optional Body:	
Body:	Crazee Pug is a member of MySpace and is inviting you to join. Crazee Pug Says: __YourMessageWillAppearHere__
	Invite
	Skip for now

Figure 7.6
Although the system prompts you to invite your friends to view your profile, it's best
to skip this step and invite friends later, when your profile is completely filled in.

Step 5: Add Your Songs

This section will give you the opportunity to upload up to four of your
songs. First, click on the Manage Songs link, as shown in Figure 7.7.
Then, choose your profile's settings for your player by checking the
appropriate boxes (as shown in Figure 7.8). Always allow users to add
your music to *their* profiles. It's free advertising for you. (See Chapter
11, "Profile Songs and Your Music Player," for more information.)

Start Adding Songs to Your Profile

Visit the **manage songs** page to upload your music.

Skip for now

Figure 7.7
Manage your songs in this next step.

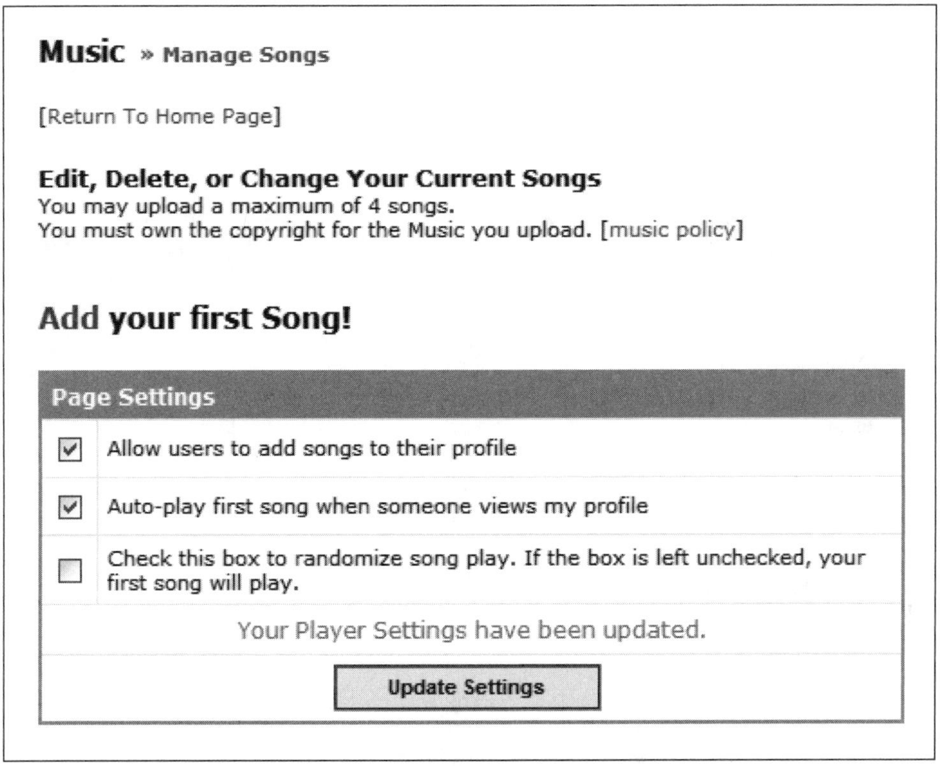

Music » Manage Songs

[Return To Home Page]

Edit, Delete, or Change Your Current Songs
You may upload a maximum of 4 songs.
You must own the copyright for the Music you upload. [music policy]

Add your first Song!

Page Settings	
☑	Allow users to add songs to their profile
☑	Auto-play first song when someone views my profile
☐	Check this box to randomize song play. If the box is left unchecked, your first song will play.
	Your Player Settings have been updated.
	Update Settings

Figure 7.8
Choose how your player will behave when visitors click on your profile.

You will also have to choose how visitors will hear your music—the first song in your player will automatically start, or you can choose to randomize it. Choose to auto-start your first song to play when you are promoting a particular single. Otherwise, let the songs play randomly.

Now, add your song's information (as shown in Figure 7.9). Enter the title, album name/year, and record label that released the song. There is a field to enter the lyrics as well. We discussed in the last chapter that you should only list lyrics for your original songs, plus author/publisher, copyright, and performing rights organization information. Lyrics are optional, of course, but users often appreciate being able to read what you're singing so they can better understand the context and theme of your music.

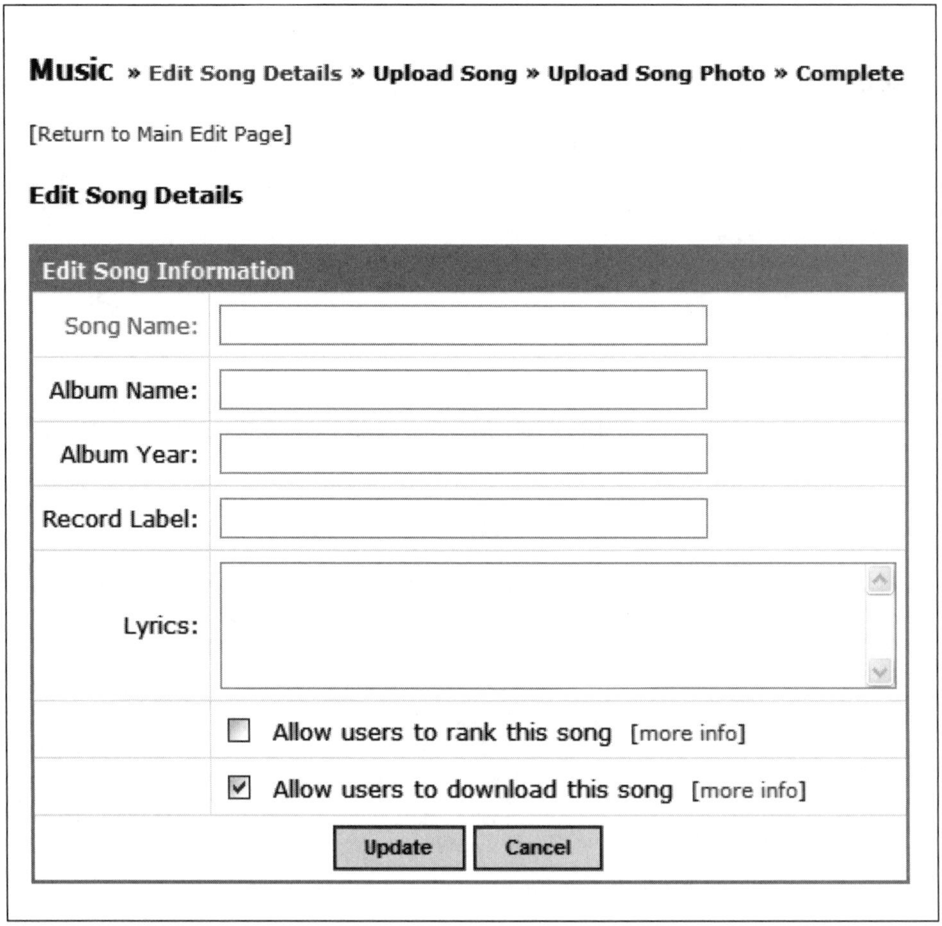

Music » Edit Song Details » **Upload Song** » **Upload Song Photo** » **Complete**

[Return to Main Edit Page]

Edit Song Details

Edit Song Information	
Song Name:	
Album Name:	
Album Year:	
Record Label:	
Lyrics:	
	☐ Allow users to rank this song [more info]
	☑ Allow users to download this song [more info]
	Update Cancel

Figure 7.9
Add the info about your song and choose whether users can rank and download it.

The last two fields are for ranking and downloading. Users can rank your song and comment if you choose to let them. (The details of this action are shown in Figure 7.10.) Many artists are afraid to allow users to rank their songs, though, fearing they might encounter negativity. But use this tool to your advantage by encouraging users to rank and comment on your songs. Not only is it useful for marketing and promotion because it gives you a concrete reason and purpose to ask fans to visit your page and listen to your song, but it also gives you important feedback. Use this feedback to critically analyze your music and make necessary adjustments. If you have people commenting that they can't understand what you're singing either because your vocals are muffled or because you're mumbling, you know what you need to fix.

Figure 7.10
MySpace's tidbits on ranking.

Lastly, you can choose to allow people to download your song for free. (The details of this are shown in Figure 7.11.) I don't recommend doing this directly on your MySpace player. The free downloads on MySpace don't allow you to collect any information on the user.

If you're going to give away your music for free, at least get the down-loader's information so you can use it to market more of your music to that person later. To solve this issue, direct visitors over to your main webpage to get them to give you their names and email info to get that free download.

Figure 7.11
MySpace's details on downloading.

The only time a free download on MySpace is a good idea, in my opin-ion, is if you've uploaded an interview or a special message to fans. You can market it as a fun freebie to get people to your profile, and then encourage them to pass the word on to their friends.

Once you've filled out the song info, you will upload your MP3 in the same fashion as you upload a photo (see Figure 7.12). Choose the MP3 file from your hard drive and submit it to the MySpace server for upload. The system will show you the progress (see Figure 7.13).

Lastly, upload the image that you want to associate with your song, as shown in Figure 7.14. An image will load in your profile player for each song. Never leave this blank. If you can't come up with distinct and separate images for each song, at least upload your album cover or a photo of yourself or your band.

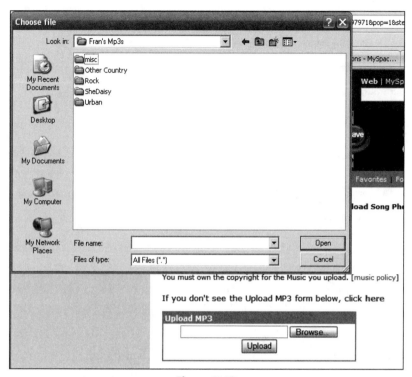

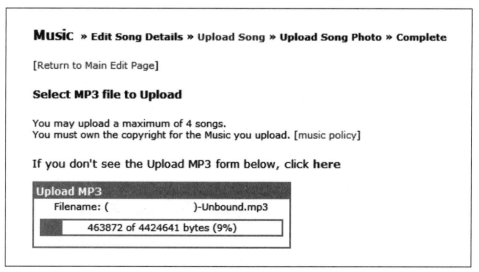

Figure 7.12
Uploading songs is a lot like uploading photos.

Figure 7.13
Your song's uploading progress will display on your browser.

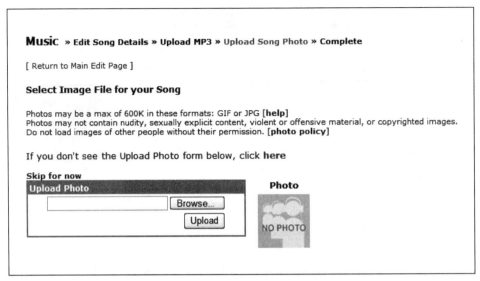

Figure 7.14
Always upload a photo to display with your song.

Your first song is now uploaded and will be ready within 24 hours (see Figure 7.15). Continue to click Add Songs until you have uploaded as many songs (up to four) as you want fans to hear.

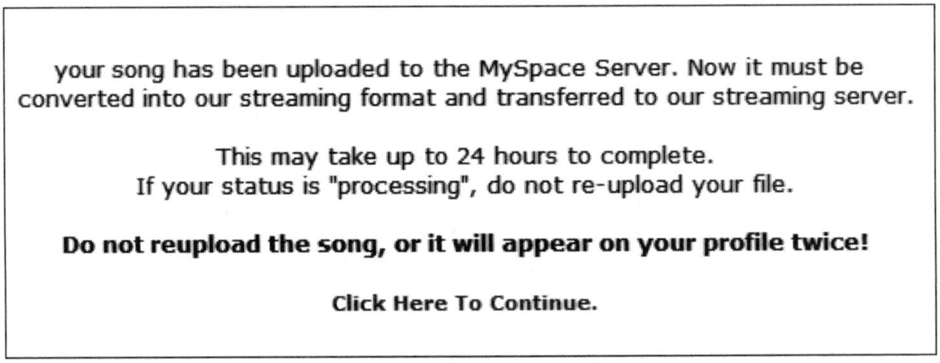

your song has been uploaded to the MySpace Server. Now it must be converted into our streaming format and transferred to our streaming server.

This may take up to 24 hours to complete.
If your status is "processing", do not re-upload your file.

Do not reupload the song, or it will appear on your profile twice!

Click Here To Continue.

Figure 7.15
Your song will be available on your profile within 24 hours.

Step 6: Populate the Profile

After this initial setup process, you will be directed to your account's control panel. From here, you will continue editing and populating your profile.

Click on Edit Profile to the right of your default account picture. You'll notice that the Edit Profile link is among many other links next to your photo that will help you edit your profile and add or delete information (see Figure 7.16).

Figure 7.16
Get familiar with the editing/managing links next to your thumbnail.

In the Edit Profile screen, you'll notice five tabs spanning the top. Click each tab to view the areas to edit.

- **Upcoming Shows.** On this tab, you will enter all the information on your upcoming shows, including date, time, location, admission, and a brief description (see Figure 7.17).

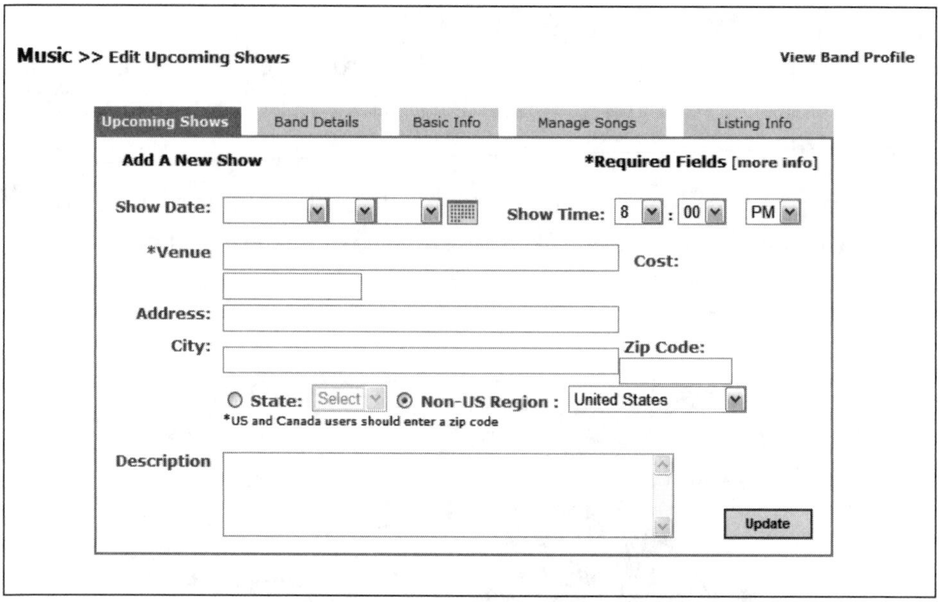

Figure 7.17
Entering your shows is simple and straightforward.

■ **Band Details.** You will get a lot of use out of this tab (see Figure 7.18). Band Details houses the parts of your profile that have the most text. These fields are also where you will plug in code to customize your layout. Fields include Headline, Bio, Members, Influences, Sounds Like, Website, Record Label, and Label Type. You'll notice that Website, Record Label, and Label Type are already filled out because you entered these fields when you started the signup process. In Chapter 6, you crafted a headline and a bio, as well as info on your members, influences, and who you sound like. Now it's time to plug that information into the appropriate fields.

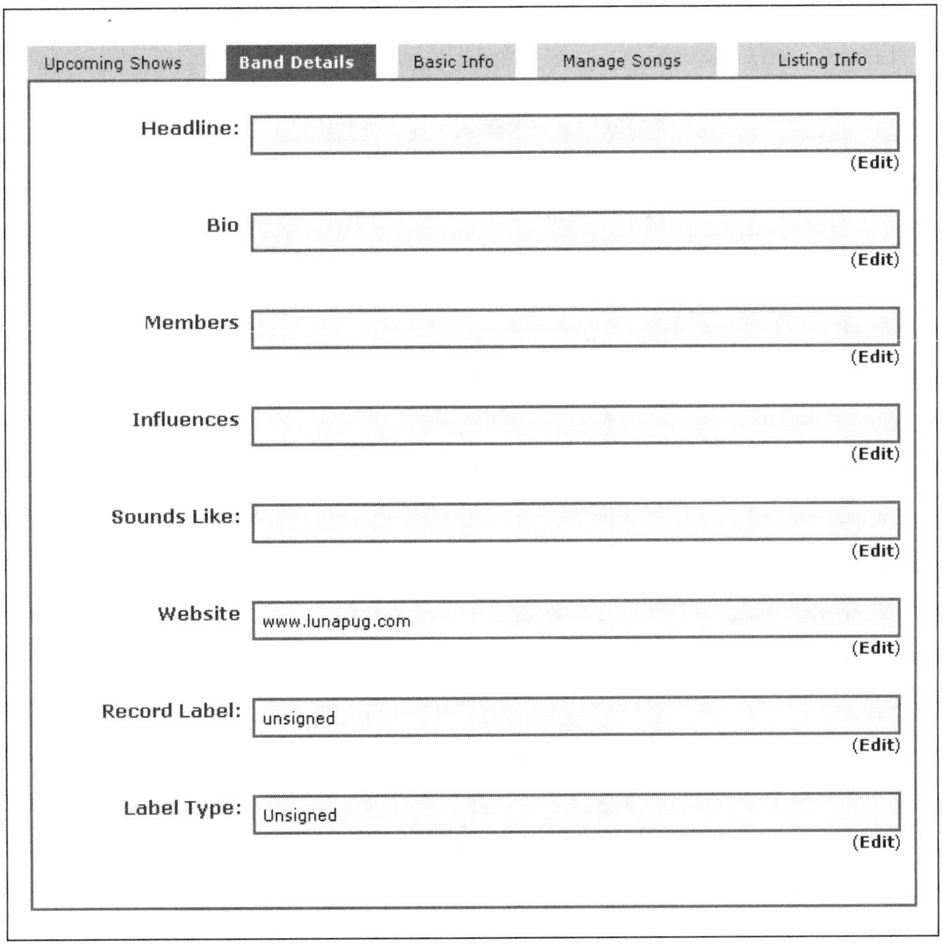

Upcoming Shows	Band Details	Basic Info	Manage Songs	Listing Info

Headline: _____ (Edit)

Bio _____ (Edit)

Members _____ (Edit)

Influences _____ (Edit)

Sounds Like: _____ (Edit)

Website www.lunapug.com (Edit)

Record Label: unsigned (Edit)

Label Type: Unsigned (Edit)

Figure 7.18
Your Band Details section features several text fields.

- **Basic Info.** Here is where you can change the name of your band and edit your location (see Figure 7.19). You can list your actual city and state, or type in another location of your choice. For instance, you may not want to enter "Sherman Oaks, California." Instead you might choose to type in "Southern Cali."

Edit Profile>>View Basic Info   **View My Profile**

| Upcoming Shows | Band Details | Basic Info | Manage Songs | Listing Info |

Band Name: Frannie V (HTML Not Allowed)

Country: United States

State/Region: -- Please select -- Or

City:

Zip/Postal Code:

Submit

Figure 7.19
On the Basic Info tab, you can customize your location.

■ **Manage Songs.** Click on this section to add and delete songs from your profile's player (see Figure 7.20).

Figure 7.20
Your Manage Songs section, which you used earlier to upload your music, will also show you what songs are in the queue.

■ **Listing Info.** Go here to tweak your genre selections (Figure 7.21).

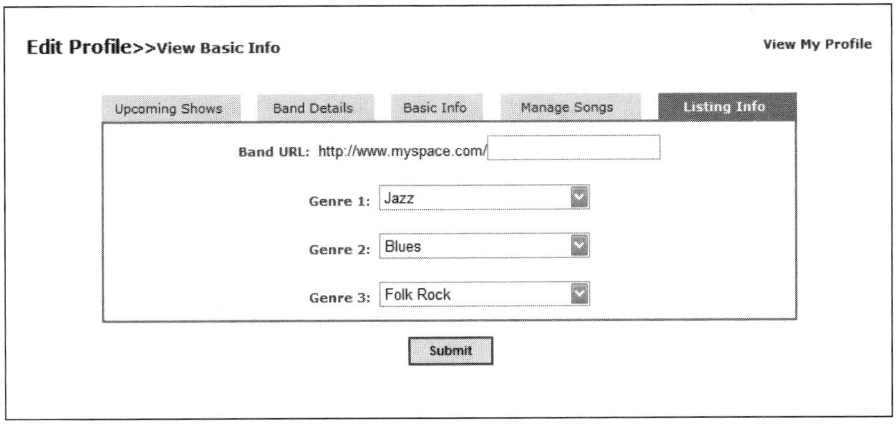

Figure 7.21
The Listing Info lets you change your genre selections.

You have just completed your initial profile! Take a preview of your profile and survey your good work. It might not be exciting to look at yet, but move on to Chapter 8, "Customizing Your Page," for info on how to make your profile unique.

 8 Customizing Your Page

Your profile has been created, and maybe you've even gone ahead and uploaded some music, written a bio, and uploaded some photos. Still, it might look a bit boring. The default MySpace page, while clean-looking, is pretty dry (see Figure 8.1). No worries, though, because now you're going to learn how to customize your page and really make it your own!

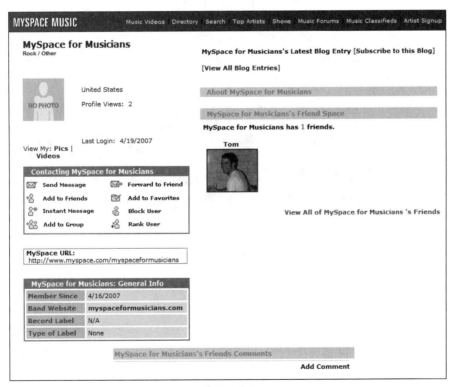

Figure 8.1
The default MySpace page, while very clean-looking, doesn't have a lot of personality.

Customizing a MySpace page, also called "pimping" it out or "tweaking" it, can go from the simple (embedding a few pictures and bolding some text), all the way to the very complicated (creating overlays that completely alter the MySpace layout and navigation until it's unrecognizable). All of these tweaks involve using some type of code, such as HTML. So, we'll start easy and work our way up.

Much of the code you'll need can be found on the Internet and you can just copy and paste it into your profile. Some code is not very hard to manipulate, and you can just write it up yourself. Still, there are other types of design alterations, such as div overlays, which are very tricky and best handled by professionals or those proficient in HTML code.

Either way, there are a few things to keep in mind while pimping your page. The first is that you must never cover up the banner ads that appear on the top of the MySpace pages (see Figure 8.2). That's how MySpace makes their money (since none of us is paying for the profiles we create). And as you can imagine, people get pretty ornery when you start messing with their bread and butter. Tampering with ads will get you kicked off the service.

Figure 8.2
The advertisement at the top of this graphic is a banner ad from a MySpace advertiser.

Second, you should never delete or alter MySpace's functional links, such as the top-of-page navigation links that take you home, allow you to browse, or allow you to click through the MySpace Music section (see Figure 8.3). This also includes the links at the bottom of the page (About, FAQ, and so on; see Figure 8.4). You will see layouts that have removed them, which often irritates fans who can't find the links they need. Leave the links alone and design around them. They're not that big of a design constriction.

Figure 8.3
These are the top navigation links. They should remain intact.

About | FAQ | Terms | Privacy | Safety Tips | Contact MySpace | Promote! | Advertise | MySpace International

Figure 8.4
These bottom links also should not be covered up or removed.

Lastly, while this chapter will introduce you to the basics of customization, it can't cover every possible tweak that one can apply to a profile. That alone would take a whole book, and even then I don't think we'd get them all. Every day, programmers around the world are coming up with new toys we can use to spice up our profiles, from custom code and manipulations to Flash animation, sound, and video tools, and everything in between. So while you'll get a primer here, the purpose is not to turn you into a master programmer. I encourage you to browse the web for more bells and whistles that we haven't covered. Visit Appendix B for lots of sites you can try out, visit the discussion forum on MySpace (click on Forums > MySpace > Customizing), or do your own web searches on "myspace tweaks," "myspace layouts," and the like.

Finding the Friend ID

Before we get to all the tweaking, you have to know how to find your friend ID and that of others. There are some cool things you can do with your profile that require you to know what a friend ID is and where to locate it.

The friend ID is your special number that MySpace assigns you when you create an account. Everyone has one, whether he or she is a regular user, a band, a comedian, or a filmmaker. It's how the system identifies you. Here's how you find it:

1. Click on a profile. Start with your own for this exercise.

2. Look at the address bar at the top of your browser. Notice the URL will have the word "friendid=" and then a bunch of numbers after it. The numbers immediately after this equals sign and before any other characters represent your friend ID (see Figure 8.5). The friend ID is usually at the very end of the address, but sometimes it might be embedded in the middle somewhere.

http://profile.myspace.com/index.cfm?fuseaction=user.viewprofile&friendID=652875

Figure 8.5
In this example, this user's friend ID is 652875.

To make sure we're all on the same page, let's look for Tom's friend ID. He's your first friend, that lone guy sitting on your friends list when you signed up, as shown in Figure 8.6. If you deleted him, go to www.myspace.com/tom. Click on Tom's profile and look in your web browser's address bar. You should see that his friend ID is 6221 (see Figure 8.7).

Figure 8.6
This is Tom, your very first friend.

http://profile.myspace.com/index.cfm?fuseaction=user.viewprofile&friendid=6221

Figure 8.7
Tom's friend ID is 6221.

When a tweak calls for friend IDs, you'll know where to look!

A Few Basics

Let's start by adding a few basic items to your profile. We will do this using HTML, which stands for *HyperText Markup Language*. HTML is a type of computer language used to create webpages. This HTML code is like a set of directions to your web browser, which interprets and then displays a webpage accordingly. Most HTML uses the < and > symbols, which are located above your comma and period keys, respectively, to enclose its directions to the web browser. Let's touch on some of the basic HTML tags you might want to use on your profile.

First, you can modify the text to make it stand out more, and you can add line spaces to break up copy. Go into your account's home control panel and, next to your thumbnail picture, click on the Edit Profile link (see Figure 8.8). Then click on the Band Details tab. Under the Bio field, click Edit. Let's experiment by typing the following text into your profile's Bio field:

> Welcome to my profile! This is my first MySpace profile. In just mere moments I am gonna rock this layout. I'll be adding photos, video, and revamping my layout completely.

Click the Preview button, and you'll see that your entry is just plain text (see Figure 8.9).

Now we're going to alter it, so click Edit. Add the following <P> and <BR> tags (which I've capitalized and bolded here so they'll be more visible) to your text:

> Welcome to my profile! **<P>**This is my first MySpace profile. **
**In just mere moments I am gonna rock this layout. **
**I'll be adding photos, video, and revamping my layout completely.

Figure 8.8
The Edit Profile link appears beside your picture in your home control panel.

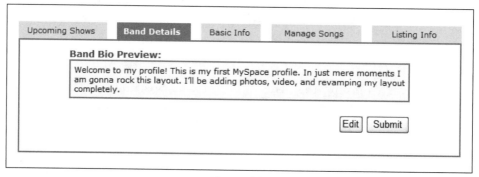

Figure 8.9
Your plain-text entry doesn't have any special formatting.

Click Preview to see how your text looks now (see Figure 8.10). The paragraph tag (<P>) added a line space, which is like hitting Enter twice in a word processor. The <BR> is a line break, which is the same as hitting return with the Shift key pressed in a word processing program. These tags do *not* require ending tags (</P> or </BR>). Although some editors and browsers add them in, they're not actually necessary.

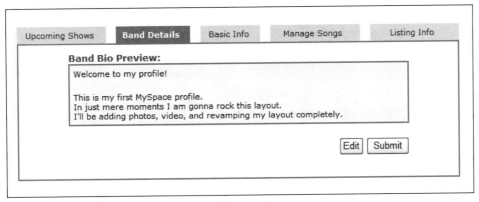

Figure 8.10
Now our text is broken up by paragraph and line breaks.

Click Edit again and add the following tags (again, capitalized and bolded here) to your text:

<H4>Welcome to my profile!</H4> <P>This is my first MySpace profile.
In just mere moments <B>I am gonna rock this layout. </B>
I'll be adding photos, video, <I>and</I> revamping my layout completely.

We just added a header format (<H4>) to the first sentence. You can apply header formats from <H1> to <H6>, with <H1> being the biggest text, and <H6> being the smallest. We also bolded part of the third sentence and italicized the word "and" in the last sentence. Notice that these tags only modify the text they enclose. Therefore, we need beginning and ending tags. Put these types of tags *around* the text you want to modify. The ending tag has a / in it, indicating to the web browser that this is where you want the modification to stop.

Click Preview to see the changes (see Figure 8.11).

Now go back to Edit and add the following bolded tags. We're not finished yet!

<CENTER><H4>Welcome to my profile!</H4></CENTER> <P> <CENTER>This is my first MySpace profile.
 In just mere moments <B>I am gonna rock this layout.</B>
 I'll be adding photos, video, <I>and</I> revamping my layout completely. </CENTER>

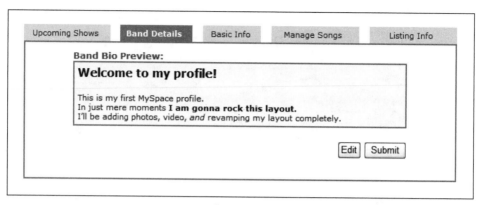

Figure 8.11
Our text is evolving to include variances in font style and size.

Now we've added <CENTER> tags so our text will be centered. Again, only the text between opening and ending <CENTER> tags will be affected. Here, we decided to center the entire passage. We had to put two sets of <CENTER> tags, however. One goes around the text before the paragraph tag (<P>). The second set goes around the rest of the text because it is only broken up by line breaks. When you use <P> tags and add a whole line space, it's wise to treat that portion separately and give it its very own alignment tags. When you preview your new HTML tweaks, they should look like Figure 8.12.

Figure 8.12
This time we took our passage and centered it.

Edit the text again, and this time we will add a hyperlink to the MySpace homepage. A hyperlink tag has beginning and ending tags also. We create a link by using the following formula:

> <A HREF="*INSERT WEB ADDRESS HERE*">Type the text you'd like to be highlighted and linked</A>

So now if we want to hyperlink the entire second sentence of our practice copy, it will look like this:

> <CENTER><H4>Welcome to my profile!</H4></CENTER> <P>
> <CENTER><A HREF="http://www.myspace.com">This is my first MySpace profile.</A>
 In just mere moments <B>I am gonna rock this layout.</B>
 I'll be adding photos, video, <I>and</I> revamping my layout completely. </CENTER>

Everything between <A HREF="....."> and </A> will appear as a clickable hyperlink (see Figure 8.13).

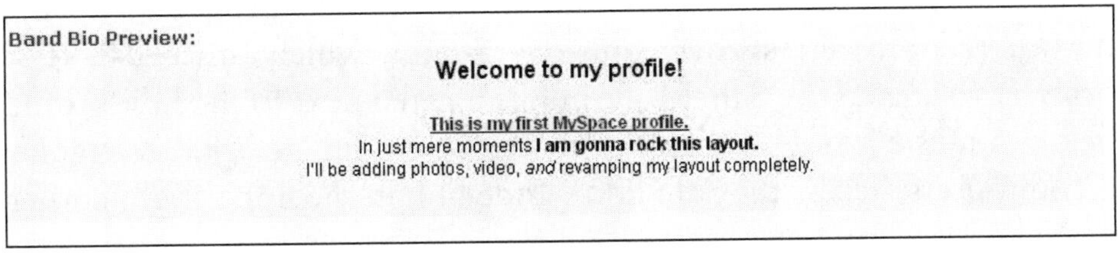

Figure 8.13
Now the second line is linked to the MySpace homepage.

I hate to make things more complicated than they should be, but because MySpace doesn't always interpret standard HTML tags and code the same way regular webpages do, you sometimes have to alter the code to fit this environment so links will work correctly. The hyperlink code as is would work in most other webpages, but in MySpace, we have to omit the quotation marks and instead make it:

> <A HREF=http://www.myspace.com>This is my first MySpace profile.</A>

Now the link will work correctly and will take you to the MySpace homepage when clicked. Go ahead and try it!

You can see that although standard HTML will have you enclose URLs in quotation marks, MySpace doesn't always interpret the HTML properly unless you omit the quotation marks. When adding code to your MySpace profile, be willing to experiment, and if something doesn't come out the way it's supposed to, check your code first for errors. Make sure you have any ending tags if needed. And if your code is correct, play with it a little bit, omit the quotation marks, or move it to a different section of your profile to see whether it will work. There are times you'll find that your code will not work at all. MySpace filters out certain tags and widgets it doesn't like, such as various types of buttons and check boxes, so not every type of code tweak will be successful.

Additionally, you can try editing your profile in safe mode, which will allow you to input HTML and text, but won't load any customizations while you're still in safe editing mode. This is particularly helpful when you are working with lots of graphics, videos, or large backgrounds, making it easier for you to do your edits without having to wait for the webpage to refresh over and over again, which can cause your browser to crash. The Safe Mode link is located next to the Edit Profile link in a music profile, which you'll see back in Figure 8.8. For regular account users, access the Safe Edit Mode link in the upper-right corner of Edit Profile mode (see Figure 8.14).

Figure 8.14
Safe Edit Mode in a regular profile is all the way in the right corner.

Back to our editing exercise…. You can submit your profile text edits now, and then view your profile so you can see what it looks like on your page. When you're on your own, it's not necessary to add HTML code in a linear fashion as we have shown here. For some, it's confusing to look at. If it's easier for you to see it as it should be laid out, you can add manual line breaks to break up your code when you type it up in your MySpace profile editor or in a text file. Either way, just hit the Enter button to bring your text to the next line, as you would if you were typing up any other document. You could break up the text like this:

```
<CENTER>
<H4>Welcome to my profile!</H4>
</CENTER>
<P>
<CENTER>
<A HREF=http://www.myspace.com>This is my first MySpace
profile.</A><BR>
In just mere moments <B>I am gonna rock this layout.</B><BR>
I'll be adding photos, video, <I>and</I> revamping my layout
completely.
</CENTER>
```

After the code has been saved in MySpace, the browser will probably run it all together anyway, so this way of editing shouldn't affect the functionality.

We've only started touching on what can be done with HTML. The next section will take a look at embedding images and videos. However, for further HTML study, there are a few great tutorials on the Web that will really school you on all things HTML. You'll find an excellent one at www.w3schools.com/html/default.asp.

Try out some online HTML editors, too. You want one that will allow you to edit in real time like a word processor. Two I use are www.zoodu.com/html-editor and www.pimp-my-profile.com/htmledit. They're almost identical in their interfaces (see Figure 8.15), but if one is swamped with traffic, you can always try the other. With editors like these, you type in the text you want, format it, add some links and photos, play with the alignment, or add tables. Then the editor will generate the code for you so you can plug it into the appropriate section in your profile. Note that these HTML editors are not for creating MySpace layouts. They are only for editing content within a specific section of your profile.

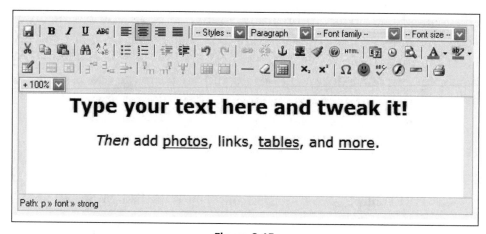

Figure 8.15
The HTML Editor at Zoodu.com lets you type in text, format it,
and even add graphics, tables, and more.

Adding Photos, Images, and Other Graphics

To embed an image, you must first create it and upload it onto a server or image hosting site. When deciding what type of format and size your image should be, consider the constraints of MySpace profiles. The sections and columns do not lend themselves to overly large pictures. Huge graphics throw your profile layout out of whack, making it necessary for visitors to scroll left to right to see everything. Therefore, a good rule of thumb is to keep your images to no more than 450 pixels wide and 550 pixels high.

Aside from dimension, images should also be in .jpg or .gif format for web viewing. The file size is best kept to 200K or less, which is already pretty large. Even then, you don't want to load your profile with too many images. Bulky-sized graphics and/or too many pictures on a profile can cause a visitor's browser to crash. It can also cause you to max out your allotted bandwidth given by the image hosting site, resulting in an error showing up instead of your graphic.

As far as where to store photos, PhotoBucket.com, ImageShack.us, and Flickr.com are three of the most popular free media hosting sites with MySpacers. After uploading your graphic, the hosting site will give you the URL link address of the image (see Figure 8.16). You'll use this information to construct an image source tag. The image source tag (<IMG SRC=…>) is one of those, like <P> and <BR> and a few others, that stands alone. No ending tag is necessary.

Figure 8.16
An uploaded image on PhotoBucket.com shows the URL where the image is located.

So go ahead and upload a photo or graphic to your hosting site of choice. Then copy and paste the given URL into the HTML image tag, as indicated here:

<IMG SRC="http://*ENTER IMAGE URL HERE*">

This HTML command directs the web browser to display the image located at the indicated http address. Remember how MySpace is a little quirky with HTML? This is another one of those instances where you might have to remove the quotation marks to get the picture to load correctly. Take the image source tag you've created and paste it into the Bio (or another) section of your profile (see Figure 8.17). Preview and submit this new addition. View your profile, and you should see the image loaded into the page at the same place you inserted the HTML directions (see Figure 8.18).

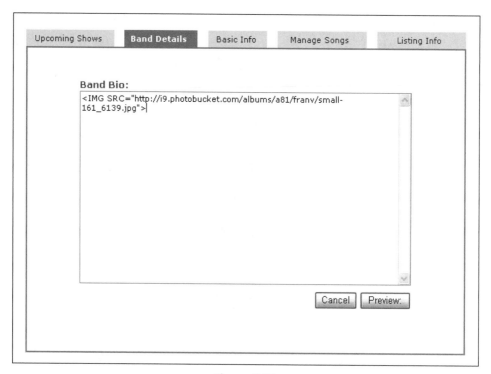

Figure 8.17
Place the image source tag in the Bio field.

Figure 8.18
The profile loads the image because the image source tag directs it to do so.

If you want to center the image, then you add the <CENTER> tags around it, like this:

> **<CENTER><IMG SRC="**http://*ENTER IMAGE URL HERE*"**>**
> **</CENTER>**

Go ahead and try it with and without quotation marks. Your picture should now be centered in the Bio section!

You can also link your photo to an outside website, such as your official website. Remember how we created hyperlinks? Instead of surrounding text with the hyperlink tags, we will surround the image tags. Your code will look like this:

> **<A HREF="**http://*ENTER WEBSITE URL HERE*"**>**
> **<IMG SRC="**http://*IMAGE URL HERE*"**></A>**

Again, you may need to take out the quotation marks so it will work correctly in MySpace. Feel free to add some text or other images/media before or after by using <P> to insert some space. This keeps everything from running together.

Special Photo Treatments

Slideshows are very popular on MySpace. They allow people to showcase a lot of pictures, but they only take up a small amount of real estate on the profile. MySpace now has a built-in slideshow feature that takes the pictures you have loaded into your account and converts them into a little presentation (see Figure 8.19). You can customize the show by adding captions and altering the dimensions of the slideshow, the colors of the borders, and even the kind of slideshow, such as a regular linear presentation or one where photos randomly "fly" in. When you're finished tweaking, you copy and paste the provided code into your profile at the point you want the slideshow to appear. To try it out, go to Add/Edit Photos from your home control panel. You'll see a link to the slideshow utility (pictured in Chapter 4, Figure 4.26).

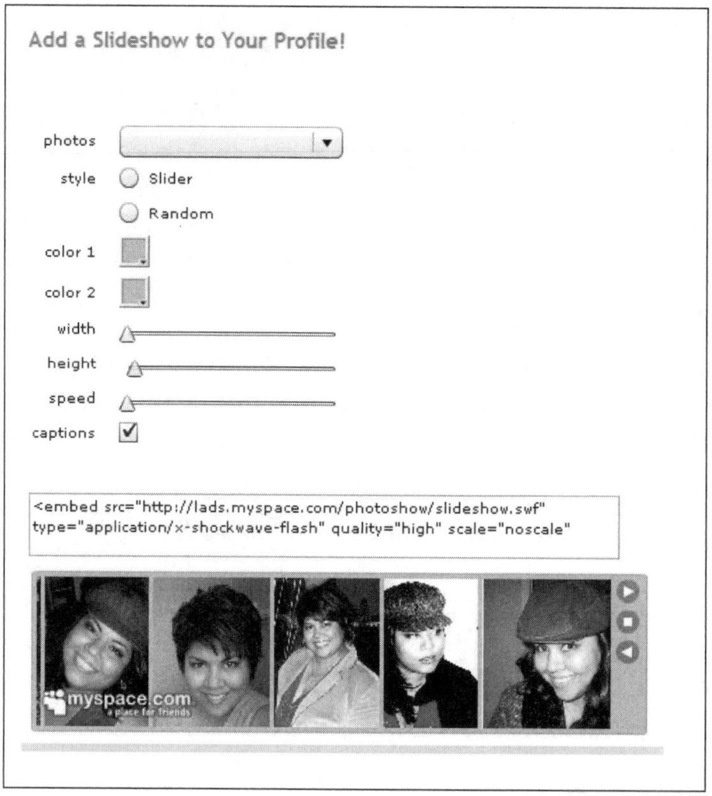

Figure 8.19
The MySpace slideshow page lets you create shows from pictures
you have uploaded to the MySpace servers.

There are some other really cool slideshows available on the web. My favorite sites for creating slideshows are PhotoBucket.com, Slide.com, and RockYou.com. All three have lots of options for customizing your show, including interesting transitions. RockYou, for instance, lets you make a show that looks like a rotating, three-dimensional cube (see Figure 8.20). Slide has one that looks like white-bordered photographs being scattered on a table (see Figure 8.21). And PhotoBucket boasts a cool skin that looks like a stylized turntable, with your pictures as the records (see Figure 8.22). All three sites are free, and you simply load your photos and choose what kind of slideshow you want. Like the MySpace slideshow utility, these sites give you code to plug into your profile wherever you want it to appear (see Figure 8.23).

Figure 8.20
RockYou.com can make a 3D cube slideshow like this one.

Figure 8.21
Slide.com has a realistic "photos on the table" slideshow.

Figure 8.22
This fun PhotoBucket.com slideshow emulates a turntable.

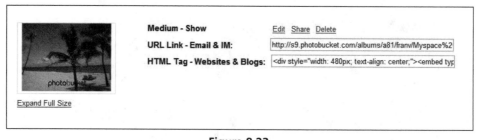

Figure 8.23
Like other slideshow providers, PhotoBucket.com provides a URL link to your slideshow.

Adding Video to Your Profile

You have the ability to upload videos into your MySpace account, or you may choose an outside website to host your videos. There are various websites out there that provide server space for video clips, which are then converted into embeddable content. YouTube.com is one well-known site that is simple to use and has a community of its own that is active in viewing and commenting on user videos. It also has special musician and comedian accounts, and you can place your YouTube videos anywhere, including on MySpace, in email, in blogs—pretty much any web-based environment. You'll find many other video hosting options in Appendix B, "MySpace Resources," as well.

Whichever hosting site you choose, the process of inserting videos into comments is a fairly simple one involving pasting and tweaking code. Let's look at uploading your videos to MySpace.

Your MySpace profile control panel has a link under your picture for View My Profile/Pics/Videos/Blog/Comments/Friends. Click on the Videos link, and on the Video page, click the Upload tab to begin processing your video clip (see Figure 8.24). At this time, both MySpace and YouTube have a 100-MB size limit for videos, so make sure your clip is within this constraint.

Figure 8.24
The Upload tab will take you to a screen where you can browse
your hard drive to find the clip you want to upload.

Let's walk through the steps as they appear on MySpace now. The first step is to title your video and add a short description that should include your name (or your band's name), the songs featured, the venue if it's a location video, and the type of music (see Figure 8.25). You can make it searchable by other MySpace users by checking the appropriate option.

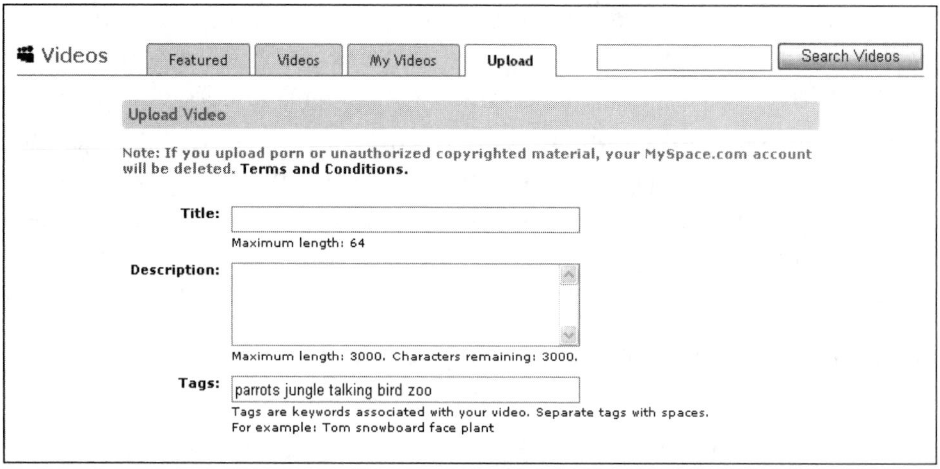

Figure 8.25
The Upload screen allows you to title your video, add a description,
and make your clip searchable.

Next, choose a category for your video (presumably Music) and add searchable tags. Tags help users find your video based on keywords. In the example in Figure 8.26, a video with talking parrots in a jungle-like zoo setting is tagged with the words "parrot, jungle, talking, bird, zoo." The tags in MySpace should not have commas between them. Keywords for your video would include similar information as that in your description.

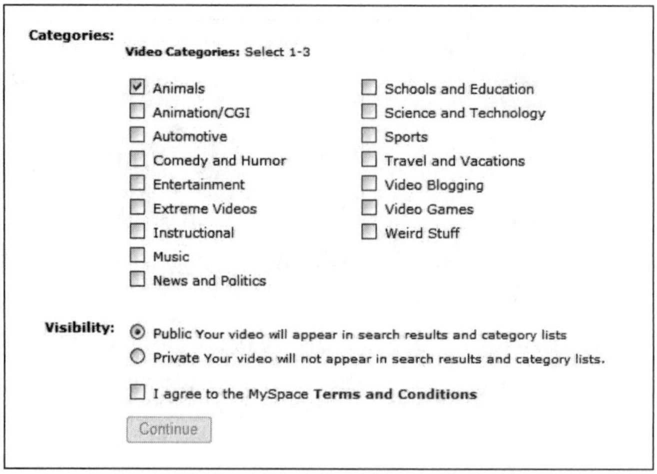

Figure 8.26
Categorize and tag your video.

Now choose your video file from your hard drive, and then click the Upload button. Notice in Figure 8.27 the many formats MySpace accepts.

Upload Video: Step 2

File Size Limit per upload: 100MB.
Acceptable formats: .avi,.asf,.dv,.wmv,.mov,.qt,.3g2,.3gp,.3gp2,.3gpp,.gsm,.mpg,.mpeg, .mp4,.m4v,.mp4v,.cmp,.divx,.xvid,.264,.rm,.rmvb,.flv,.mkv,.ogm.

Note: If you upload porn or unauthorized copyrighted material, your MySpace.com account will be deleted. **Terms and Conditions.**

Upload Film

[Browse...]
[Upload]

Are you having problems uploading videos? **Try our new awesome uploader!**

Figure 8.27
Now it's time to upload your video. Note the acceptable file formats.

The video is now in processing mode. It will take a few minutes for it to upload and then be converted to a playable web format. When it is complete, a thumbnail of the video plus additional information will appear in your My Videos tab (see Figure 8.28).

Figure 8.28
Your video is now ready to plug into a comment or your profile.

To get the code you'll need to insert the video into a web environment, such as a profile, comment, or webpage, click on the thumbnail picture of your video. You'll be taken to a screen that will not only allow you to view the video, but will also provide details about that clip, including the needed code. Scroll down and see two types of code— Video URL and Video Code. The video URL is simply the address where your video is being stored, and this address can be emailed to friends who may want to click to see your clip. However, in order to embed the video, we need the Video Code (see Figure 8.29).

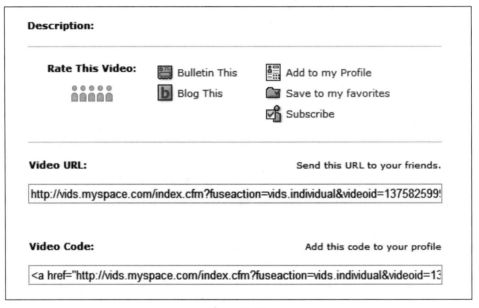

Figure 8.29
Copy the Video Code into your computer's clipboard.

Click once on the Video Code box, and you will see the code is now highlighted. To copy the code, right-click with your mouse and choose Copy, or on your keyboard use the shortcut Ctrl+C. Then, as you did for pictures and slideshows, insert this code into the spot on your profile where you want your video to appear.

The process for uploading videos into a YouTube.com (or other video hosting) account is similar to MySpace. Both ask you to title, describe, tag, categorize, and finally upload your clip.

YouTube.com, like many other video hosting sites, will give you embedding video code that looks something like this:

```
<object width="425" height="350"><param name="movie"
value="http://www.youtube.com/v/a5ujuBgk0Q01"></param>
<param name="wmode" value="transparent"></param>
<embed src="http://www.youtube.com/v/a5ujuBgk0Q01"
type="application/x-shockwave-flash" wmode="transparent"
width="425" height="350"></embed></object>
```

Again, paste this into your profile where you want it to appear.

More Video Tips

A great touch for your profile is to display one of your videos, and then below it provide the code in a text box. Encourage users to display the video on their pages by copying and pasting the code into their profiles. Make it easy for them by showing the code in a scrollable text box (see Figure 8.30).

Figure 8.30
Fans can copy the video code in your text box, and then paste it
right into their profiles. It's free advertising for you!

The code will look like this:

```
<textarea cols="30" rows="5" wrap="hard" readonly="yes">
INSERT YOUR VIDEO CODE HERE </textarea>
```

You can change the column height and row width to make the box smaller or larger. Since the text box is set to read only, users can only copy the code from it; they cannot alter it in any way.

Try this same tactic when displaying banners that you want users to display on their profiles. For more on banners, see the "Profile Banners" section further on in the chapter.

Also be aware of conflicting audio and video on your profile. If your music player is set to begin playing automatically, you should not have any videos on your profile that also play automatically. Obviously, it creates a sound collision when everything starts playing at once. Should your video play as soon as your page is loaded, and you don't know how to stop it from doing so, try to edit your settings from within your video hosting service, or switch to a different video host.

Revamping Your Profile Layout

While adding media and a few text formats are important things to know, it's overhauling your profile's look that you're probably most interested in! You may be wondering how you are going to add an awesome background and different colors to your page. This section will show you how you can completely revamp your profile.

In Chapter 6, I suggested you start thinking about what you want your profile to look like so that it jives with who you are and the music you make. Hopefully you wrote some ideas down because now you'll need them to shake up your MySpace default page.

One of the best ways to get a feel for what you do and don't like is to look at a lot of profiles. Take note of what strikes you as attractive and what looks positively ugly. Which profiles inspire you? What kinds of features do you covet? Which ones make you question the sanity of the profile owner? You may notice fairly quickly that there are many really cluttered pages on MySpace. Some of them work, but most are just such a mess you want to navigate away from them as quickly as possible, as with the one in Figure 8.31, with a background so busy you can't read the too-light text. Flashing graphics, glittery text, dark type on dark backgrounds, white type on light backgrounds, super-busy backgrounds, so many photos and videos your browser is incapable of loading them all, lots of blinky logos in every corner... the eyestrain is enough to give a person a migraine.

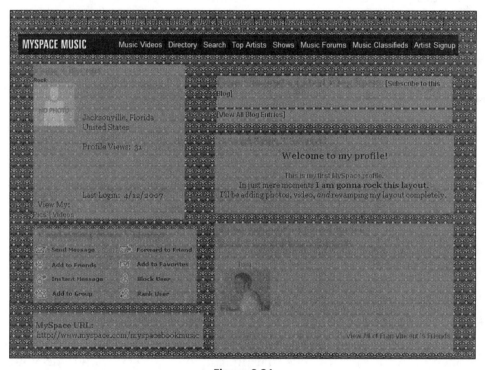

Figure 8.31
This ugly profile has a busy background, but the rest of the profile is rendered transparent, and the font colors are too light to stand out.

My recommendation is to go ahead and try out lots of toys and tweaks, but test, test, test. Spend the time looking at your profile as a fan would. Try it out on Internet Explorer, Mozilla Firefox, and Mac Safari. Get your friends and family to visit it and rate it honestly. If it takes forever for you to load your page, it's going to bog down everyone else, too. Having trouble reading your text? Change your background or your text color so there is enough contrast to make reading easy.

Go for higher contrast. Keep the number of text colors and font styles and sizes to a minimum. Watch for overly busy backgrounds and obnoxious, animated artwork. Your profile can have some really cool features, but it must be usable.

Using Style Sheets

Most of the customized MySpace profiles out there are created using Cascading Style Sheets. CSS, as it's commonly referred to, is a type of programming language that defines how various HTML elements should be formatted. For example, if you want all of the headers in your profile to be kelly green and an 18-point font size, then you can specify that once in your style sheet, instead of going through and changing each and every header to this specification. CSS cuts down the work and streamlines the code.

We won't dive into the ins and outs of this style sheet language. We'll leave that to programmers. Instead, we'll learn how to find ready-made style sheets and how to use editors to create your own. For those who really want to learn how to do it manually, try out www.w3schools.com/css/default.asp for an excellent tutorial.

Pre-Made Layouts

The web abounds with ready-made layouts for MySpace profiles. Some of them are great, and some are hideous. The first thing you should do is start shopping for layouts. They're free, so you can download as many as you want and try them all on for size. Peruse Appendix B for a list of sites that offer layouts and codes. Or, do your own web search for "myspace layouts."

A word of caution about layout sites… most are heavily laden with annoying banner ads, sponsored links, pop-ups, and other types of advertisements. Unfortunately, some may also be carrying adware or spyware. Before you go layout shopping, make sure your virus scan is in working order. Delete your cookies (in the Tools > Internet Options screen for Internet Explorer users) and run a malware scan with a free software product such as Ad-Aware (www.lavasoft.com).

When you find a profile that you like, copy and paste it into a text file and save it on your hard drive so you can go back to it later. To try it out in your profile, paste the provided layout code into the bottom of your Bio field (for bands) or your About Me field (for regular users). Save changes and reload your profile to see how it looks. Not quite right for your image? That's okay, keep shopping!

Should you find something that has the color scheme you like, but perhaps you're not loving the main or table backgrounds, save it in a text file anyway. You can tweak it to suit your needs by removing the offending background or replacing it with one of your choosing (such as a picture of yourself). Here's how to tackle this....

Search through the code (or use the "find" function in your text program) to locate the "background-image" phrase. It should be fairly near the beginning of the code:

```
background-image:url('http://LOCATION OF BACKGROUND IMAGE');
```

We're going to replace whatever is in the pre-made layout with a background picture of you. The *maximum* size of your background should be 800 pixels by 700 pixels (see Figure 8.32). Load this into your favorite photo hosting site. Take the provided URL and paste it into the code in place of the URL that's already there. Now, take the entire layout style sheet, with your new background, and paste this code into the Bio section of your profile. Load it up and see how it looks!

Let's say you don't want a background image at all. Search for the same code and just remove all the text between the parentheses:

```
background-image:url();
```

If you decide later that you want to add a background image back in, simply put the URL of your new background location between the parentheses.

You may see a couple of instances of "background-image" in the code. The one toward the top is likely the main background image. Another occurrence of "background-image" is likely to be a table background.

Figure 8.32
Artist India.Arie has a, 800×700 pixel background on her profile. Notice that her image only appears on the far left side, and the rest of the background was left white.

You can remove/replace backgrounds that appear in the section boxes (tables) in your profile by following the same procedure.

Recall the ugly profile with the busy background in Figure 8.31? Once we take out the background, it starts to look a lot cleaner (see Figure 8.33).

Layout Editors/Generators

Pre-made layouts might not be your thing, so try creating your very own profile layout from scratch by using an online layout editor. Two I like are located at pimp-my-profile.com/generators/myspace.php and www.pulseware.com.au/site_pi.asp?p=wpa-167088. The one at pimp-my-profile.com (see Figure 8.34) is very comprehensive, though you can't see your layout as you build. The generator at www.pulseware.com.au (see Figure 8.35), however, does less, but its WYSIWYG interface lets you see what your layout will look like as you build it, which is great for beginners.

Figure 8.33
Without the horrible background, this profile is starting to look better.

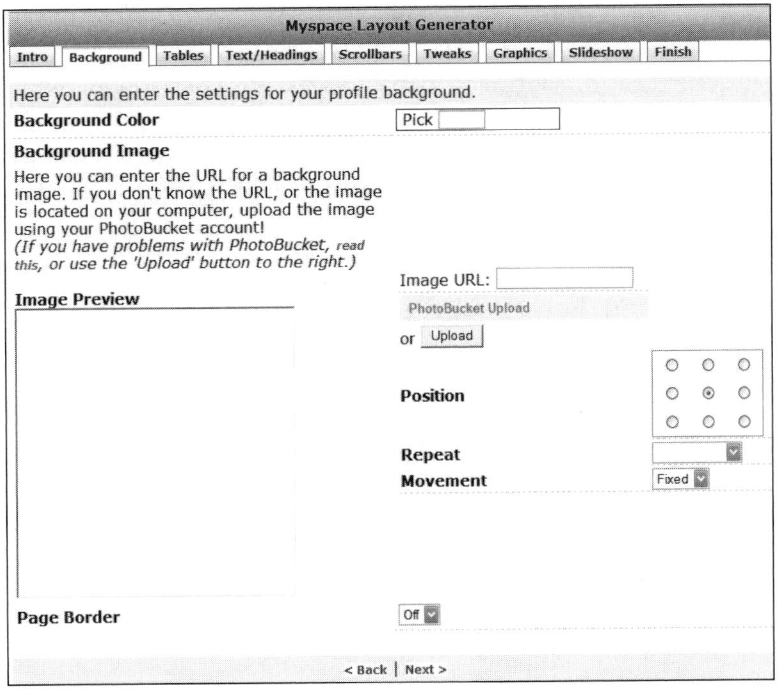

Figure 8.34
This pimp-my-profile.com layout editor has a lot of options to make your profile shine.

Figure 8.35
The www.pulseware.com.au editor is great for beginners because
you can see the changes as you make them.

Layout editors (also called *layout generators*) are excellent tools to help you get your profile to look exactly as you want it to. So, if you have the time and the creative initiative, then develop your own layout!

Div Overlays

Div overlays, also called *div layouts*, are a much more intricate way to alter your profile. They sometimes include Flash animation, too. The code in the overlay completely covers up the way MySpace profiles are currently structured and lets you make your profile look like just about anything you want. Figures 8.36 and 8.37 are just two amazing examples of what div overlays can do.

Working with div overlays is not for the beginner. However, it is an option that's available to you. First try out one of the many free div overlays available at Groups.MySpace.com/Freedivs. If you decide you want to create your own, I've provided links to several div overlay generators in Appendix B. You can also look to a professional designer to create a custom div layout or Flash animation for you.

Figure 8.36
This photographer's profile at www.myspace.com/phillmphoto is completely different
from the default structure, making it ideal for showcasing his photography.

Figure 8.37
Joss Stone's profile is so different that it's barely recognizable as a MySpace page.

More MySpace Tweaks

There are so many more ways to alter your profile that it'll make your head spin. In this section, we'll touch on a few that musicians might need to maximize their pages.

Adding Interest Tables

Regular MySpace accounts have a section called Interests, where users can list general interests, movies, music they like, and so forth (see Figure 8.38). Although bands do not have a place to list interests, they do have an area called General Info, where you'll find details about band members, the official website, and the record label (see Figure 8.39).

Fifi's Interests	
General	Watching TV and surfing
Music	Green Day, Sublime, Front 242
Movies	Blue Crush, The Godfather

Figure 8.38
This is a sample of an Interests table from a regular MySpace account.

Fran Vincent: General Info	
Member Since	10/7/2006
Band Website	[insertwebsitehere].com
Band Members	Ellen Mets (guitar/vocals) Jeff Honcho (drums)
Influences	Staind, 3 Doors Down, Evanescence, Aerosmith
Sounds Like	Hole, Seether, Veruca Salt
Record Label	unsigned
Type of Label	None

Figure 8.39
Bands have General Info tables, which behave the same way as Interests tables.

For layout tweaking purposes, both of these areas are referred to as Interests tables, and you are not limited to the fields MySpace gives you. You can add more fields of your choosing. The code to accomplish this looks like:

```
</td>
</tr>
<tr>
<td valign="top" align="left" width="100" bgcolor="b1d0f0">
<span class="lightbluetext8">INSERT TABLE TITLE</span></td>
<td style="WORD-WRAP: break-word" width="175"
bgcolor="d5e8fb">
INSERT TEXT OR MEDIA HERE
```

So let's put it to practice. For this example, we'll add Collaborators to your band's General Info section after Band Members. Here's how it's done....

Go into Edit Profile mode > Band Details > Members. Paste the following code at the bottom of the Members field, below any text you want to appear in the Members section (see Figure 8.40).

```
</td>
</tr>
<tr>
<td valign="top" align="left" width="100" bgcolor="b1d0f0">
<span class="lightbluetext8"> Collaborators </span></td>
<td style="WORD-WRAP: break-word" width="175"
bgcolor="d5e8fb"> Sly Winkert (charts)<br>
April Tu (string arrangements) <br>
Chad Millar (producer)
```

When you hit Preview, the resulting page will look odd, but don't worry because it's not a true representation of what it will look like in your actual profile (see Figure 8.41). Click Submit, and then reload your profile to see the changes. You'll notice that the new Collaborators field appears below the Band Members field and has taken on the formatting and style of whatever layout code you've previously entered into the Bio section (see Figure 8.42). Use the aforementioned code to add as many fields as you like. You can even add small images instead of text using <img src> tags, if you prefer.

Figure 8.40
Create a new field in your General Info table by adding the
appropriate code after your bio.

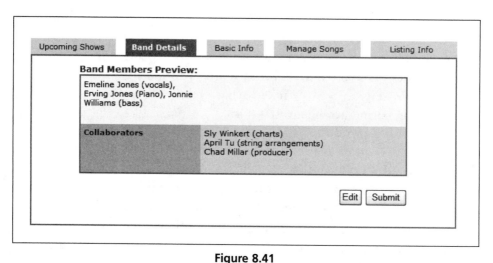

Figure 8.41
The Collaborators field appears in the preview. It won't look
quite like this in the actual profile, however.

Fran Vincent: General Info

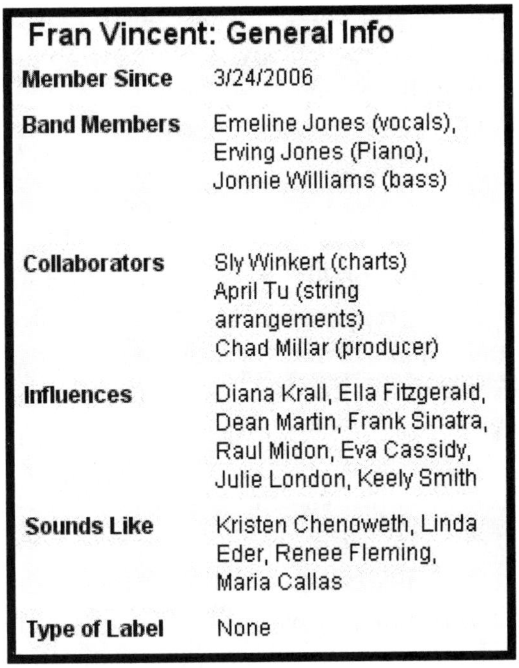

Member Since	3/24/2006
Band Members	Emeline Jones (vocals), Erving Jones (Piano), Jonnie Williams (bass)
Collaborators	Sly Winkert (charts) April Tu (string arrangements) Chad Millar (producer)
Influences	Diana Krall, Ella Fitzgerald, Dean Martin, Frank Sinatra, Raul Midon, Eva Cassidy, Julie London, Keely Smith
Sounds Like	Kristen Chenoweth, Linda Eder, Renee Fleming, Maria Callas
Type of Label	None

Figure 8.42
Now Collaborators appears below Band Members in the General Info table.

Adding Content Tables or Sections

The sections that appear throughout regular and band profiles are also referred to as *content tables*. The About (or Bio) section is an example of a default content table in a music profile. In a regular profile, About Me and Who I'd Like to Meet are default content tables. Again, you are not restricted to these default sections. You can create more and call them whatever you want! Here's the code to do it:

```
</td>
</tr>
</table>
</td>
</tr>
</table>
<br />
<table bordercolor="ffcc99" cellspacing="0" cellpadding="0"
width="435" bgcolor="ffcc99" border="0">
<tr>
```

```
<td class="text" valign="center" align="left" width="300"
bgcolor="ffcc99" height="17" style="word-wrap:break-word"
>   <span class="whitetext12"> INSERT
SECTION TITLE HERE</span></td>
</tr>
<tr>
<td>
<table bordercolor="000000" cellspacing="3" cellpadding="3"
width="435" align="center" bgcolor="ffffff" border="0">
<td valign="top" align="center" width="435" bgcolor="ffffff"
style="word-wrap:break-word">
INSERT TEXT OR MEDIA HERE
```

Similar to constructing another interest table, the content table code
will be placed in the field after which you want the new section to
appear. In a music profile, there's really only one main section—that's
About, also called Bio. For our example, we'll add a section for Media
to our band page. Paste this code at the end of your Bio section, as
shown in Figure 8.43:

```
</td>
</tr>
</table>
</td>
</tr>
</table>
<br />
<table bordercolor= "ffcc99" cellspacing="0" cellpadding="0"
width="435" bgcolor="ffcc99" border="0">
<tr>
<td class="text" valign="center" align="left" width="300"
bgcolor="ffcc99" height="17" style="word-wrap:break-word">
   <span
class="whitetext12">Media</span></td>
</tr>
<tr>
<td>
```

<table bordercolor="000000" cellspacing="3" cellpadding="3" width="435" align="center" bgcolor="ffffff" border="0">
<td valign="top" align="center" width="435" bgcolor="ffffff" style="word-wrap:break-word">
Excerpts from interviews, positive reviews, etc. would appear here.

Band Bio Preview:

Paste your band's bio here.

Media

Excerpts from interviews, positive reviews, etc. would appear here. .

Edit   Submit

Figure 8.43
The preview of the new Media content table appears here.

This new Media table now appears on your profile (see Figure 8.44). You can put whatever you want in this section, from text to images, videos, or Flash animation. You may have noticed that the code for both interest and content tables contains "bordercolors" and "bgcolors." The values inputted here tell the tables to take the colors of the default MySpace profile. However, any pre-made or custom layout codes loaded into your profile will override these default values.

About Fran Vincent

Paste your band's bio here.

Media

Excerpts from interviews, positive reviews, etc. would appear here. .

Figure 8.44
Now you have a new field in your profile. It will take the formatting of whatever layout codes you have input.

Customizing Contact Tables

Your contact table is that small section containing links to Send Message, Add to Friends, and Forward to Friend, among others. You're not stuck with the default. You can actually create your very own contact table or use a pre-made one.

To make your own contact table, you obviously have to be pretty good with graphics programs. So, assuming that you are, your contact table should be about 300 pixels wide and 155 pixels tall. A default contact table appears in Figure 8.45. You'll have to keep the same position of these links in your new contact table. The fun part is that you can call these links whatever you want. The system will maintain the links in the same location. All you have to do is create the artwork. Figure 8.46 is a contact table I created. As you can see, I played with the wording. You can add a background image or color to your contact table design if desired.

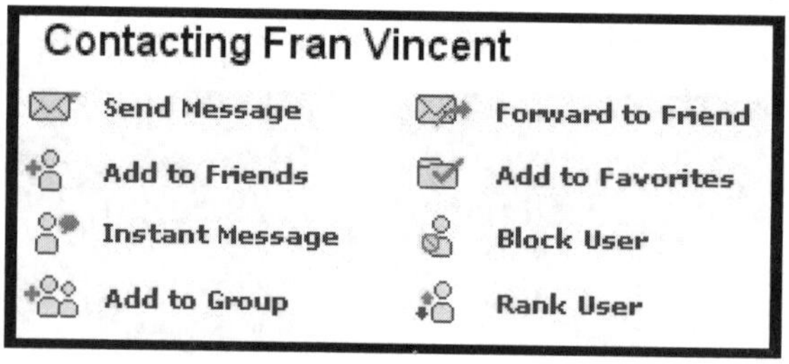

Figure 8.45
The default contact table always contains these same links.
Your new contact table must do the same.

Figure 8.46
This is a custom contact table. Note that the links are in the same place, but they are labeled in a more fun way.

If you don't have graphic software to create a contact table, you can go to a site that will help you create it. I find that www.ifihad.com/myspace-code-generators/contact-tables does a nice job. You'll see in Figure 8.47 that the site lets you switch up the fonts, change the contact table text, and load a background image. It then gives you the code to plug into the Bio section of your profile.

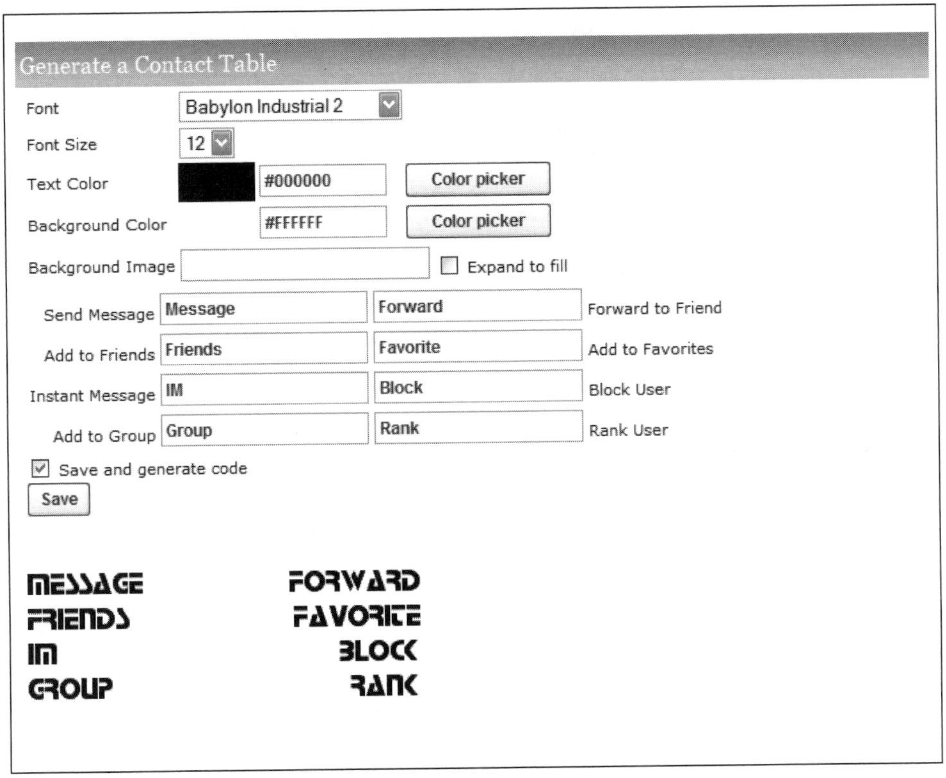

Figure 8.47
The contact table generator at Ifihad.com does a good job of helping you create your very own contact table.

Even if you create your contact table on your own graphic software at home as I did, you can still use this very same link at Ifihad.com to get the code to load your contact table. When you are finished designing your contact table, save it as a JPEG or GIF image and load it up to your photo hosting site of choice. Copy the URL location. Go to the Ifihad.com link, and, where it asks for a background image, provide the URL of your newly designed contact table. Delete the text from the fields Send Message, Forward to Friend, and so on (see Figure 8.48). Click the Save and Generate Code check box, and then click the Save button. On the next page, you will see the code you need to make your contact table appear on your profile. Paste this code into your bio section below your bio text, but before any other code.

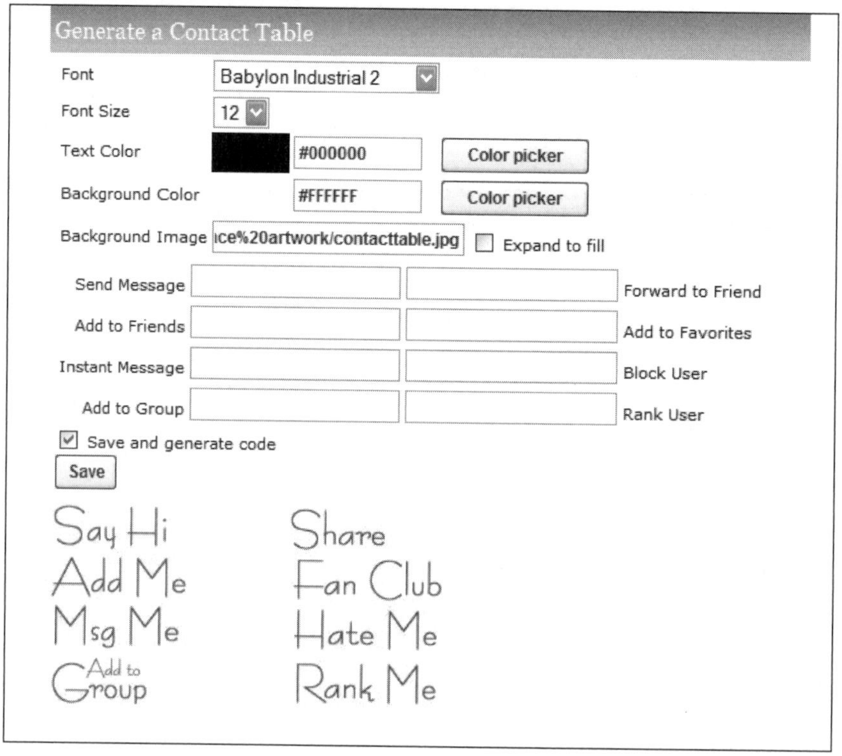

Figure 8.48
You can use the Ifihad.com generator to get the code for a contact table you created yourself. Just be sure to delete all the text from the generator's text fields.

Profile Banners

Adding banners to your profile can help you use up underutilized space and advertise new albums, merchandise, song downloads, and more. This section will show you a few different types of banners and how to use them.

Top Banners

Bands seem to love to add their own snazzy banners above the MySpace banner advertisement that appears atop every page. These are referred to as *top banners*. Browse through major label artists' profiles, and you'll see many top banners. First you have to create a banner, and then you can pop it into your profile. Use this code to do it:

```
<style type="text/css">
body{background-position:top center;margin-top:
ENTER HEIGHT OF BANNER IN PIXELS HERE;}
div.topbanner {top: 0;left: 49%;margin-left: -225px;
width: 100%;height: ENTER HEIGHT OF BANNER IN
PIXELS HEREpx;position: absolute;}
</style>
<div class="topbanner"><a href="INSERT LINK TO YOUR
OFFICIAL WEB SITE"><IMG SRC="INSERT URL OF YOUR
BANNER IMAGE" border="0"></a></div><br>
```

The first time you are asked to enter the height of the banner in pixels, insert a number only, without *px* after it. The second time the code calls for it, enter the same number with *px* right after it (for example, 150px). The margin-left: value is used to position your banner left to right. The lower the value, the farther left the banner will be. In the example, we used -225px, which placed our banner for Ariel's Closet in the center of the profile (see Figure 8.49). You will have to play with the value to get your banner example where you want it. Place the code into the very bottom of your Bio field. Load it up and see how it looks. Play with the margin-left: values as needed.

Extended Network Banners

Consider replacing the "extended network" text with a banner. This extended network section appears on every profile, and most consider it wasted space (see Figure 8.50). Don't let it just sit there. Make a banner announcing when your new album is coming out or create an image banner that fits into the look of your layout.

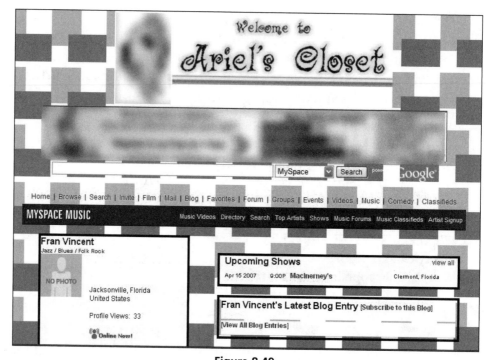

Figure 8.49
The top banner for Ariel's Closet is placed above the MySpace
advertisement and doesn't interfere with it in any way.

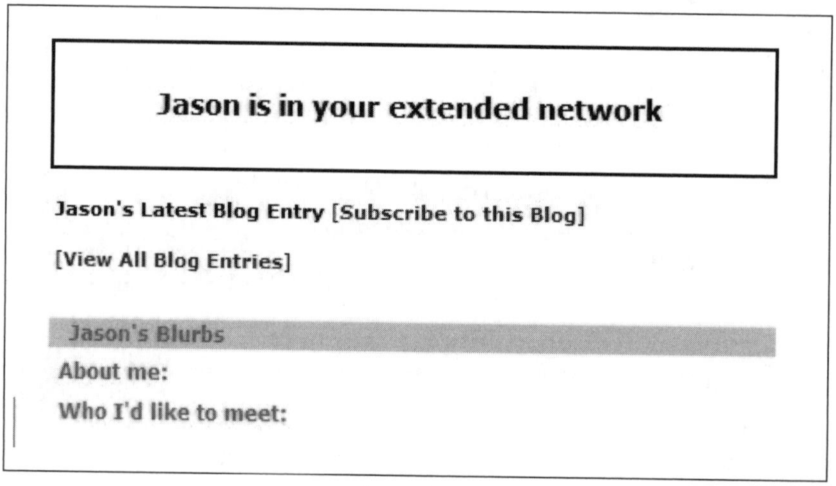

Jason is in your extended network

Jason's Latest Blog Entry [Subscribe to this Blog]

[View All Blog Entries]

Jason's Blurbs

About me:

Who I'd like to meet:

Figure 8.50
The extended network banner is another MySpace constant,
but it can be covered up with a more useful banner.

You can create your own banner with your graphics program, or you can use a banner generator online. To create your own banner, keep the width between 435 pixels and 475 pixels and the height between 60 and 75 pixels. Use the code below:

```
<style type="text/css">
table table table td {vertical-align:top!important;}
span.blacktext12 {visibility:visible!important;
background-color:transparent;
background-image:url("ENTER THE URL OF YOUR
BANNER IMAGE");
background-repeat:no-repeat; background-position:center center;
letter-spacing:-0.5px; width:ENTER BANNER WIDTHpx;
height:ENTER BANNER HEIGHTpx;
display:block !important; } </style><br>
```

Change the values as indicated and paste this code into the end of your Bio section.

You can also make extended network banners with the help of online generators. Try www.mywackospace.com/extended-banner-editor to design yours (see Figure 8.51). After you've made your unique banner, the site will generate the code you need to place it in your profile.

Other Banners

You can pop banners anywhere in your profile. Advertise merchandise or link to your official website or download sites that carry your music.

MyBannerMaker.com is a flexible generator that makes banners of all different sizes (see Figure 8.52). You can use these banners anywhere in your profile.

In the "Adding Video to Your Profile" section, you learned how to add a text box to your profile so users could grab your video code and embed your video into their profile. You can do the same thing with banners. Want fans to display your banners on their site? Give them the code by using the text-box tweak discussed earlier.

Figure 8.51
The extended network banner generator at MyWackoSpace.com
shows you just what your banner will look by using a sample profile.

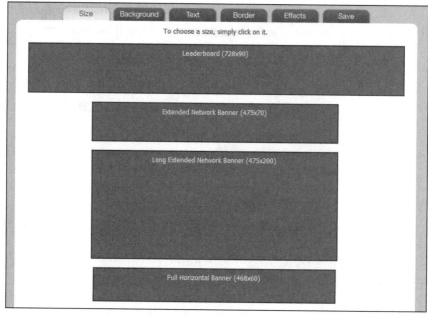

Figure 8.52
MyBannerMaker.com makes banners of many different sizes.
You can use these almost anywhere on your profile.

More MySpace Toys

Is your new layout all finished? Well, before you get comfortable, check out this list of other things you could do to your profile. For links, check out the appendixes or run your own web searches for code.

- **Move stuff.** Don't like where your music player sits? Visit Pimpwebpage.com/band.php for codes to move around the music player and other elements of your profile.

- **Online Now icons.** Ditch the default Online Now icon and try one that says "Rockin' Out!" instead.

- **Image filters.** These filters change the way your profile's images behave. For instance, you can make an image blur or flip when a mouse pointer hovers over it.

- **Hide last login.** Trying to evade stalkers? Get some "hide last login" code to mask your MySpace activities.

- **Add an email signup list.** Plug an email form into your profile or create a link to your main mailing list signup on your official website.

- **Sell your music downloads.** Use the MySpace/SNOCAP store or pick from dozens of other music download sites. The link to open your store is located in your artist home control panel.

- **Wireless alerts and voicemail.** Let fans leave messages for you or sign up for your text message alerts. Visit Saynow.com and Mozes.com.

- **Podcast.** Link to your podcast and let fans stream or download your very own radio show.

- **Sell merch.** Direct fans to where they can buy your tees, caps, and hoodies. Cafepress.com is a good place to start.

- **Offer ringtones and mobile content.** Get fans to purchase your ringtones, mobile videos, and wallpapers. Oodles of mobile marketing sites are popping up all over the Net.

- **Add another MP3 player.** This is really cool for regular account users. Flash-based MP3 players are all over the web in various styles. Some look like iPods, and others like '80s boom boxes. Surf over to MyFlashFetish.com.

So many tweaks, but only so many hours in the day. Looks like you've got a lot of work ahead of you! Don't take a break just yet. Head over to Chapter 9 and learn how to add friends and customize your friend space.

9 You Gotta Have Friends

People often wonder how a website started by two guys looking to keep their buddies in the know about the L.A. club scene could balloon into a community of tens of millions in just a few short years. The answer is friends. What started as a select few grew as their immediate pals invited their friends, who invited more friends, and so forth. This grassroots type of marketing is what makes MySpace and other social communities so attractive. People go where their friends are. And they make that community thrive by persuading more of their real-life friends to join, as well as making new online contacts. As a musician, you will be doing the same.

This chapter is all about friends—what a friends list is, how to add and deny friends, how to customize and manage your friends list, and how to block abusive friends. In this chapter, we will discuss how to:

❏ Make a list of people you know, including friends, family, coworkers, classmates, and industry contacts

❏ Use MySpace to search for friends by email address

❏ Add your favorite bands, comedians, and filmmakers

❏ Add other musicians in the same genre as you, as well as complementary genres

❏ Add the friends of the aforementioned musicians

❏ Employ the use of a friend adder (optional)

❏ Have a plan to add friends regularly

The Friends List

In the MySpace world, everyone has a friends list. It is a compilation of people who have requested that you add them to your list and those who have approved your friend request. The list appears as a collection of thumbnail pictures just above the comments section of your profile page. Some may be actual friends that you know, while others may be strangers you only know in the Internet world. Adding and requesting friends is how you build a following in this online community.

Building a strong friends list is important because this list becomes your marketing audience. You can post bulletins, which are like broadcast emails, to everyone on your list at once. And you and your friends can leave comments for each other on your profiles. You can encourage the friends on your list to add your music to their profile, tell others about you, and more. Plus, being on a friends list is like being a part of an exclusive club. Always remind yourself that building a strong following through your friends list is the goal of every MySpace marketer.

My Friend Space and Tom

In your profile control panel, you'll see a section at the bottom-right called *My Friend Space* (see Figure 9.1). This is where thumbnail pictures of your friends and fans will appear. The options in the My Friend Space section allow you to control various functions of your friends list, including deciding who appears on your profile, deleting and organizing friends, and viewing their birthdays. It also shows how many friends you have accumulated. Users visiting your page will see your friends list as well. Your profile will only display so many friend thumbnails at once, but visitors can click on View All to see more.

If you've just opened up a musician account, you'll notice a mysterious stranger in your friends list. Hmmm… you don't remember adding him? This is Tom and he is everyone's very first MySpace friend. Tom is one of the site's founders and appears automatically in every new account that is created. You'll also have an email from him, welcoming you to the community. From time to time, Tom will post bulletins and notices to keep the community informed about new MySpace developments, system glitches, and the like—as well as the occasional hilarious video or joke!

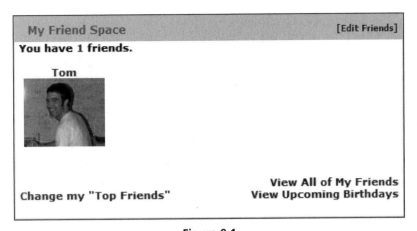

Figure 9.1
Your My Friend Space allows you to control aspects of your friends list
and shows pictures of all of your friends, including Tom, your first MySpace pal.

Finding Friends

Now that you've met Tom, it's time to fill in your friends list!

Start with the People You Already Know

The very first step in building your friends list for your new MySpace profile is to gather email addresses of your current real-life friends, family, and acquaintances. Click on the Invite option located on the medium-blue navigation bar and paste the email addresses of everyone you know in the To field. Write up a short message letting your friends know you now have a MySpace profile and you'd like to add them to your friends list. Send it off by clicking the Send Invite button (see Figure 9.2). If someone already has a MySpace account using that email address, the system will find that person. And if your email buddy doesn't have a profile, MySpace will invite that person to join. Once the person joins, he or she will be automatically added as your friend. It's a nifty little process that saves a ton of time in searching for people one by one.

MySpace also allows you to search for emails manually by entering in addresses one by one. The medium-blue navigation bar that appears toward the top of the page has a link for Search. Click on this page, and you will see a section to help you Find Someone You Know (see

Figure 9.3). Be sure to pick the search-by-email option, and then enter email addresses from your personal address book. MySpace will find current users or allow you to invite non-users to join MySpace and be a part of your friends list.

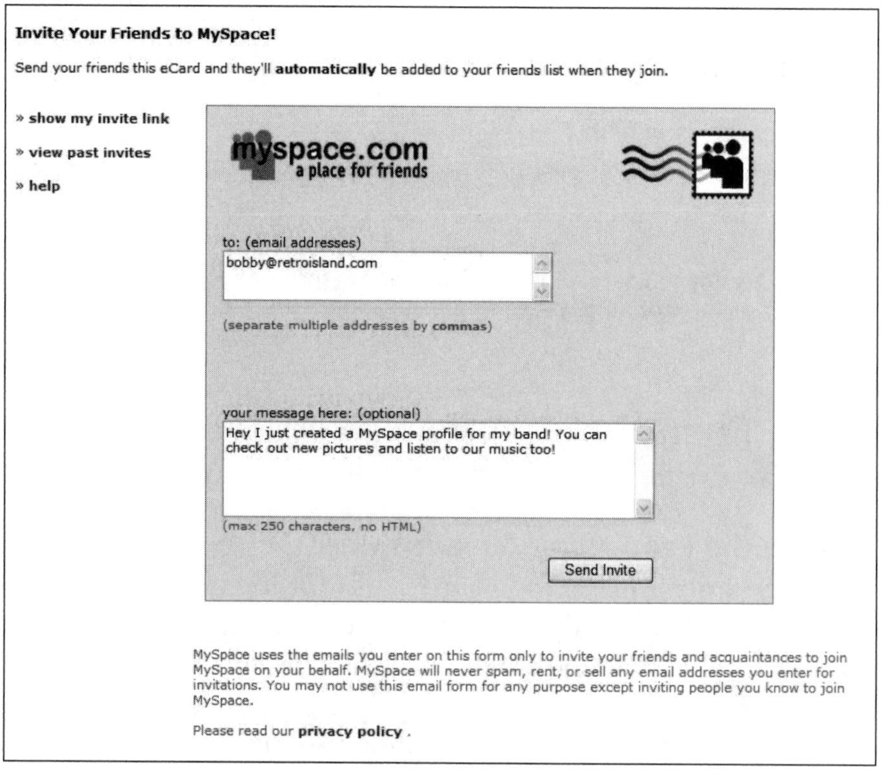

Figure 9.2
The invite page lets you copy and paste the email addresses of your
real-life friends to see who is on MySpace.

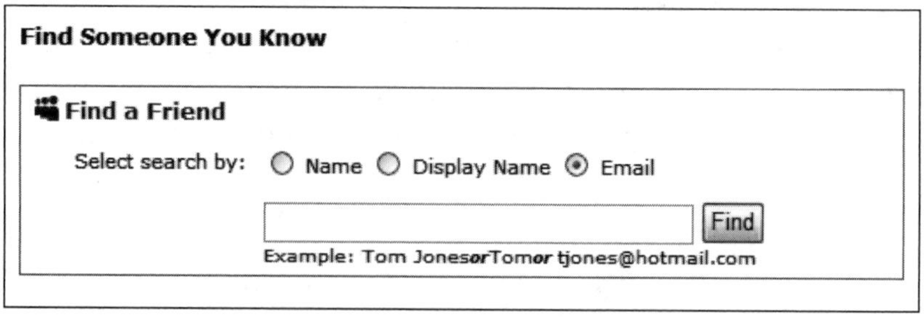

Figure 9.3
This search option allows you to find individuals by their
email address, real name, or MySpace handle.

For whom should you search? Friends, family, acquaintances, and entertainment industry contacts—such as venue managers and artist managers whom you have met along the way—are all good candidates for your friends list. Remember to look for your current fans. Enter emails you've gathered at gigs and from fans who have provided their email address to you through your website email list or by purchasing online merchandise or music from you.

Sending Friend Requests

When you search by email address, the results page will show the person's thumbnail picture (if the person has a MySpace account) and a few brief details, such as where the person is located, as well as some options on what to do next (see Figure 9.4). You'll notice there is no option to add that person as a friend. The only way to request that the person be your friend is to click View Profile and send the person a request from his or her page.

Find a Friend

Nazia **Headline:** "Mahalo!"
Location: Washington DC, US
Profile Updated: Sep 26, 2006 12:56 PM

View Profile
Send Message
Send Instant Message
Forward to a Friend
Add to Blog Preferred List

Nazia

Figure 9.4
A successful search will return results that look like this.
Clicking on View Profile is the next step in adding a friend.

Once you're on that person's profile, there will be a contact box (sometimes called a *contact table*), usually located below the person's picture. This contact section appears on every profile and contains all the functions related to contacting the user or saving his or her information for later reference. To send the person a friend request, click on Add to Friends (see Figure 9.5). Note that the contact box seen in Figure 9.5 is the standard-style box provided by MySpace. However, users can create customized contact boxes that may say something similar, such as Add Me or Be Friends. The words may be different, but the function is the same.

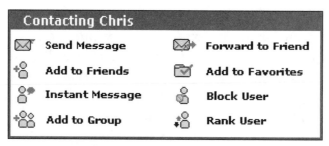

Figure 9.5
Send a friend request by clicking Add to Friends in the contact box.

The system will ask you to confirm that you want to add this person as your friend. Click Add to Friends to proceed. MySpace will notify the user that you have requested to be added as a friend. The MySpacer will then have the option to accept or deny your request. Some users have an additional privacy setting that requires requesters to know either their last name or their email address. The system will prompt you for that information if it is required.

Expanding Your List

Now that you've sent friend requests to people you know in the real world, it's time to venture out and make new friends. By this point you hopefully have built up a respectable-sized friends list filled with people you know and fans who already know you. But if you don't know many people and you are a new band with few contacts, you needn't worry. We'll explore ways to build up that friends list to rock-star proportions!

Start with the Entertainers You Know and Love

The ugly truth is that people like to join band profiles that already have a lot of friends. They click on a profile, and if it says, "Rock Band has 15 friends," the impression is that this profile and the music aren't all that interesting. Yet you have to get people to join in order to have a lot of friends that will attract others in the first place. It's sort of a teenage party—no one wants to go if they don't think there'll be a lot of people there. It may be unfair and reek of a high school popularity contest, but when you are new to MySpace, you have to work at building up your friends list quickly.

The fastest way to do this—after starting with people you already know, of course—is to seek out bands, comedians, and filmmakers whose work you like. Most entertainers will add anyone who asks. So go after them first! Almost all of the major label artists and entertainers you know and love will be on MySpace (see Figure 9.6).

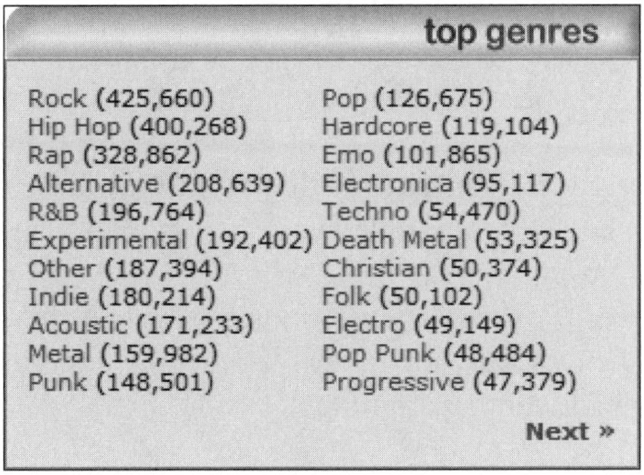

top genres

Rock (425,660)	Pop (126,675)
Hip Hop (400,268)	Hardcore (119,104)
Rap (328,862)	Emo (101,865)
Alternative (208,639)	Electronica (95,117)
R&B (196,764)	Techno (54,470)
Experimental (192,402)	Death Metal (53,325)
Other (187,394)	Christian (50,374)
Indie (180,214)	Folk (50,102)
Acoustic (171,233)	Electro (49,149)
Metal (159,982)	Pop Punk (48,484)
Punk (148,501)	Progressive (47,379)

Next »

Figure 9.6
Browse the genre directory in the MySpace Music section.
Look for bands that are similar or complementary to yours.

Your Friends Are My Friends

Pay close attention to artists in the same or a complementary genre as your music. For example, if you're an R&B singer, add R&B, gospel, hip-hop, and rap artists, too. Their audience is your audience. Once you are their friend, send friend requests to people on their lists as well. Do not, however, approach this in an assembly-line fashion. It is important to actually look at each person's profile, paying close attention to anything that would indicate he or she won't add anyone who doesn't have the courtesy to offer a polite hello. There are many people on MySpace who do not appreciate getting friend requests from strangers who don't bother to send them an introductory email (see Figure 9.7). They see these requests as an insincere intrusion, meant only to rack up thumbnails on a list. Instead of offending someone's sensibilities and raising their ire, respect their wishes and send them a brief but sincere email saying you saw them on so-and-so's profile and you thought they might like your music too.

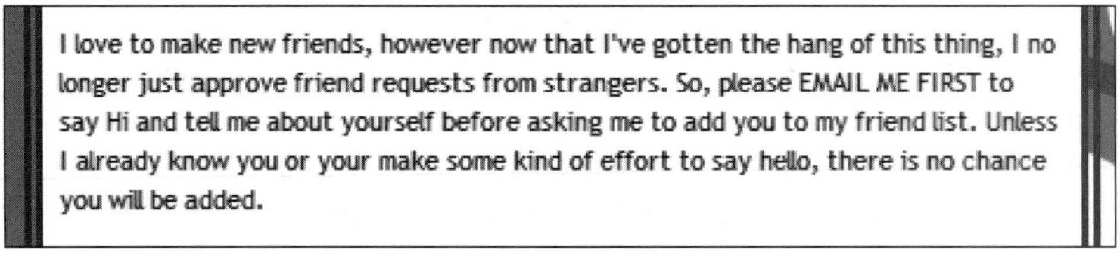

> I love to make new friends, however now that I've gotten the hang of this thing, I no longer just approve friend requests from strangers. So, please EMAIL ME FIRST to say Hi and tell me about yourself before asking me to add you to my friend list. Unless I already know you or your make some kind of effort to say hello, there is no chance you will be added.

Figure 9.7
Picky potential friends won't tolerate a friend request from a stranger,
so pay attention and remember to say hello first!

So start browsing the music, comedian, and film directories for your favorites as well as compatible-genre artists and send them friend requests. Make a concentrated effort in the beginning to add friends quickly, followed by a consistent ongoing plan to contact new people every week. Then watch your friends list grow into a happening party that everyone will want to attend!

Friend Bots, the Incredible Adding Machines

For the serious music marketer with little time to spare, the use of a friend bot can be a great way to add lots of friends in a short amount of time. A friend bot is a program that crawls through MySpace searching for friends that fit a predetermined set of criteria, much in the same way a search bot weaves its way through the Internet catalog sites for search engines. Your friend bot can then email prewritten messages and automatically send friend requests on your behalf. Some bots even allow you to post comments to many friends at once, saving time and hassle. Another perk is that many of them will keep backups of your friends list so that if your account is ever compromised or deleted and you need to start all over, you know who was on your list and you can add the same people back in.

Friend bots are often referred to as *friend adders*. Very few, if any, are free, so it is a small investment to make toward marketing and promotions. Because they tend to come and go, I'll refrain from listing one here. Instead, do a web search for "MySpace friend adder" to see what's available.

It's important to note that, per the terms of use, MySpace does not allow the use of bots to add friends or send mass messages or comments because of spamming concerns. So, you're technically not allowed to use these types of programs, and MySpace seems to be cracking down on developers who offer adders to the public. You want to make sure that if you use an adder program or some other bot program, you do not add, send, or comment to more than 100 to 150 friends in one day. Some people may tell you that 250 to 500 per day is acceptable, but the truth is anything over 50 will start to draw attention to you. Anything more than 100 to 150, and you are likely to be flagged as a spammer; your account may be frozen, suspended, or deleted.

All Aboard the Friend Train!

Some people add the masses to their friends list by using a friend train. It's also called a *MySpace train* or a *whore train*. (We won't even go into why it's called that last one!) When you "ride" a friend train, you post the friend train code into a bulletin and send it out to your friends, asking them to add everyone on the train. You will now show up on the train, and people will post similar bulletins asking everyone to add you. I personally don't recommend taking this approach. First, MySpace seems to be employing more filters to disallow the kind of code needed for a friend train bulletin post. Second, although you can inflate your friend numbers, it doesn't necessarily mean you're actually targeting people who might be interested in your music and who will attend a show or make a purchase. However, if you're bent on giving it a go, do a web search on "myspace train," "friend train," or "whore train," and you'll find many to choose from.

Add Me Groups

There's a discussion group for everything! There are even groups whose sole purpose is to get everyone to add the members to your friends list. Like friend trains, you're not getting any kind of targeted audience, but your friends list numbers will grow. For some, this is a beginning tactic just to have *some* friends so their list doesn't look so empty and won't scare away would-be fans. To find Add Me groups, go to the Groups link in the medium-blue navigation bar. Toward the bottom of the resulting page is a groups search box. Type "add me," and voilá! You'll see many groups that are dedicated to adding friends. Follow the group's instructions, which are usually just posting a message that says "add me!"

Add Me Links

Another way to encourage friend adds is to post an "Add to Friends" link on your profile below your bio text. You can also post this type of link in any comments you make to others or embed it into emails you send out to non-friends. It's just another way to put your add link out there so it's readily available for users to find.

In Chapter 8 we took a look at how to create links and how to locate a friend ID. And in Chapter 10, "Comments, Anyone?" we will look at posting comments in more depth. You can consult this how-to information for more instruction on embedding the link in a profile or comment. Basically, this is the HTML you'll need:

1. First, create an <img src> tag for the Add to Friends icon. We will use the same graphic that appears in the contact table of your profile. Currently, the Add to Friends artwork is located at http://x.myspace.com/images/profile/friend_1.gif. Windows users find this by right-clicking on the graphic and then clicking Properties.

2. The tag will therefore look like <img src=http://x.myspace.com/images/profile/friend_1.gif>.

3. Now, take this link and add your friend ID where the Xs are: http://collect.myspace.com/index.cfm?fuseaction=invite.addfriend _verify&friendID=XXXX. Your ID number may be longer than four numbers. (For help finding your ID, see Chapter 8 under "Finding the Friend ID" section.)

4. Enclose the <img src> tag with a hyperlink tag using the formula above, and with your friend ID in place of the Xs. We'll also center it. Now the tag will look like this: <a href=http://collect. myspace.com/index.cfm?fuseaction=invite.addfriend_verify& friendID=XXXX> <img src=http://x.myspace.com/images/profile/ friend_1.gif></a> .

5. Note that the code above does not include any quotation marks (" ") around the URLs. This works best for the MySpace environment.

6. Take the above code and embed it into your profile or a comment. Users will then see the Add to Friends icon (see Figure 9.8), and when they click it, they will be able to ask you if you'd like to be that user's friend!

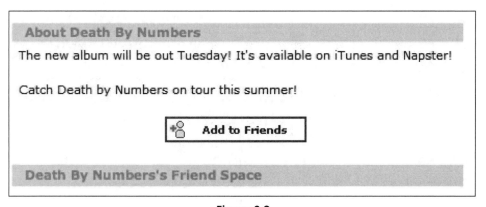

Figure 9.8
Your Add to Friends icon embedded in your profile copy will look something like this.

It's Not You, It's Me

One's friends list is a dynamic entity. It changes all the time. People come and go. They lose interest or become overwhelmed with their burdensome lists and start to clean house. Often, bands they don't follow regularly are the first to get the ax. When you have tons of friends, you may see the number of them fluctuate here and there. But with so many on the list, you probably won't notice who has left.

Then, there are those who from the beginning have blocked all friend requests from bands and musical artists in their Account Settings. Usually this is because they don't want to be inundated by requests from bands they don't know. In this case, you can opt to send them a pleasant email introducing yourself, asking them to check out your music and add you if they like. However, if they're not interested, don't take it personally—just move on. You have almost 200 million other people from whom to choose!

Approving and Denying Friends

Requesting friends is a natural and expected part of being in the MySpace community. You are sure to get requests from people who happen upon your page while browsing the music area, see you in another's friends list, or hear about your music from others. You will also likely get requests from people who are interested in selling you products and services, including porn and live webcams. While you are in the business of promoting your music, you don't have to approve every request that comes your way. Use your discretion.

When someone asks you to be their friend, you will see a notification in your profile control panel's My Mail section (see Figure 9.9). Click on the notice to go to the Friend Request Manager.

My Mail

☒ **New Friend Requests!**

inbox	friend requests
sent	post bulletin

Figure 9.9
You have friends! MySpace lets you know when others want to be your friend.

You will see a picture of the person requesting your friendship, as well as their handle and buttons to Approve, Deny, or Send a Message (see Figure 9.10). This is the same screen others see when you send them a friend request. Most of the time you will be approving requests, but when you get one that looks fishy, as if it's for product or service with which you don't want to be associated, hit the Deny button. The requester does not receive notice that you denied the request. The system is discreet in that regard. The request to you simply disappears from the person's console. Often, that is that. Sometimes the persistent ones will keep sending you friend requests and emails. You have the option of blocking them from ever contacting you again, which is explored at the end of this chapter, under the "Deleting and Blocking" section.

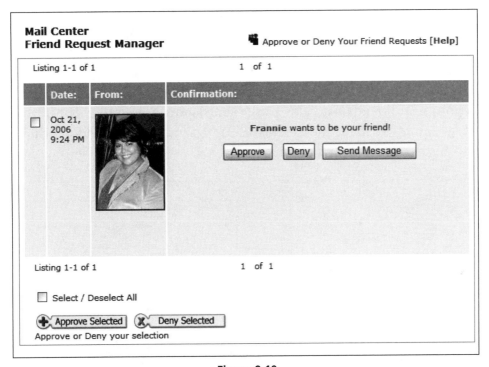

Figure 9.10
The Friend Request Manager keeps track of everyone wanting to be in your inner circle.

It is easy to approve or deny several requests at once by checking off the users in your Friend Request Manager and then hitting the Approve Selected or Deny Selected button at the bottom of the console.

The Top of the Heap

Once upon a time, MySpace allowed you to designate your "Top 8" friends who would appear on your profile's first page. It is considered a coveted spot to be in the Top Friends area of someone's profile. MySpace has since expanded options to allow Top 4, 8, 12, 16, 20, or 24 friends. How many people and whom you choose to display on your profile's My Friend Space is entirely up to you. Those who don't appear there are accessible when users click on View All of My Friends.

By default, friends generally appear in the order they were added. To reorganize your top friends, click on the link Change My Top Friends in your control panel's My Friend Space section (see Figure 9.11). Choose the number of top friends you want to display from the drop-down menu on the page that appears. You'll see all your friends' thumbnail pics displayed. Browse through your pages or use the search option to find and place friends in the order you want them to appear in your Top Friends list. The Top Friends spots are highlighted in red. Once you're satisfied, click the Save Top Friends button, and your new Top Friends list will be complete!

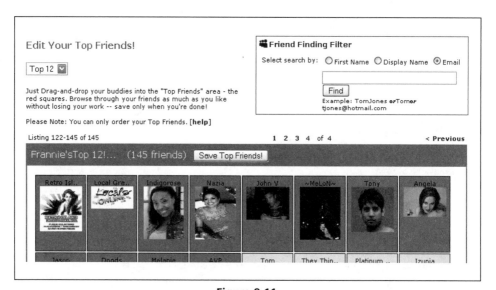

Figure 9.11
Change your Top Friends list as often as you like. Even use the list to reward loyal fans.

Customizing Your Friends List

Your friends list doesn't have to look like everyone else's friends list. There are a few ways to make yours unique.

The Possibilities

While MySpace gives you the option to change how many and which friends appear on the first page of your profile, it doesn't allow you to customize that list further. The Internet is full of websites that will generate code to change the look of your friends list. Some options include creating a Top Friends list of more than 24 friends; tweaking the number of friends that appear in a row or column; changing the word "friends" to "fans" (or any other word); altering the names of friends from their actual profile alias to a name of your choice; choosing which of your friends' pictures you want to show on your profile; making two friends lists; and reversing the order, scrolling, and hiding friends.

How and Where to Find Code

There are many ways to customize your friends list by manipulating the code. Let's take a look at the possibilities.

Tweaking Your Top Friends List

You don't need to know any kind of HTML or other programming language to generate custom code for your profile. Plenty of resourceful people have already done the work for you. What you need is a code or script generator (sometimes called a gen) that will ask you to input your friends' information, and then will create the code for you. My favorite friends list code generator is Top 16+ Code Generator / Editor for MySpace Profiles (www.locohost.net/myspace_top16); see Figure 9.12. It is easy to use with a very simple interface. Even though the title is "Top 16," it will actually generate lists up to 80 friends strong to turn your default Top Friends list (see Figure 9.13) into a new, custom list (see Figure 9.14). Paste the newly generated code (see Figure 9.15) into your profile as directed by the generator to see the results.

** This code will completely replace your "top 8" when your profile is viewed. **

Friend Space Heading (OPTIONAL):   Frannie's Fan Club

View All Friends URL (OPTIONAL):   (Click on the View All Friends URL on your profile and paste the URL here)

Friend Count (OPTIONAL):   tons o'

Friend #1 Name:
Friend #1 Profile URL:
Friend #1 Image URL:

Friend #2 Name:
Friend #2 Profile URL:
Friend #2 Image URL:

Figure 9.12
The code generator at www.locohost.net/myspace_top16.

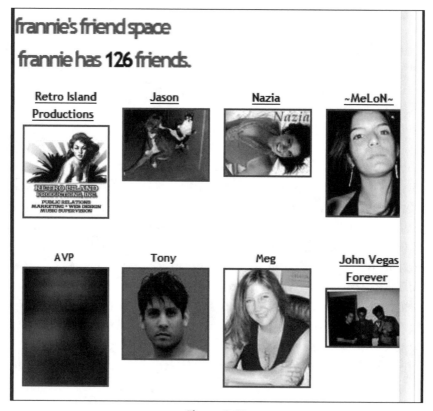

Figure 9.13
A default MySpace Top Friends list.

Figure 9.14
The new MySpace Top Friends list, altered by custom code.
Notice that the layout, aliases of friends, and pictures have changed,
as well as the headers for the friends list.

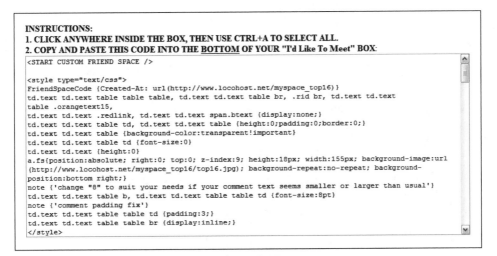

Figure 9.15
The new code for a friends list to be pasted into one of the user's
profile fields while in Edit Profile mode.

Another excellent friends list code generator is located at http://r4wr.com/ friends. It has slightly different options focusing on style formatting and text alignment. If the recommended code generators don't suit you, do a web search for "MySpace friend list codes," and you will be amazed at the dozens and dozens of results.

A fun way to alter your Top Friends list is to split it into two. You can have a regular Top Friends list as well as another list for "special" people, such as a VIP list or a Fan list. You can denote the second list any way you like. It sets these friends apart from the others and is a great way to reward your street team and fan clubbers with a coveted spot on your profile. An easy-to-use VIP friends list generator can be found at www.coshed.com/generators/vip-friends-list-generator.php. This site has tons of other excellent scripts and tweaks for MySpace.

The code generator will usually include instructions on where to paste the code while you're in Edit Profile mode. However, these code generators are made for regular MySpace accounts, and musicians' profiles are set up a little differently. You may not be sure where to paste the code, but here are few tips:

1. First, paste the code into the end of the Bio section, save changes, and view your profile to see if the changes took.

2. If the code doesn't execute correctly, make sure you don't have any broken HTML tags in that section. Broken, missing, or incorrect tags, which are noted by < >, would include opening tags but no closing tags (for example, <center> but no </center>) and vice versa, as well as misspelled tags. Note that <img src>, <br>, and <hr> do not require closing tags. These are used by themselves.

3. Check the rest of the profile's fields to be sure there are no other tag problems.

4. Other code in a field can sometimes cause conflicts. Remove all previous code in the field and paste in only the Top Friends code. Save and check for correct execution.

5. Still doesn't work? Try pasting the code into another field.

6. If it still does not work, create a new field or section in which you can paste code. (See Chapter 8 for details.)

MySpace can be buggy, and customizing profiles is often hit or miss. Being flexible, patient, and willing to try new things will yield the best results in your customization efforts.

More Friends List Tweaks

Try some of these other friends list code gens:

- Hide your friends: www.xgenerators.com

- Reverse your friends (place them on the other side of your profile—usually the left side): www.kazspace.com

- Scroll your friends: www.myspacescripts.com

Deleting and Blocking

Now that your friends list is getting bigger, you'll need to spend some time managing it. Here are a couple of things to keep in mind.

Most bands will not make a habit of deleting friends, but there may be times when you need to do so. Stalker types, hate mailers, inappropriate comment writers, and people who leave long profile and blog comments promoting themselves are possible candidates for deletion. Deleting friends is easy. In your profile's control panel, Edit Friends is located in the My Friend Space section. Click here and delete friends at will.

For those users who really are becoming too weird for you to handle, blocking is an appropriate measure. Blocking a MySpace user not only removes that person from your friends list, but also bars him or her from ever contacting you again through the blocked profile. Go to the offending MySpacer's profile, and in the contact box, click Block User. Manually delete any comments the user has left for you on your profile. If a user threatens you, MySpace recommends you call law enforcement immediately.

Now that your friends list is in place and growing, it's time we talked about commenting.

10 Comments, Anyone?

One of the most integral parts of being a MySpacer is leaving comments for your friends. As you browse around the place, clicking on various people and perusing their comments, you'll notice that the comments section is used as a community bulletin board of sorts. Friends old and new remark on the happenings of the weekend, make inside jokes, and of course tell their favorite bands how much they love their music. Artists leave comments for fans, announcing gigs and thanking people for adding them to their list.

The comments section, as public as it seems, is really a sort of walled garden. You can see it, but you can't get access to it... unless you are a friend, as Figure 10.1 shows. By now you have realized the importance of building a strong friends list and hopefully you have begun to assemble your own. It's time to start cementing relationships with your friends and making them a part of your community through commenting.

This chapter will explore the basics of commenting, embedding media into your comments, and using marketing tips to maximize your commenting efforts.

Error: You must be someone's friend to make comments about them.

Back

Figure 10.1
Only friends can leave comments.

The Basics

There are three main types of comments—profile comments, which are left on a MySpacer's profile homepage; image (or picture) comments, which are left in response to a posted picture or graphic in the View Pics section; and blog comments, which are left in response to entries in the user's blog section. This section provides a rundown of the various types of comments, where to find them, how to leave them for others, and how to approve/deny/delete those left for you.

The Profile Comment

The starting point for all comments is the profile. Users who employ custom layout codes may move their friends' comments, rename or reorganize the way the comments section looks, or hide it all together. However, when a profile is in default mode and unchanged by any formatting scripts, profile comments appear below your My Friend Space (see Figure 10.2), where all the little thumbnail pictures of one's friends are gathered.

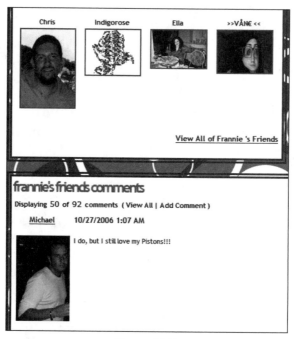

Figure 10.2
Profile comments appear just below your collection of friends in your Friends Comments section, which contains various links and information related to comments.

This section is aptly named "*[Your alias]*'s Friends Comments." At the present moment, you may only have 50 or fewer comments, all of which are displayed directly on your profile. Eventually, you'll accumulate so many that they'll spill over into subsequent pages.

You'll also notice in this area that MySpace keeps a running count of how many comments you have and how many are displayed, and provides links to View All. Clicking on this link will do several things. First, it lets visitors see all of your comments. Second, clicking on this link within *your own profile,* while you are logged in, allows you to delete comments left for you by others (see Figure 10.3). This is handy when you want to delete a comment that you deem inappropriate or too long, or one that contains a graphic that has distorted the look of your profile layout. In addition, clicking this link on a *friend's profile* allows you to delete comments you left for that person. This is convenient if you accidentally hit the Submit button twice and left the same comment over again!

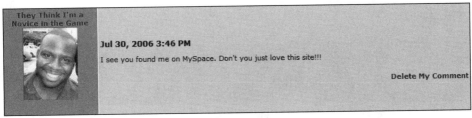

Figure 10.3
Clicking on View All on your own profile allows you to delete comments from friends.

Leaving Text Comments

Now you'll learn how to leave basic text comments for friends, by starting with the profile comment. The process is nearly identical for image and blog comments.

At the top of the Friends Comments section is the Add Comment link. On some custom layouts, the link appears at the very bottom of the comment section and can be easy to miss on pages with many comments.

Figures 10.4 and 10.5 show you both types of Add Comment links. Be sure to scroll all the way down to the end if you don't see the link at the top!

Figure 10.4
The default MySpace Friends Comments section.

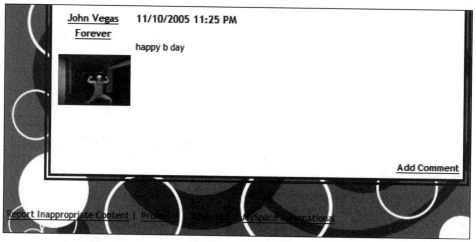

Figure 10.5
In this custom layout, the Add Comment link appears
at the bottom of a MySpacer's comment section.

When you want to leave a profile comment for a friend, you click on Add Comment. A page will come up that will allow you to type in your comment, as shown in Figure 10.6.

When you are finished, click Post a Comment. The system will give you an opportunity to review your comment once more and edit it if necessary (see Figure 10.7). When you are satisfied, click Post a Comment again.

Figure 10.6
Type your comment into the text box.

Figure 10.7
Confirm or edit your comment.

Depending on your friend's account settings (see Figure 10.8), your comment either will post immediately on the profile or will be sent to your friend's inbox for approval (see Figure 10.9). Figure 10.10 shows the notice you'll receive indicating that approval is required.

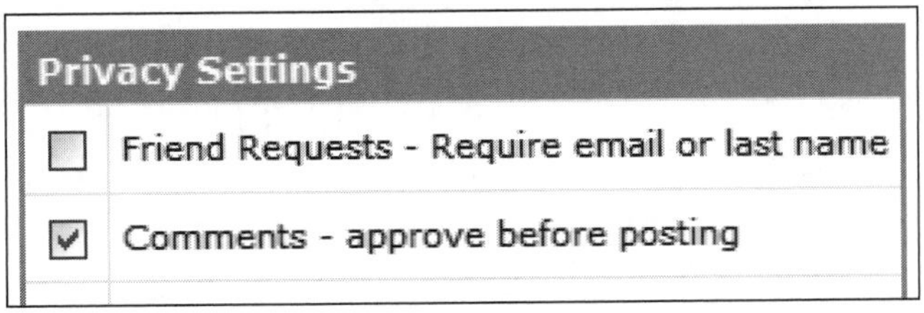

Figure 10.8
MySpacers who opt for it can approve all comments before they are posted to their profile.

Figure 10.9
Notification of a pending comment appears as a new message.

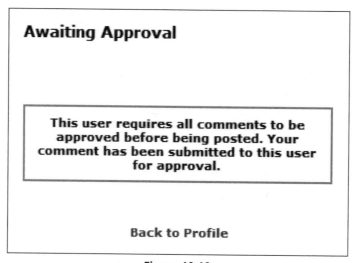

Figure 10.10
If your friend requires comment approval, you will see this message.

Your comment will be sent to your friend as an email, as shown in Figure 10.11, with buttons allowing your friend to approve or deny it (see Figure 10.12). If your friend chooses to approve your comment, it will post to his or her profile, as shown in Figure 10.13. If denied, the message will not be returned to you, nor will you be notified—the comment will simply not be posted to your friend's profile.

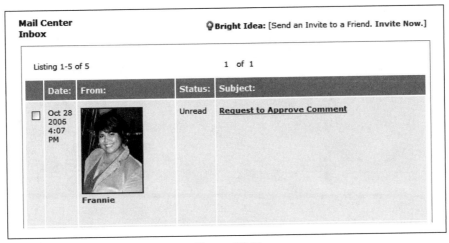

Figure 10.11
The comment approval message goes to one's inbox.

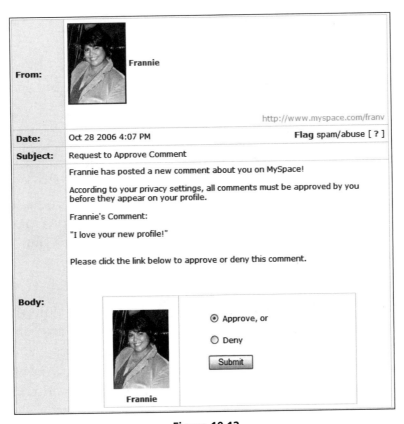

Figure 10.12
The user will see the comment request displayed like this,
with options to approve or deny.

Figure 10.13
The approved comment will appear on the profile.

Of course, you will go through the same process when someone leaves you a comment!

The Image Comment

MySpacers are given space to upload a number of pictures to their accounts (up to 300 at the time of this book's printing). These pictures are then accessed via the View My Pics link of one's profile, located near the top of the profile, below the user's main photo, as indicated in Figure 10.14. Friends can click on this link and view your photos (see Figure 10.15), and even remark on the uploaded photos and graphics, called *image* or *picture comments*.

While you can embed graphics and photos hosted on a non-MySpace server into your profile's code, only photos uploaded onto the MySpace server can be commented upon. You'll see that each photo has a set of options below it, the first one being Post a Comment. Click on this link, and the process is the same as leaving a profile comment, except the image comments will appear below the photo, as shown in Figure 10.16.

Figure 10.14
Friends can comment on photos loaded into the View My Pics section.

Figure 10.15
Uploaded photos will appear on your profile like this.

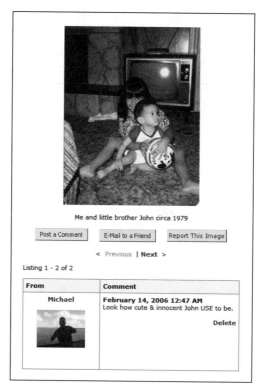

Figure 10.16
A finished image/picture comment.

Just like profile comments, image comments left for you will go to your inbox for approval. Even if you approve them, you can still delete them later. Clicking on your own profile's View My Pics link while logged in will allow you to delete unwanted comments. You can also delete your image comments left for others by visiting the picture and clicking Delete My Comment.

The Blog Comment

Every MySpacer has the ability to post *blogs* (short for *Web logs*), which are online entries that can be used like a journal or a bulletin board that appears on your profile. The user can then choose to allow the entire MySpace public to comment on his entries, or he can limit it to all of his friends or a preferred list of users. Blogs are located near the top of the profile, as shown in Figure 10.17. (For more details on how to use blogs, see Chapter 13, "Blogging in the MySpace World.")

Figure 10.17
The blog section of a profile.

To leave a blog comment, click on the blog entry and scroll to the bottom. If the user is allowing others to leave their thoughts, you will see the Add Comment link (see Figure 10.18).

> *** This internship is unpaid and for credit only. You must be enrolled in a college or university and receive credit for the internship. ***
>
> **12:30 AM - 0 Comments - 0 Kudos -** <u>Add Comment</u>

Figure 10.18
This user allows comments to be left in response to his blog entry.

Clicking here will take you to a special text box meant only for blogs, which you can see in Figure 10.19. This is different than the other types of comment text boxes because you can format your entry with options such as bold, italic, centering, and more. Blog comments also allow you to give kudos if you like, which are like a thumbs up.

The biggest difference between blog comments and profile or image comments is not just the HTML text editor. Blog comments do not allow you a final chance to edit your remarks, nor do they allow you to delete your comments later. So be absolutely sure of what you want to say before you hit Post!

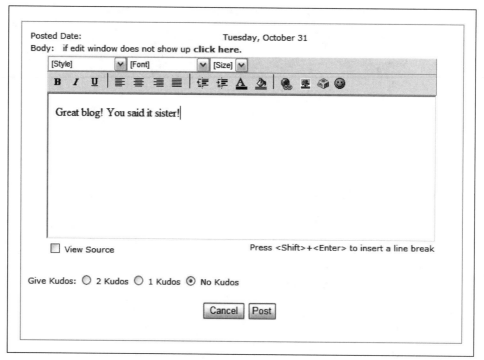

Figure 10.19
The blog comment text editor.

From here, the process is the same as for other types of comments. The user will receive notification of your comment and will approve or deny it.

Leaving HTML Comments

Unlike plain text, HTML code allows you to leave comments containing images, videos, hyperlinks, and more. Not only can you make your comments for friends more fun, but with embedded graphics and links, you can also use comments to build your brand among fans.

In Chapter 8, you learned about basic HTML and how to use it when customizing your MySpace profile. The HTML needed for adding links, photos, and video to comments is identical.

This section will focus on embedding images, hyperlinks, and media in comments. Please see Chapter 8 for further information on HTML tags and using images and video within MySpace.

Embedding Images

Leaving image-embedded comments is an excellent way to catch the eye of visitors. Photos and graphics can be used to generate even more interest in you as an artist, or as a way to advertise gigs and special events.

Keep images less than 200KB, no wider than the average comment section column (about 250 to 400 pixels), and no longer than 550 pixels. Users who are left comments with large embedded images—even if those images are short in width but long in length, leaving the profile layout intact—are apt to delete them without posting. No one wants to feel like an advertisement is sucking up all their comment real estate.

While Chapter 8 will give you the basics of how and where to upload content, as well as the HTML code, here are the necessary steps for including an image in a comment:

1. Create/edit an image and save it as a JPG or GIF in a manageable size.

2. Upload the image to an outside server.

3. Locate the URL of your image.

4. Insert the URL into an <img src> tag (see Figure 10.20).

5. Place code and any introductory text into the comment box.

6. When you are finished, click Post a Comment, review, edit if necessary, and click Confirm (see Figure 10.21). Your approved comment will appear on the profile, as shown in Figure 10.22.

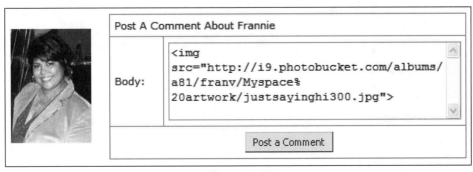

Figure 10.20
The< img src> HTML tag as it appears in the comment box.

Figure 10.21
Confirm that your image appears properly by reviewing the Confirm Comment screen.

Figure 10.22
The comment with embedded image as it appears on a profile.

Hyperlinks

Our next task is to create a hyperlink in a comment. This is a great way to direct people to your home website or music download shop. Leaving a comment with a clickable URL is the same as embedding a hyperlink in a profile. See Chapter 8 for details on creating hyperlinks.

If we were leaving a simple text message that included a website address that was not clickable, it would look like what you see in Figure 10.23.

Figure 10.23
Our comment entered in plain text only.

In plain text, the URL to the website would not be activated (see Figure 10.24). As marketers, however, we want to make it very easy for our fans to access our website, so we want to create a hyperlink that a visitor can click and be transported to our website. When we add HTML tags, our comment will now be inputted as you see in Figure 10.25.

Figure 10.24
The website will not appear as a link because no HTML tags were included.

Figure 10.25
Our comment is now formatted to create a hyperlink for www.retroisland.com.

You can surround any text with hyperlink tags. Let's say we want to link the name of the website. It would look like this:

> Hey thanks for the add! Visit our Web site at
> <a href="http://www.retroisland.com">www.retroisland.com</a>
> for more info on how to market your music!

Take a look at Figure 10.26 to see how your comment will look in the MySpace environment with HTML encoding, and the final result as it appears on a profile in Figure 10.27.

Figure 10.26
Now we can see that the website address has been turned into a link.
Users who click on it will be taken to the site.

You can hyperlink graphics as well as text. The hyperlink tags remain the same, but instead of enclosing them around text, you will enclose them around HTML image tags.

Figure 10.27
The final comment appears in a profile like this.

Figure 10.28 shows a sample of what the HTML of a linked image would look like.

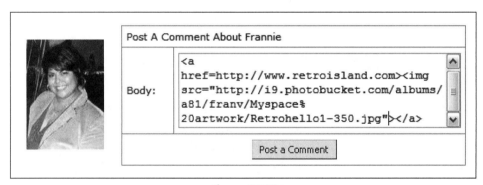

Figure 10.28
The hyperlinked image as it appears in HTML.

Be sure to double-check all of your tags to ensure that you have included </a> at the end of every item you want to hyperlink! The final comment pulls the image from the server where it's stored and links it to the retroisland.com website. The border around the image indicates that it is hyperlinked. See what it looks like in Figure 10.29.

Figure 10.29
The final comment featuring a hyperlinked image.

Embedding Video

Friends often love leaving humorous videos in comments for each other. As a music marketer, however, you must be very judicious when using video on another's page. Post no more than one video in a comment and always aim to use video code that does not automatically start playing when the page is loaded. Consider using video clips of your live shows, recording-studio B-roll, interview footage, and even promotional music videos. Whichever you choose, be sure your clip not only has good visual quality, but also has excellent audio quality. This is especially important when you are using live show footage, which can sometimes look dark and grainy and sound distorted. Also be sure that your videos do not contain any pornographic content. Most hosting sites, including MySpace, will delete your accounts if you upload porn.

Whether you upload your videos onto MySpace or use another provider, such as YouTube.com, you'll need to copy (Ctrl+V) the video code to paste into the comment, as shown in Figure 10.30.

Figure 10.30
MySpace video code is pasted into a comment box.

Go to a friend's profile where you wish to leave a comment containing your video and click on Add Comment. When the comment box comes up, paste this copied code into the box by right-clicking with your mouse and choosing Paste, or by pressing the Ctrl+V keyboard shortcut.

You can leave the comment like this or add some introductory text, as shown in Figure 10.31. To add text before the video, put your cursor before the tag (which starts with <a href=...>) and type in your text. After you have finished your introduction, type the tag <p> on the next line to add some space between your text and the embedded video.

The resulting comment will look like Figure 10.32.

Figure 10.31
Add introductory text to your comment.

Figure 10.32
A comment with introductory text and a video clip.

Chapter 8 contains more details on video.

More Comment Settings

Some MySpacers do not allow HTML comments to be left in their profiles (see Figure 10.33). If you paste HTML code into a comment box where it is restricted, the code will not be processed. Instead, it will be displayed as plain text, tags and all. The user's account will warn you ahead of time that HTML comments are not allowed for this profile. Leave plain text comments only.

You can also set your account to notify you when you receive a profile, image, and/or blog comment. Access your Mobile Alert Settings through Account Settings to modify these options.

Figure 10.33
This user does not allow HTML comments.

Customizing Comments

There are three main ways to customize commenting—mass commenting, scrolling comments, and the use of profile comment boxes. Some MySpacers like to hide their comments, but as a music marketer you won't want to do that. User interaction is vital in growing a fan base. Comments should remain visible.

Mass Commenting

In Chapter 9 we talked about friend adder programs that automate the process of finding and adding friends by using bots. These types of programs sometimes incorporate mass commenting and mass bulletins. Because many of the comments you will be leaving will be the same for all your friends, a mass commenter that will automate the arduous task of leaving many comments can really help you maximize your marketing efforts. The cost normally runs between $30 and $70, depending on the features of the program. The time it saves is well worth it, though you run the risk of losing your account if MySpace discovers it.

Remember that the MySpace powers-that-be do not like bots and adder programs, so be frugal in the number of comments you leave in a 24-hour period. More than 50 begins to attract attention, and you have a higher likelihood of being flagged as a spammer by the MySpace system. You always run that risk when using bots. If you decide to be a marketing daredevil, be sure to always save copies of any custom code you used to alter your profile, and use the bot program to back up your friends list on a regular basis. If MySpace freezes or deletes your account, at least you'll have all of your profile info and a comprehensive friends list handy should you need to start over.

Comment Boxes and Scrolling Friends

Earlier in the chapter we learned that leaving a comment starts by clicking the Add Comment link on a friend's profile. Some users prefer to remove this extra step and plug in code to create a profile comment box. This box appears right on your profile, near your comment section, and consists of a text box and a submit button. Visitors will no longer have to find the Add Comment link, click it, and then leave a comment. Should you see this feature on a friend's page, you'll know what to do.

Integrated profile comment boxes, as shown in Figure 10.34, are an added convenience that MySpacers love. Plus, they serve as visual encouragement for fans and friends to leave comments for you. Let's discuss how you can incorporate a comment box into your music profile.

The code to create a comment box can often be bundled with the ability to scroll through comments and friends at the same time. It basically takes the friends list and comments sections of your profile and partitions them off so they become a scrollable section all their own. This is helpful when you want to show off a ton of top friends and lots of comments, but you don't want to force visitors to scroll endlessly to the bottom of your profile. People tend to lose interest that way, so this set of code packages friends and comments into a tidy, manageable segment.

My favorite comment box/scrolling friends code generator, shown in Figure 10.35, can be found at www.myspace.nuclearcentury.com/commentbox.php. I like it because it's super easy to generate, and even the least Web-savvy person can use it. It's pretty basic and will give you a comment box and scrolling friends/comments (see Figure 10.36).

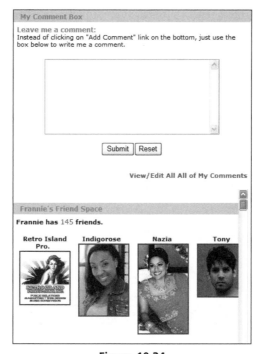

Figure 10.34
An example of an integrated comment box with scrolling friends/comments.

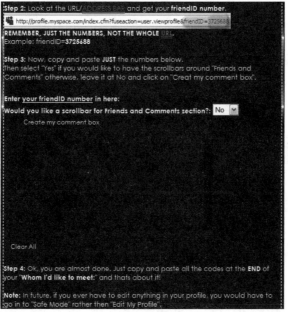

Figure 10.35
The comment box generator at Nuclear Century.

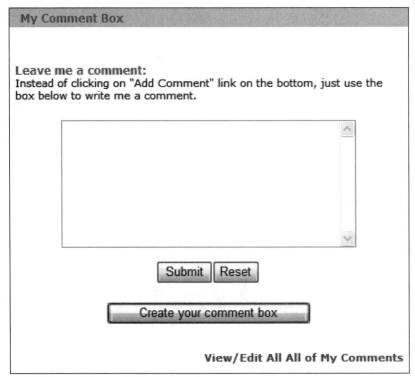

Figure 10.36
The comment box as it appears on a default music profile.

Want to get fancy? Try customizing your comment box with colors, various fonts, custom button text, and backgrounds. A simple-to-use generator is located at www.htmate2.com/commentbox. I like this one because it has little in-browser pop-ups that explain the various fields for those who wonder what they all mean (see Figure 10.37). It also generates color codes for you, shows you fonts to choose from, and allows you to preview your comment box first, so you can tweak it if it doesn't look exactly how you want. However, this comment box doesn't have a scrolling feature bundled with it. Try using a picture of your band or a logo as the comment box background, and integrate colors that fit with your band's image. Figure 10.38 shows an example of a customized comment box.

A web search for "myspace comment box" will kick out many other possible generators for you to use.

Textarea Background Color [   ] <u>Click here to choose Color</u>

Words In Box by Default [   ]

Address URL to Background Image [   ]

Button background Color [   ]

> Right Click on the Image you want to find out
> Select 'Properties'
> on the new window, right next to 'Address URL',
> Copy the link (beginning with 'http://...' and put it in
> this box, that's it!

Button text Color [   ]

Color of text in the box [   ] <u>Click here to choose Color</u>

Choose a Font:

○ Arial
○ Courier New
○ *Comic Sans MS*
○ Georgia
○ Verdana
○ Lucida Console
○ Times New Roman
○ Helvetica
○ **Impact**
○ Trebuchet MS
○ Small Fonts
○ *Monotype Corsiva*
○ Garamond
○ Tahoma

Figure 10.37
The custom-designed comment box generator at htmate2.com, with pop-up instructions.

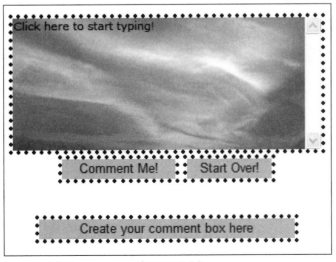

Figure 10.38
An elaborate comment box on a default profile.

In the musician profile, these comment codes should be placed at the end of the Bio section. Once you have put comment box code into your profile, you may need to do all future profile edits in Safe Mode. Also, be aware that some codes do not play well together. You may be able to have a comment box, but the custom Top Friends list may stop working. It's buggy, so if you're plugging in code without professional help, there may be times when features won't behave as they should and you will have to decide which feature is most important to you to keep.

Comment Spam

Why must a few evildoers ruin a good thing? Yes, even comments contain spam. It was inevitable, I suppose, considering that spammers are *everywhere* these days. Comment spam happens when someone bombards your comments with the same message over and over again. Often it's offers for meds or cell phones, photos of hot chicks, or some pyramid-scheme business opportunity. And sometimes it's an overzealous musician who thinks leaving 20 identical comments for the same person saying "Listen to my music" is actually going to attract new fans to his profile. (Hint: It doesn't.) This type of bombardment is aptly named "comment bombs." These bombs are sometimes sent by bad people, but some are sent by users who have no idea it's happening because their account was commandeered by a virus or a hacker. It's gotten so bad that some of these comments are programmed so they stay at the very top of your comments list, and you cannot delete them by normal methods.

First, never allow comment spam to remain on your profile. It is an absolute turnoff to all the legitimate fans who visit your page. Delete the offending comment spam by going into Safe Mode editing and deleting the comments from there.

Second, always enable comment approval in your Account Settings > Privacy Settings. This way, no comments will get posted to your page without you seeing and approving them first. Third, delete anyone on your friends list who is spamming you. And lastly, change your password every month or two (or more often if you suspect someone might have compromised your account) by going into Account Settings.

Hackers can spam your friends when they gain access to your account, so changing your password often will keep them guessing.

Making Comments Work for You

Using comments to your advantage is the best way to build a relationship with your fans and attract new ones. Of course, you don't want to abuse your relationship by bombarding friends with too many remarks, lest you be regarded as a weird stalker musician. Plan on leaving no more than one comment a month, unless something super newsworthy happens. Can't think of what kind of messages to leave or what you might say? Here are some great reasons to leave comments for your friends and fans:

- **When you add, or are added as, a new friend.** Leave a comment thanking your new friend for the add or just saying hello. Invite your friend to check out your profile, listen to your songs, and leave a comment telling you which is his or her favorite. You may even create a graphic to embed in the comment.

- **When someone leaves a comment for you first.** It's polite to return the favor and say "thanks for stopping by." Plus, it gives you one more opportunity to build a relationship and possibly attract new friends.

- **When it's holiday time.** This is when software for mass commenting comes in handy. Again, it's one more opportunity for exposure. Why not say "Happy Thanksgiving!" to everyone on your list?

- **When you change your profile layout or main website or you add new content.** Let friends and their visitors know that you have an awesome new profile or website and you have just added T-shirts for sale!

- **When you upload new music.** Ask friends to listen to your new songs and comment on which ones they like best. Ask them to add their favorite to their profile.

- **When you want to announce gigs, tour dates, personal appearances, and CD listening/release parties.** Have you just posted gigs for the next two months? Or maybe a summer tour? In-store appearances and TV and radio interviews are also ideal opportunities to leave comments. You can create a graphic or post a simple, "Hey, we're playing at a bunch of places the next couple months. Check out the schedule and see whether we'll be in your area!"

- **When you want to announce a special giveaway or contest.** Tell everyone you're giving away a CD to the person who refers the most friends to you this month.

- **When you need support.** Vying for the top spot in a battle of the bands? Perhaps you need people to vote for you for best artist. Mass commenting is a great way to ask everyone to support you in your time of need.

- **When you have news.** Did the local paper or a CD reviewer give you a great write-up? Or maybe you're one of the top artists on MySpace or another music site. Brag a little with, "Hey, we were just voted the best new band. Check out our profile for all the details." Press coverage, awards, changes in band lineup, CD sales milestones, and the like are all newsworthy tidbits.

- **When you post new photos or videos.** People love checking out photos and video clips.

- **When your music is available for sale on a new site.** If your music is now available on iTunes or any other download service, your friends will want to know!

- **When you want to recruit street team members.** Advertise that you're looking for people who love your music to help you promote your CD and gigs in their area.

Now that we've covered almost all there is to know to get you started with commenting, it's time to move on to the next step... profile songs.

11 Profile Songs and Your Music Player

Regular users can add music to their profiles from their favorite MySpace musicians, giving the artist exposure to new listeners. But to take advantage of this free promotion, you, the artist, must first ensure that your music player is set to allow adds. This chapter will explore how to use your music player and profile songs to market your music and encourage promotional buzz.

The Basics

The music player that appears on your artist profile can hold up to five songs as of this writing (recently up from four; see Figure 11.1). Users can click on any song in the player to listen to your music. Depending on your settings, listeners may also have the option to download, rate, view comments, read lyrics, or add one of your songs to their profile (see Figure 11.2).

Visitors who choose to add your song to their profile do so by clicking the Add link on the song of their choice. The song will automatically appear in the mini-player on the user's profile, along with your name and a link to your profile (as shown in Figure 11.3). This mini-player only holds one song at a time, making it pretty important real estate on a fan's page. If a fan adds your song to their page, it means he or she had to discard someone else's music to make room for yours. Figure 11.4 shows a song confirmation.

Figure 11.1
MySpace now allows artists' music players to hold up to five songs, plus
accompanying artwork. Here, artist Cary Brothers has four uploaded to
his music player (www.myspace.com/carybrothers).

Figure 11.2
These options appear below each song in your music player.
The Add option should be activated so users can add your song to their profile.

Figure 11.3
A regular MySpacer's profile will display your added song in this mini-player.

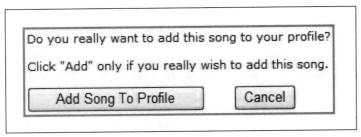

Figure 11.4
When a user adds your song, he is asked to confirm the choice.

This means that every visitor to that person's page will hear your music playing, which exposes your songs to hundreds, even thousands, of pairs of ears, depending on how much traffic that profile gets. Multiply this by the oodles of fans who all have your song playing on their profiles, and you can quickly see the potential for viral promotion and free exposure.

This can't happen unless you activate the add option in your artist music player. As a rule, you should always allow listeners to add your song to their profile. You are presented with this option when you upload music to your profile's player. But, you can always go back anytime to correct the oversight if you neglected to allow listeners to add your songs to their profiles.

Log into your MySpace account. On your home control panel, click Edit Profile, then go to the Manage Songs tab. Here you'll see the main settings for your player. The first check box in the Page Settings section is Allow Users to Add Songs to Their Profile. Always make sure this is checked, as in Figure 11.5.

For more information on managing your music player and settings, please refer to Chapter 7.

Profile songs are crucial page elements for active MySpacers. The song one chooses for his or her page not only is reflective of that person's musical interests at that time, but it also sometimes hints at the person's social and emotional moorings and values. It even sometimes coincides with the visual theme of the person's MySpace profile (for example,

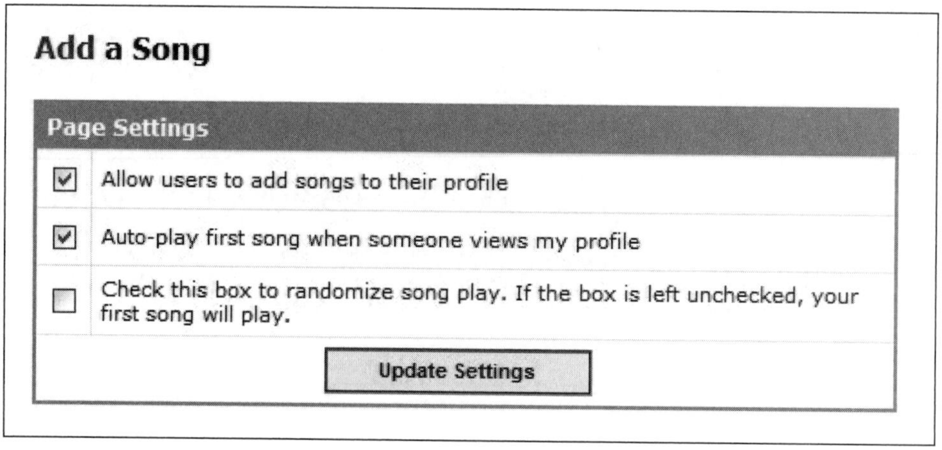

Add a Song

Page Settings

☑ Allow users to add songs to their profile

☑ Auto-play first song when someone views my profile

☐ Check this box to randomize song play. If the box is left unchecked, your first song will play.

Update Settings

Figure 11.5
Make sure the first option (to allow users to add your songs)
is checked in your account settings.

the Beach Boys with the island theme). The song a person chooses is a very personal choice and says something about the person, even if the person himself is unconscious of an overt revelation. We often make judgments about a person we don't know based on what the person looks like, what his profile looks like, what he writes in his blogs and profile text, and what kind of music and videos he features. It's a first impression of sorts.

A person doesn't need to be your MySpace friend to add your song to his profile. Anyone in the MySpace community can feature your song on his page. Your job as a marketer is to encourage visitors and friends alike to listen to your songs and add them to their profiles.

Encouraging Listens and Adds

There are a number of ways to encourage people to listen to your songs and add them to their profiles. The key is to be interactive. Just because you have music on your profile doesn't mean your job is done. Ask people to listen, rate, comment, and add. Let's take a look at a few ways you can get fans interested in your song clips.

Ask Nicely

Sometimes we take it for granted that people will know exactly what we want them to do. But unless you ask, a person might not think to add your song to his or her profile. Encourage visitors to your page to listen to your newest song, rate it, comment on it, and add it to their profile. Let them know you appreciate their support. You can embed your request right into your profile's text, near the top of the About section. It might look something like this:

> Check out our latest single, "Life in the Afterglow." Let us know what you think…. You can rate "Life in the Afterglow" and leave us a comment. If you like it, please add the song to your profile and tell your friends. Thanks again for your support!

Whenever possible, encourage fan interaction with you and your music. An interactive environment makes you seem more real and less like a faceless marketing department behind a profile. This encouragement can be done directly on your profile, in bulletins, through emails, by leaving comments for friends, and in your blog entries. Ask fans to listen to your music and give their thoughts and feedback. Invite them to leave you comments and recommend you to their friends. If you don't ask, you don't get. So ask, and ask often.

You can get would-be and current fans to visit your profile and listen to your songs through using comments, posting bulletins, posting blogs, and adding text to your profile. Following are a few additional ways to use your music player features and profile songs to your advantage using these communication methods:

- **Solicit feedback.** Leave comments on friends' pages and post bulletins. "Hey, we just uploaded a new song, 'Go West Girls,' and we'd really like to know what you think of it! Take a listen and leave us a comment!"

- **Set goals.** Tell everyone via profile text, comments, bulletins, and even email that you're trying to get 100 profile song adds this week. Invite them to listen to your song, add it to their profile, and leave you a comment. Promise you'll comment back for anyone who does this. Then follow through.

- **Use your rank song/comment settings on your music player.** Get the word out that you are now allowing your songs to be rated (see Figure 11.6) and asking for comments to be left (see Figure 11.7). Ask people for critiques. Check each of your songs' settings under the Manage Songs function to make sure you have allowed ratings/comments (see Figure 11.8).

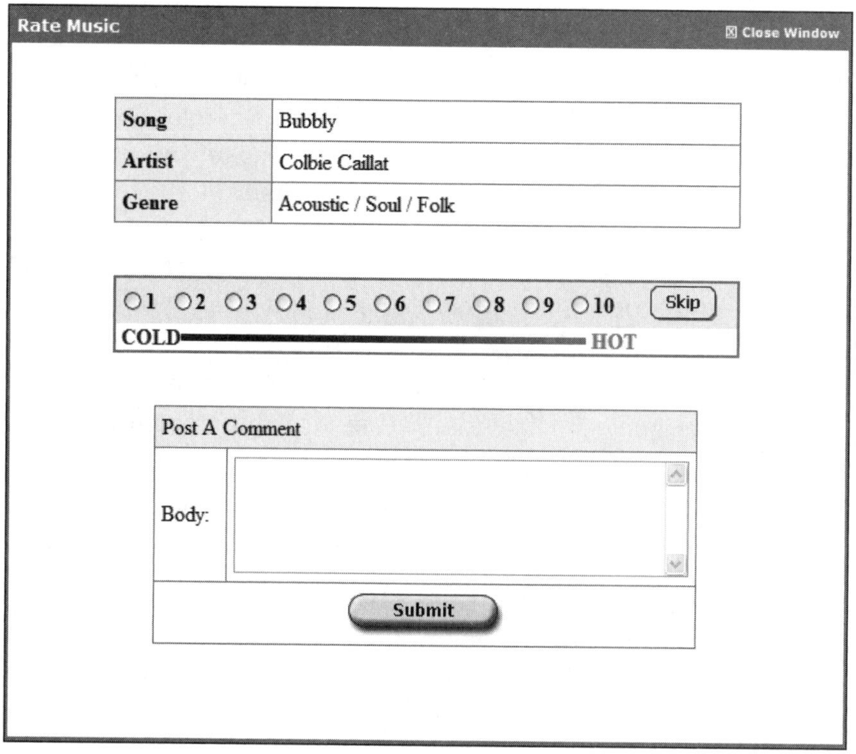

Rate Music   ☒ Close Window

Song	Bubbly
Artist	Colbie Caillat
Genre	Acoustic / Soul / Folk

○1 ○2 ○3 ○4 ○5 ○6 ○7 ○8 ○9 ○10   Skip
COLD━━━━━━━━━━━━━━━━ HOT

Post A Comment

Body:

Submit

Figure 11.6
An artist ratings page looks like this. Users can rate from 1 to 10 and add comments.

- **Pick favorites.** Ask friends to vote for their favorite song of yours and leave you a comment with their pick and why it's their favorite. Ask them to add their favorite to their profiles.

- **Brag.** Have you gotten great comments, feedback, radio play, or even press coverage on your songs? Spread the news and get others interested in seeing what your music has to offer.

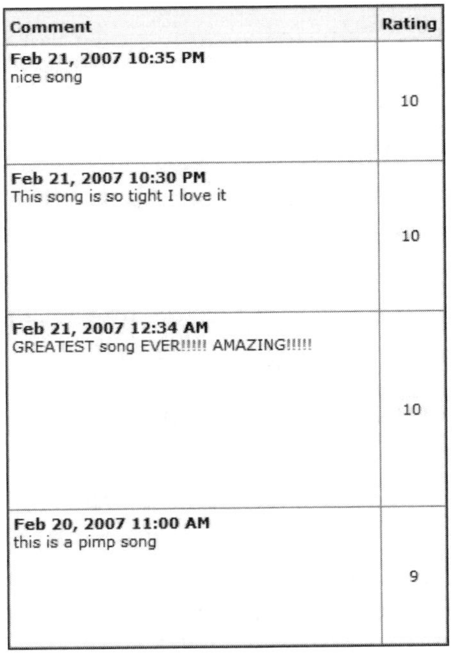

Comment	Rating
Feb 21, 2007 10:35 PM nice song	10
Feb 21, 2007 10:30 PM This song is so tight I love it	10
Feb 21, 2007 12:34 AM GREATEST song EVER!!!!! AMAZING!!!!!	10
Feb 20, 2007 11:00 AM this is a pimp song	9

Figure 11.7
Comments left when rating a song can be read by others only from
the Comments link within your music player.

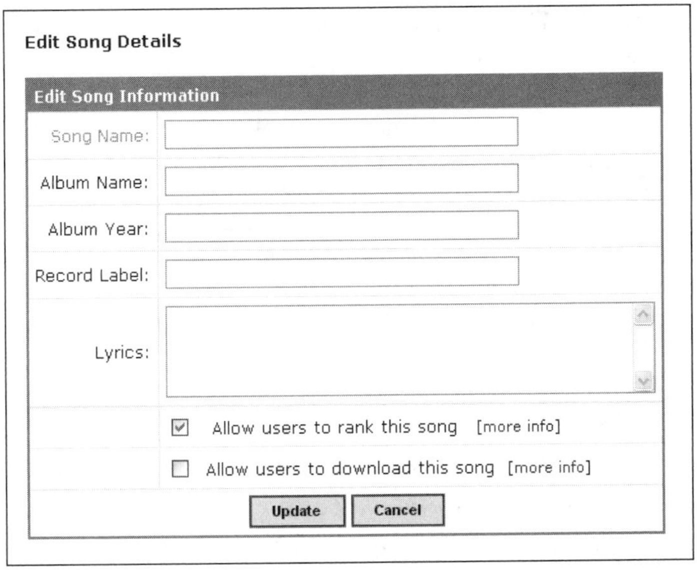

Edit Song Details

Edit Song Information

Song Name:	
Album Name:	
Album Year:	
Record Label:	
Lyrics:	

☑ Allow users to rank this song   [more info]

☐ Allow users to download this song [more info]

Update   Cancel

Figure 11.8
Set the ranking (also called rating) option within each song selection,
under the Manage Songs link in your account.

- **Post lyrics.** Announce that your lyrics are now available within the music player and that you are responding to the many requests for them. Ask fans to comment on your songwriting.

- **Strive for the top.** Rally your fans and friends to listen to your songs, leave comments, add your music to their profiles, and spread the word... all because you're striving for a Top Artist spot. MySpace non-scientifically decides on top artists based on who's getting the most buzz and contributing interesting music, so it definitely takes a village to catch their eye.

- **Use outside contests, rankings, and awards.** Indie music and ranking sites such as GarageBand.com (see Figure 11.9) and TopsinAmerica.com offer contests, weekly awards, and rankings competitions for musicians. Invite friends and fans to listen to you and vote for you and your music. Then post your award results (see Figure 11.10) in bulletins and on your profile.

ENTER THE CONTEST
Musicians Only : Register Band : Enter Contest : Host MP3s : Sell Album

Get your music heard around the world!

- Every song gets written feedback from listeners
- Top songs climb the charts, win exposure from Clear Channel & more!
- Dozens signed by labels so far

Figure 11.9
GarageBand.com offers chances for artists to enter contests and receive recognition for the best of the week and overall rankings.

- **Offer free downloads.** I don't normally advocate offering free downloads through your MySpace music player. It's better to direct users to your main website, where you can gather some contact information, and *then* give a free download. Either way, though, it *is* a great promotional hook. You could even use B-roll type of audio footage, a remix, or an acoustic version of one of your songs instead of the album version. Offer a free download to the first 150 people who add your song to their profile and post a bulletin on your behalf.

Rank	Active contest: #1 of 277 in Alternative Pop All-time: #1 of 5,466 in Alternative Pop Best #1 of 365 on 21Apr2007
Awards!	Track of the Day on 11Nov2004 in Alternative Pop Track of the Day on 17Dec2004 in Pop Track Of The Week on 30Aug2004 in Alternative Track Of The Week on 11Nov2004 in Alternative Pop Track Of The Week on 27Dec2004 in Pop Best Production in Alternative, week of 29Mar2004 Best Production in Alternative, week of 30Mar2004 Best Lyrics in Alternative, week of 29Mar2004 Best Lyrics in Alternative, week of 30Mar2004 Best Melody in Alternative, week of 29Mar2004 Best Melody in Alternative, week of 30Aug2004 Best Mood in Alternative, week of 29Mar2004 Feel Good Track in Alternative, week of 24May2004 Chill-Out Track in Alternative, week of 23Aug2004

Figure 11.10
An artist's GarageBand.com awards.

Keep your text conversational, light, and sincere. Encourage friends to repost your bulletins by including an auto-bulletin button or by simply asking nicely (see Chapter 12, "Bulletins and Event Invitations"). Include auto-comment buttons on your profile so visitors can easily post your requests to their friends (refer to Chapter 10). A mass commenting or friend adder program with commenting capabilities will help you leave many comments at once. Remember, however, to fly under the radar by not posting more than 30 to 50 comments a day. Some say you can do more than that without being caught, but I recommend a conservative approach so as not to risk losing your entire profile and all your hard work. After all, MySpace's terms of use disallow such programs.

You're on your way to building a fan base that helps you market your music. Now let's learn more about bulletins and event invites....

12 Bulletins and Event Invitations

In this chapter, we'll take a look at using bulletins to communicate with your friends and fans, as well as using event listings and invites to get people to your gigs.

Your Virtual Bulletin Board

In your MySpace home control panel, you'll notice a section toward the bottom where your bulletins are kept, called *My Bulletin Space* (see Figure 12.1). Much like an actual bulletin board, people post messages that are viewable only by those on their friends list. This is a quick and easy way to communicate with all your friends at once.

When MySpace was but a youngster in social networking, bulletins were very effective in getting the attention of friends and encouraging them to check out a profile, hop over to the official website, or attend a local gig. Over time, however, many argue that bulletins have lost some of their impact. Most people have a fair number of friends, and the more friends a person has, the more bulletins he'll see appearing in that little window in the control panel. This saturation of real and spam bulletins and the tendency to over-post have caused some users to glaze over when they see posts... or ignore them entirely.

This doesn't mean, however, that you shouldn't bother using bulletins. They can still be effective if approached correctly. We'll look at how to post and how to strike a proper balance between getting on the radar of your audience and keeping in their good graces.

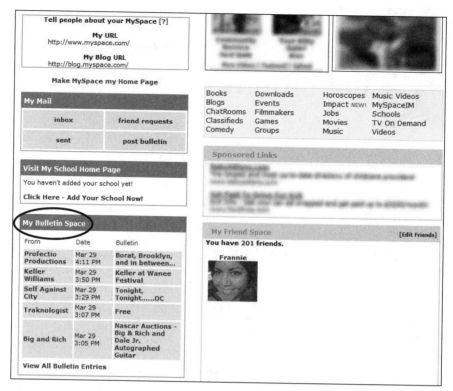

Figure 12.1
Keep track of all of your bulletins in My Bulletin Space.

The Basics of Bulletins

The first thing we'll do is look at where your bulletins are located, how to access them, and how to create and post your own. Then we'll explore how you might use them in your marketing endeavors.

You'll notice that your My Bulletin Space window only holds a few posts at a time (see Figure 12.2)—five to be exact. That's not very many. If there are a lot of bulletin posts going through, some will never see the light of day in this window. When that happens, the poster has to rely on the viewer clicking the View All Bulletin Entries link to see the rest of the posts (see Figure 12.3). You'll need to post often enough to get into the window and be seen, but not so often that you're sending out meaningless bulletins that aggravate your audience. We'll tackle this more later in this chapter, in the "Bulletin Ideas" section.

My Bulletin Space		
From	**Date**	**Bulletin**
Royalty - TV "NEW SHOW" DAILY	Apr 20, 2007 11:44 AM	**PAGE INSPECTION!!! .WO ULD U PASS??...GET ON ROYAL TV!!!**
The Dresden Dolls	Apr 20, 2007 11:35 AM	**Final day of voting - show your love for The Dolls & Amanda!**
Harry and the Potters	Apr 20, 2007 10:58 AM	**A message from the HP Alliance re: Virginia**
Harry and the Potters	Apr 20, 2007 10:55 AM	**Brooklyn Tonight! Philly Tomorrow! FUN!!!!!**
Analog Missionary	Apr 20, 2007 9:36 AM	**Sonicbids feature; Anne Rice gig; sold out albums; DRUM! mag**
View All Bulletin Entries		

Figure 12.2
Your bulletins window only holds a few bulletins at a time, making it prime real estate.

Listing 1-10 of 250		1 2 3 4 5 >> of 25	Next >
From	**Date**	**Subject**	
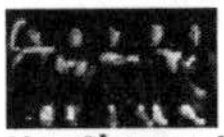 **Hawthorne Heights**	Apr 18, 2007 8:26 PM	**Reminder!!!!**	
 **DAUGHTRY**	Apr 18, 2007 8:25 PM	**Daughtry in Battle of the Videos!**	
 **Eric Michael Hopper**	Apr 18, 2007 8:13 PM	**Last FULL night to get your votes in!Famecast ends Thurs 9pm**	

Figure 12.3
The rest of your bulletins are accessed by clicking View All Bulletin Entries.

For now, let's learn how to post our first bulletin. It's really quite a painless process. In your My Mail section, click on Post Bulletin, as shown in Figure 12.4. Here you are presented with a subject and body field to enter your bulletin text (see Figure 12.5). As of now, MySpace does not provide an HTML editing interface to allow you to customize your bulletins. You can do that on third-party editing sites (addressed later in this chapter, in the "Spicing Up Bulletins" section). But for now, we'll just work with a simple text bulletin in the provided text editor.

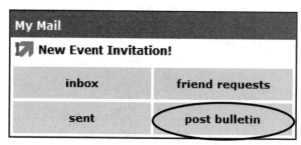

Figure 12.4
Send out your own bulletins any time by clicking Post Bulletin
in your home control panel.

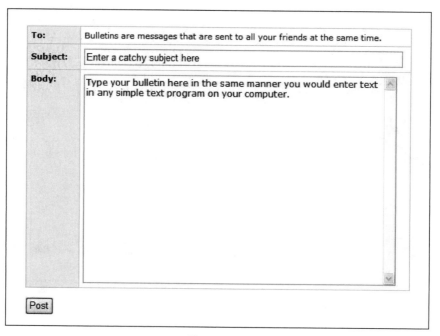

Figure 12.5
This is your MySpace bulletin editor, where you can enter text and code.

After you've entered your text, click Post. Now you'll be asked to confirm your bulletin (see Figure 12.6). Check it over and make sure you've got everything in there that you want. If so, click Post Bulletin, and away it goes to everyone on your friends list.

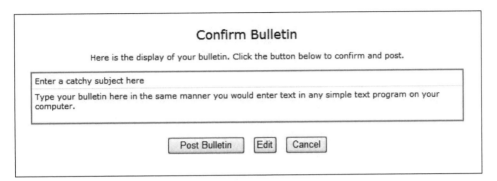

Confirm Bulletin

Here is the display of your bulletin. Click the button below to confirm and post.

Enter a catchy subject here

Type your bulletin here in the same manner you would enter text in any simple text program on your computer.

Post Bulletin   Edit   Cancel

Figure 12.6
The confirmation screen gives you a chance to edit your bulletin before posting.

Let's pretend, though, that you want to add more to it. Click Edit instead. In the provided text editor, you can use regular carriage returns to create line spacing. You don't need to enter HTML tags to accomplish this. In the example shown in Figure 12.7, we added a second paragraph and are now satisfied with the post.

Now our post is finished, and when we click Post Bulletin, it will go out to all of our friends. It sometimes takes a few minutes for your post to become available as a bulletin (see Figure 12.8). When it does, it will look like Figure 12.9. Notice your thumbnail pic doesn't appear in the main bulletin window, but only when someone chooses View All Bulletin Entries. When a friend clicks on your post, he'll see something that looks like Figure 12.10.

But let's say you change your mind and you want to remove your post. Not a problem. You can access all of your bulletin posts in a few ways. If you are on the page where you view all bulletin entries, click on the Show Bulletins I've Posted link on the right side (see Figure 12.11).

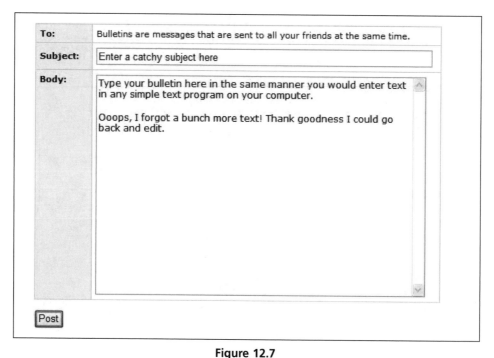

Figure 12.7
This text bulletin has been tweaked to add another paragraph.
No HTML tags are needed to create line spaces.

Bulletin Has Been Posted

Your bulletin has been posted to MySpace. Please allow up
to **five minutes** for your bulletin to appear.

Return to Bulletin Board

Figure 12.8
MySpace shows you this screen to let you know
your bulletin has been successfully entered.

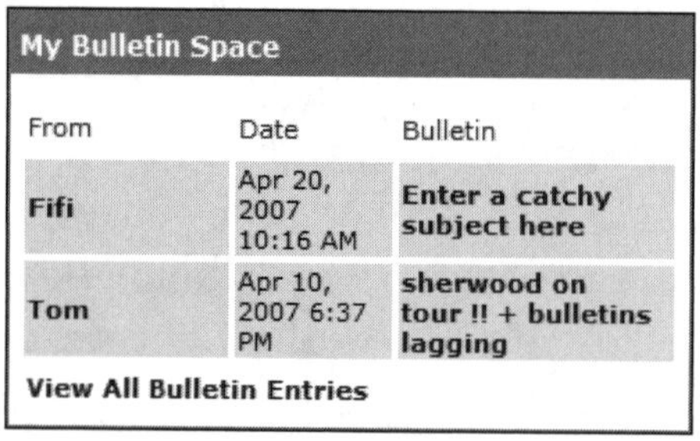

My Bulletin Space		
From	Date	Bulletin
Fifi	Apr 20, 2007 10:16 AM	**Enter a catchy subject here**
Tom	Apr 10, 2007 6:37 PM	**sherwood on tour !! + bulletins lagging**
View All Bulletin Entries		

Figure 12.9
Your bulletin goes into the queue, and hopefully will appear in everyone's
My Bulletin Space, depending on how many other bulletins it has to compete with.

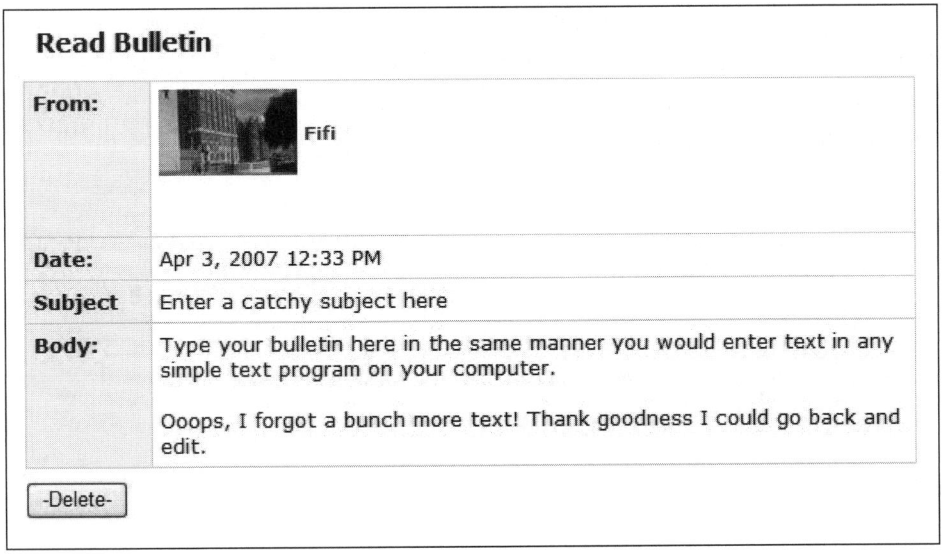

Read Bulletin

From:	Fifi
Date:	Apr 3, 2007 12:33 PM
Subject	Enter a catchy subject here
Body:	Type your bulletin here in the same manner you would enter text in any simple text program on your computer. Ooops, I forgot a bunch more text! Thank goodness I could go back and edit.

-Delete-

Figure 12.10
Your bulletin post looks like this to your friends.

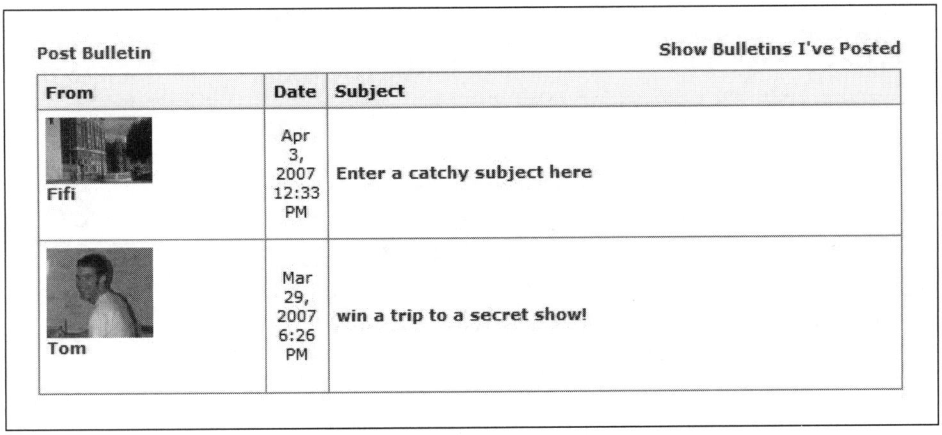

Post Bulletin   **Show Bulletins I've Posted**

From	Date	Subject
Fifi	Apr 3, 2007 12:33 PM	**Enter a catchy subject here**
Tom	Mar 29, 2007 6:26 PM	**win a trip to a secret show!**

Figure 12.11
While viewing your list of bulletins, you may decide you want to withdraw one of your posts. Click on Show Bulletins I've Posted to view your entries only.

Here you'll be able to see all of your bulletin posts and mark the ones you want to delete (see Figure 12.12). You can also reach this page from your home control panel. The far-right box with the date and the number of your profile views has a link to Bulletin Posts (see Figure 12.13).

This link will take you to the same place. Or, you can delete your post while you are reading it, utilizing the Delete button below the post (see Figure 12.14). Note, however, that although you can delete your own posts, you cannot delete bulletins posted by others. They'll stay in the system for 10 days.

Post Bulletin			Return to Main Bulletin List
	From	**Date**	**Subject**
☐	Fifi	Apr 3, 2007 12:33 PM	**Enter a catchy subject here**

☐ Select/Deselect All

▣ Delete Selected
Delete selected bulletins.
You can only delete your own bulletins.
Regular bulletins expire in 10 days

Figure 12.12
Delete any or all of the posts you've written. Use the check boxes
to choose the ones you want to mark for deletion.

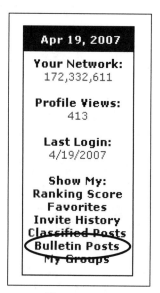

Figure 12.13
You can also access your bulletin posts from your home control panel.

Figure 12.14
While reading a post you've written, you can simply hit the
Delete button to get rid of it.

In the same way that your friends view your posts, you also view theirs. You'll notice that there is a button at the bottom of every post you're reading that lets you reply to the poster (see Figure 12.15). This makes it easy to ask a question or put in your two cents on the topic at hand, unless you find the poster irritating. In that case, you can hit the Delete from Friends button!

You've now mastered the technical basics of bulletin posting. But what if you want to jazz up your post with videos and pics? Read on!

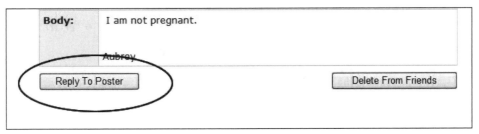

Figure 12.15
The Reply to Poster button allows for instant interactivity.

Spicing Up Bulletins

There are a number of ways to snazz up your bulletins with pictures, videos, bold text, and more. In Chapter 8, we went through how to add these elements to your profile and tweak your text. The process is the same for bulletins.

If you are comfortable with adding in HTML tags on your own to customize your text and embed visual elements, then you can do so right in the bulletin body field in MySpace (see Figure 12.16). When you click Post and are presented with the confirmation screen, you'll see the HTML tags executed into a visual display (see Figure 12.17).

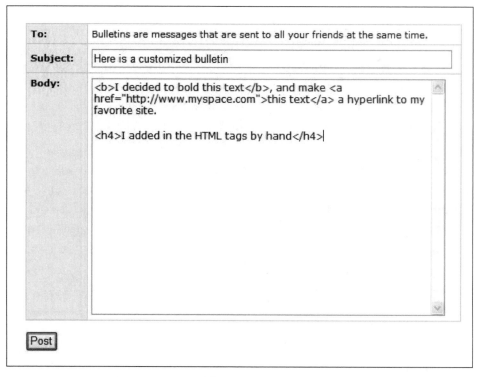

Figure 12.16
HTML tags have been added to this bulletin by hand, right in the provided text editor.

Confirm Bulletin

Here is the display of your bulletin. Click the button below to confirm and post.

Here is a customized bulletin

I decided to bold this text, and make **this text** a hyperlink to my favorite site.

I added in the HTML tags by hand

[Post Bulletin] [Edit] [Cancel]

Figure 12.17
Once you click Post, you'll be able to see your HTML tags rendered on
the confirmation page.

But if you're not ready to take that DIY route, you can always try out
one of the many bulletin editors available on the Internet. A good one
is located at www.projectmyspace.com/codes/bulletineditor (pictured
in Figure 12.18). I like this one because it has most of the HTML
editing bells and whistles you might need in one convenient online
application. All you do is enter your text and then manipulate as you
please. You can change the font, size, style, and text color; boldface text;
add bullets and indents, tables, and hyperlinks; and more with a press
of a button. You'll see the changes in real time, as you would in a word
processing program (see Figure 12.19).

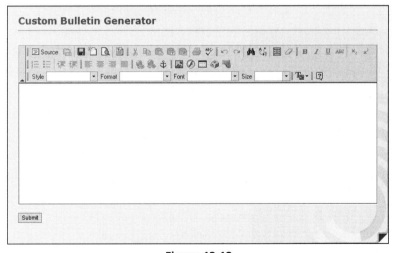

Figure 12.18
The Bulletin Editor from ProjectMySpace.com is a great tool for
customizing your bulletins.

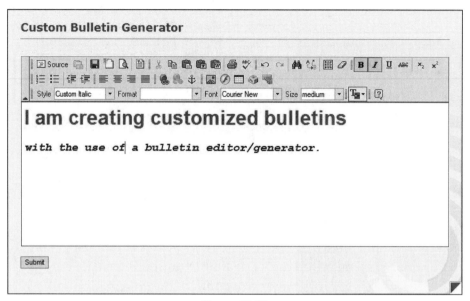

Figure 12.19
In this bulletin editor, what you see is what you get.

You can also embed photos and Flash animation in your bulletin. (Remember that your photo or Flash module must already be stored somewhere on the Internet first.) When you are finished sprucing up your bulletin, click Submit, and the code will be generated for you. You can copy and paste this into your MySpace bulletin body or use the Post Bulletin Direct to MySpace button, and the application will post it for you (see Figure 12.20). Note, however, that MySpace sometimes blocks these types of actions by third-party sites, and posting directly may not always work. Be ready to rely on good old-fashioned copying and pasting instead (see Figure 12.21). Should this recommended bulletin editor not suit you, simply do a web search for "myspace bulletin editor," and you'll find many others from which to choose.

One other item to note when using outside bulletin editors: Most do not have a quick-and-dirty button for embedding video codes. It's easy to get around this. All you have to do is get the code for the video you want to post (as shown in Figure 12.22), and then paste that into your

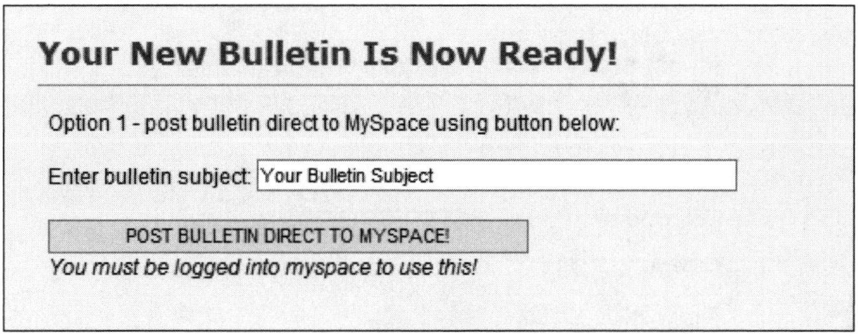

Your New Bulletin Is Now Ready!

Option 1 - post bulletin direct to MySpace using button below:

Enter bulletin subject: Your Bulletin Subject

POST BULLETIN DIRECT TO MYSPACE!
You must be logged into myspace to use this!

Figure 12.20
This bulletin editor gives you the option of letting them post the bulletin for you.

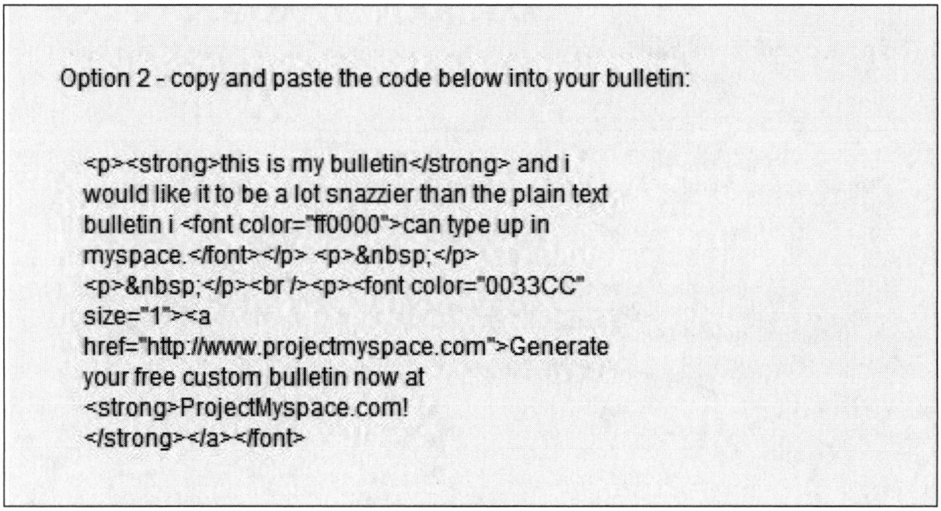

Option 2 - copy and paste the code below into your bulletin:

```
<p><strong>this is my bulletin</strong> and i
would like it to be a lot snazzier than the plain text
bulletin i <font color="ff0000">can type up in
myspace.</font></p> <p> </p>
<p> </p><br /><p><font color="0033CC"
size="1"><a
href="http://www.projectmyspace.com">Generate
your free custom bulletin now at
<strong>ProjectMyspace.com!
</strong></a></font>
```

Figure 12.21
You can also simply copy and paste the code into MySpace yourself.

MySpace bulletin body at the point where you want the video to appear (see Figure 12.23). The video should then appear at the place you specified, which you'll see when you confirm your post (see Figure 12.24). It works the same way as embedding video into your profile or comments. Please refer to Chapter 8 for more details on editing HTML.

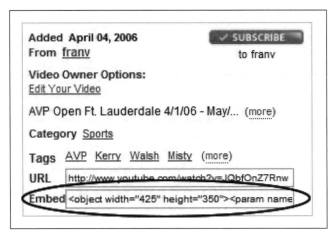

Figure 12.22
This circled code from YouTube.com is needed to embed your video into a bulletin.

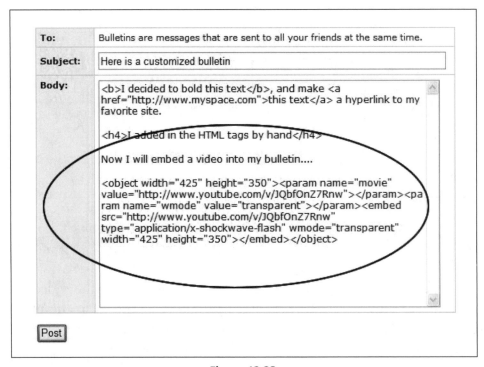

Figure 12.23
Here's what the embedded video code looks like in a bulletin.

Figure 12.24
When processed, the HTML code now pulls the video into the bulletin for all to see.

Auto Bulletins and Repost Buttons

One way to encourage friends to repost your bulletins to *their* friends is by using auto bulletins and repost buttons. This involves creating "widgets" and embedding them in your profile or bulletin posts. A widget is a basic tool in a graphical interface. It's something that users can interact with in order to perform a task, such as a button, check box, slider bar, or dialog box. I should tell you first that although auto bulletins and repost buttons were easy to do in MySpace for a long time, the service now often blocks these widgets. This means that the repost and auto-bulletin code you generate may not work at the time you try it. Still, it's important for you to know that these options exist so you can employ them when MySpace lifts their sometimes ban on certain widgets.

An auto bulletin and a repost button could be used at the bottom of your posted bulletin, encouraging friends to repost your message to their friends list. You could also use a repost button right in your profile and ask people to post your bulletin announcement to their friends. This is useful for when you've got a gig coming up and you need to pack the house, or if you've got a new release available for download.

Creating an auto bulletin and repost button is best done by using a code generator website, such as www.profilepimp.com/generators/auto-bulletin.php (shown in Figure 12.25). The code will make a handy little button that, when pressed by a logged-in MySpacer, will plug your predetermined bulletin text into the MySpacer's bulletin editor. All that person has to do is confirm this post and submit it. It will then go out to all of his or her friends.

In lieu of working widgets, you can also ask your friends to repost your bulletin by simply copying and pasting it into a bulletin post of their own (see Figure 12.26). This works well with text posts only. The more people who see your bulletin, the better. But remember to ask sparingly and for things that really matter. Too many posts about trivial topics may cause people to stop taking notice.

Bulletin Spam

Bulletin spam is a reality on MySpace. You may notice a friend sending out unusual posts that seem out of character. Or, you may notice bulletins appearing in *your* name that you know you didn't post! When hackers or phishers get access to your account, they post spam bulletins to your friends, commonly for ringtone offers, surveys, mortgages, or sexy pictures. If you see an unusual post by a friend, email your friend right away and let him know you thought the post was odd and that he should look into it. Should you be the victim of a hacker, immediately change your MySpace password and delete the offending posts. You may want to then make a follow-up post to your friends list, letting them know those bulletins for erectile dysfunction drugs were not made by you!

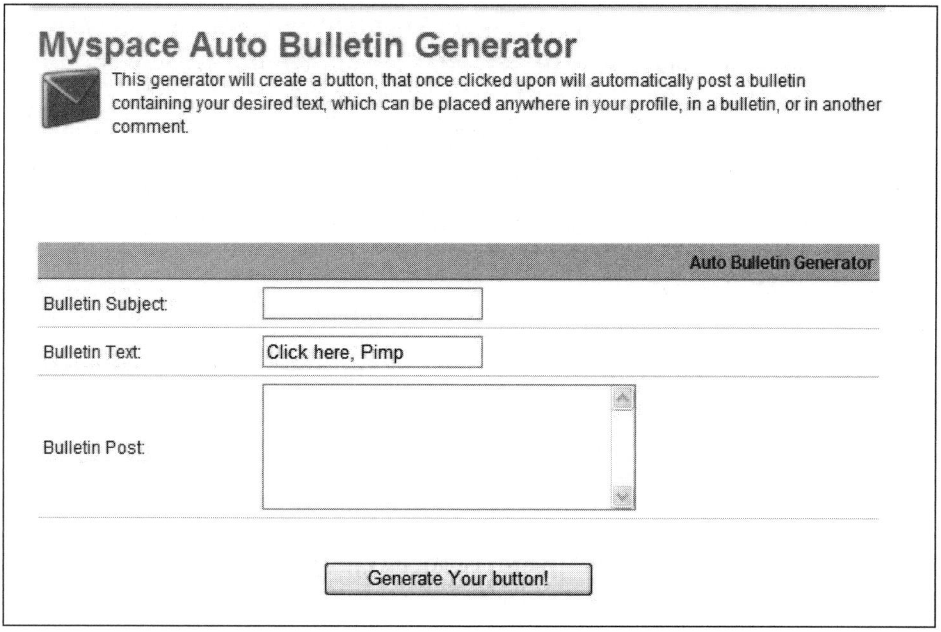

Myspace Auto Bulletin Generator

This generator will create a button, that once clicked upon will automatically post a bulletin containing your desired text, which can be placed anywhere in your profile, in a bulletin, or in another comment.

	Auto Bulletin Generator
Bulletin Subject:	
Bulletin Text:	Click here, Pimp
Bulletin Post:	

[Generate Your button!]

Figure 12.25
This auto-bulletin generator from ProfilePimp.com will create a handy button for you that, when pressed, generates a new bulletin with text you've specified.

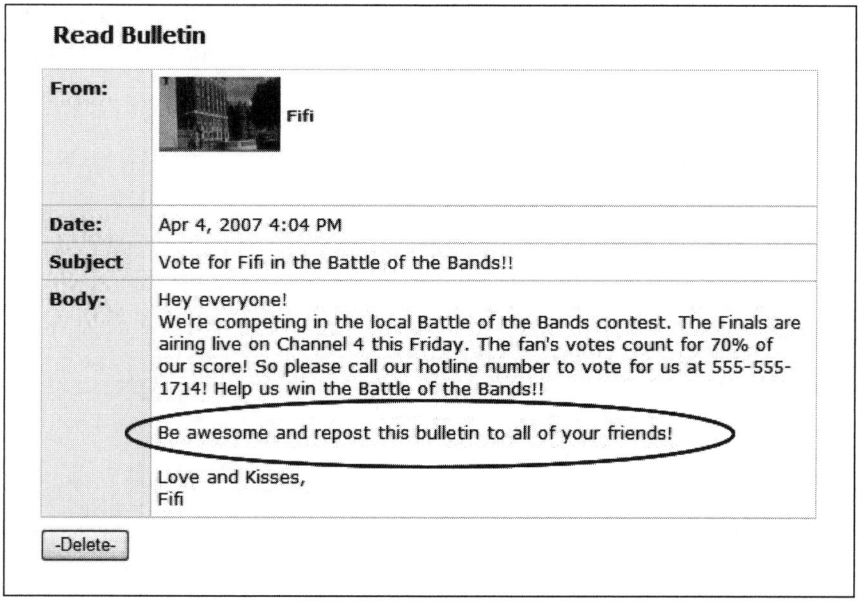

Read Bulletin

From:	Fifi
Date:	Apr 4, 2007 4:04 PM
Subject	Vote for Fifi in the Battle of the Bands!!
Body:	Hey everyone! We're competing in the local Battle of the Bands contest. The Finals are airing live on Channel 4 this Friday. The fan's votes count for 70% of our score! So please call our hotline number to vote for us at 555-555-1714! Help us win the Battle of the Bands!! Be awesome and repost this bulletin to all of your friends! Love and Kisses, Fifi

[-Delete-]

Figure 12.26
Because auto-bulletin buttons don't always work properly in the MySpace environment, simply asking friends to repost can do the trick.

Bulletin Ideas

Bulletin topics are similar to blog topics (see Chapter 13, "Blogging in the MySpace World"). In fact, you can also use bulletins to direct traffic to your blogs. Notify your list that you've entered a new blog entry and what it's about, especially when you have a blog that is a bit lengthy. Some don't like this approach, but I think it works.

Try to keep your bulletins short and sweet. Nobody wants to read pages and pages of a bulletin. That's what blogs are for! Here are a few topic ideas:

- Advertise your gigs and public appearances.

- Ask friends to listen to your newly uploaded songs, rate them, and vote for their favorites.

- Encourage people to add your new single to their profiles.

- Let everybody know that your music is available for sale and download and how they can get it.

- Tout new profile features.

- Announce promotional partnerships, merchandise for sale, and fan contests.

- Post album and performance reviews, plus favorable news clips.

- Embed new video clips or direct fans to your profile to view them.

- Dispel rumors or address gossip.

- Herald new official website features.

- Ask fans to sign up for your official email list and be eligible for special offers.

- Recruit a street team.

- Solicit votes for contests in which you may be entered.

- Check in with fans while you're on tour, offering tidbits about your experiences.

- Post links to new photos.

- Ask fans to leave you comments.

There are additional ideas peppered throughout this book, and you'll likely be inspired by posts from other bands on your friends list too. Some artists, such as MySpace queen bee Tila Tequila who boasts almost two million friends as of today (see Figure 12.27), post often and post personal topics that many people can relate to (see Figure 12.28). She doesn't just send out messages about her career, but also regular musings on how she's happily put on a couple of pounds, what she's doing for the weekend, and even goodnight messages in which she recaps her day and encourages fans to be thankful for all they have in their lives. This might not sound like what most entertainers do, but that's the beauty of it. Tila relates to her audience on a personal level and draws them into her life, portraying herself as a regular girl despite her model good looks, celebrity friends, and gritty rap style. She also makes for a very interactive artist, something that fans love and don't often find.

Figure 12.27
MySpace celebrity Tila Tequila is a master of gathering friends
and making a name for herself in this cyber-environment.

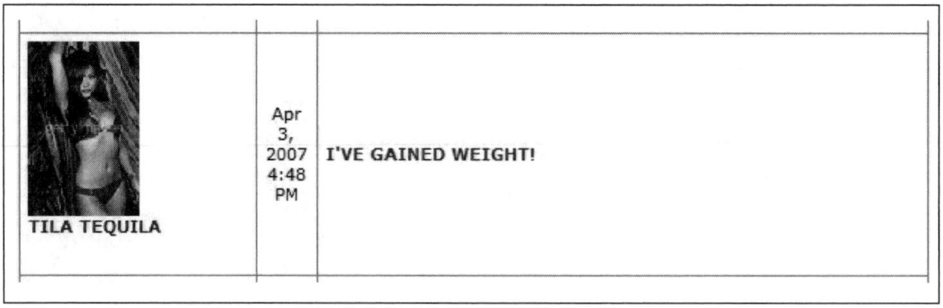

Figure 12.28
Her posts are often personal, and she talks to her audience like she would
her closest friend. This helps to build a loyal fan base.

One of the keys to keeping yourself in your fans' good graces is to post relevant topics, even if they're personal, and to stay away from "junk" posts; too many or redundant posts; inflammatory, hateful, or derogatory tirades; and controversial, non-relevant content. People do indeed delete others off their friends lists because of ridiculous posts. And you don't want to be one of those who is kicked to the curb.

So, here are a few tips to help keep you in the clear:

- Keep your hatred and vitriol to yourself. Nobody likes a Negative Nellie. If you've got a problem with a real-life friend or acquaintance or you despise some celebrity or government official, just put a lid on it. It's a bad reflection on you. I once kicked off an artist who posted a series of rants that were vulgar and disgusting, detailing what horrible, violent things he'd like to do to a media figure he hated. Not cool.

- It's okay to get on your soapbox about music and entertainment industry issues, but be careful about political issues. Remember that half your audience off the bat will likely be on the opposite side. And most of your fans are entertaining themselves on MySpace in the hopes of escaping the daily media saturation of partisan politics. Let your music speak your views for you.

- Don't post for everyone a message meant for one. This is particularly annoying. A post that starts with "Hey Jimmy, here's that video I promised I'd send you" should have been sent to Jimmy only, not the 2,000 friends on your list who don't know Jimmy and couldn't care less.

- Be careful of posting a lot of acronyms. I know it's how kids write. However, not everyone on your list may get your text-message speak. So real words and sentences please.

- Steer clear of junk posts. These are posts that are completely meaningless and bulletins you only sent out because you were bored. Things like, "Dude, I made mac and cheese and it was awesome." Yes... and? Now you've just sucked up a precious piece of real estate in the bulletin window that someone else could have had. Plus, the fans who clicked on that bulletin and were disappointed by its lack of content are lamenting that 30 seconds of lifespan they'll never get back. Keep it interesting.

- Plan out your posts. If you've got a gig coming up, you definitely want to advertise it. But you don't want to be the guy who posted "Come to my concert Friday" five times a day for a week. That's overkill. Figure you can safely post once a day the week before the concert. For more stretched-out projects, say months down the road, once a week or less will do.

- Don't overpost. Along with the previous tip, think about your overall number of posts in a day. *Relevant* content three times in one day is all right, but shouldn't be done every day. Usually one relevant post a day is considered tolerable. Irrelevant content over and over again is just going to train your fans not to click on your posts anymore. If you've got a ton happening in one day, think about how you might be able to break it up over a three- or four-day period if possible. Perhaps not every topic is urgent for that day.

Bulletins are a type of email marketing because they go to everyone on your friends list. You want people to remain open to what you have to say. Respecting their time and resources is the first step. You should also take your bulletin entries and post them as blogs so new friends and page visitors can see what they've missed.

People also often wonder whether they can block all posts or posts by certain people. If you don't want to read posts by a certain someone, that person probably shouldn't be on your friends list. As for a reliable, easy way of blocking posts, I haven't found it. There are probably programmers out there who could accomplish this, but I haven't yet found a simple way to do this that the average MySpacer could implement.

Event Planning

Now let's check out the use of Event Invites for getting friends and the public at large to attend gigs and other promotional shindigs.

To access your events page, click on Events on the right side of the medium-blue navigation bar (see Figure 12.29). This link transports you to your MySpace Events page, where you can view events in your area and post your own (see Figure 12.30).

Figure 12.29
This Events link leads to the hub of all the local social activity.

You'll see from this main Events page that there are dozens of events in your area alone, in categories such as Band Shows, Theater & Comedy, and Arts & Culture (see Figure 12.31). Going out of town? Just change your location and find out what's hip and happening in any area you plan to visit. In this same way, fans will locate events that you post (see Figure 12.32).

On the left side of the page toward the top are your Events navigation links (see Figure 12.33). Let's start with Create New Event.

On the Create New Event page, fill in the details of your event plus your contact email (see Figure 12.34). The more information you provide, the better. You can keep your event private and viewable only by those you specify, or you can make it public so anyone searching events in your area can access the invitation. This works well for gigs and CD release parties, because you usually will want as many people as possible to attend.

Figure 12.30
This main page of MySpace Events shows featured events
and lists happenings around your area.

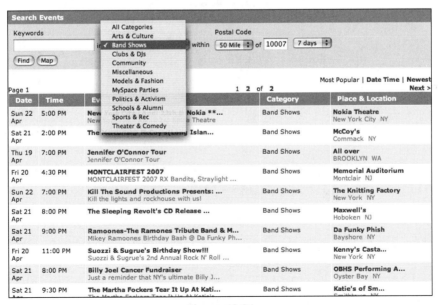

Figure 12.31
Fans will find your performances and parties by
searching for Band Shows in their area.

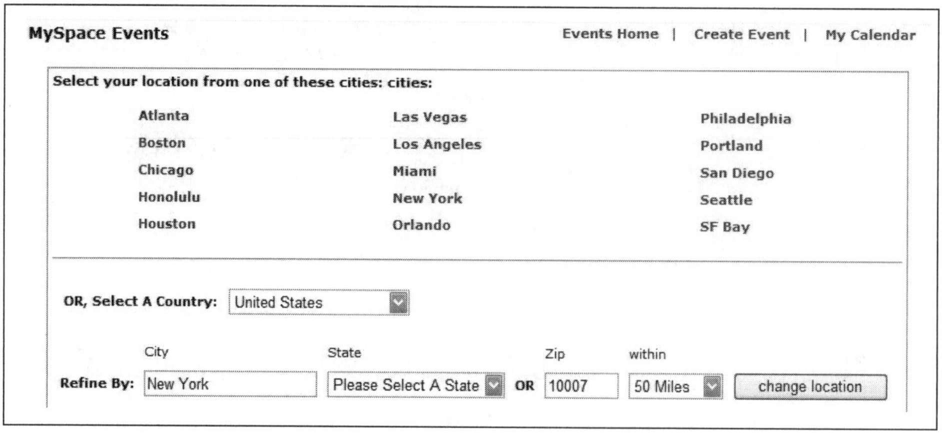

MySpace Events   Events Home | Create Event | My Calendar

Select your location from one of these cities: cities:

Atlanta   Las Vegas   Philadelphia
Boston   Los Angeles   Portland
Chicago   Miami   San Diego
Honolulu   New York   Seattle
Houston   Orlando   SF Bay

OR, Select A Country: United States ⌄

            City   State   Zip   within
Refine By: New York   Please Select A State ⌄ OR 10007   50 Miles ⌄   change location

Figure 12.32
Fans can search by metropolitan area or by a specific city/zip code.

Figure 12.33
Click here to create your event invitation.

Be sure to enter a great description to entice people to attend. You can enter a short text description or, if you prefer, you can alter your text with HTML to tweak font sizes and colors, embed photos, and more (see Figure 12.35). Try using a bulletin editor for this purpose, and then copy and paste the resulting HTML code in the appropriate Event description box.

The second invite screen lets you specify details and invite MySpacers (see Figure 12.36). When you're finished, your invite will look something like Figure 12.37. Be sure to upload an image, such as your band photo or album cover, to really make the invite stand out. You can always edit your event or invite more people at any time, or even cancel it if your plans change.

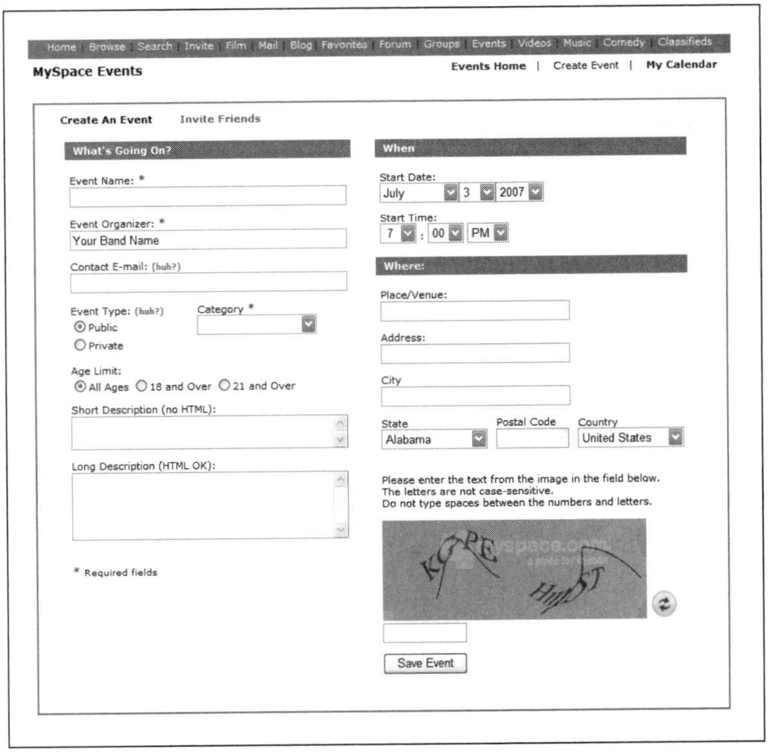

Figure 12.34
This invitation page asks for all the info on your event. Fill in as much as you can so even strangers will have the details they need to come to your show.

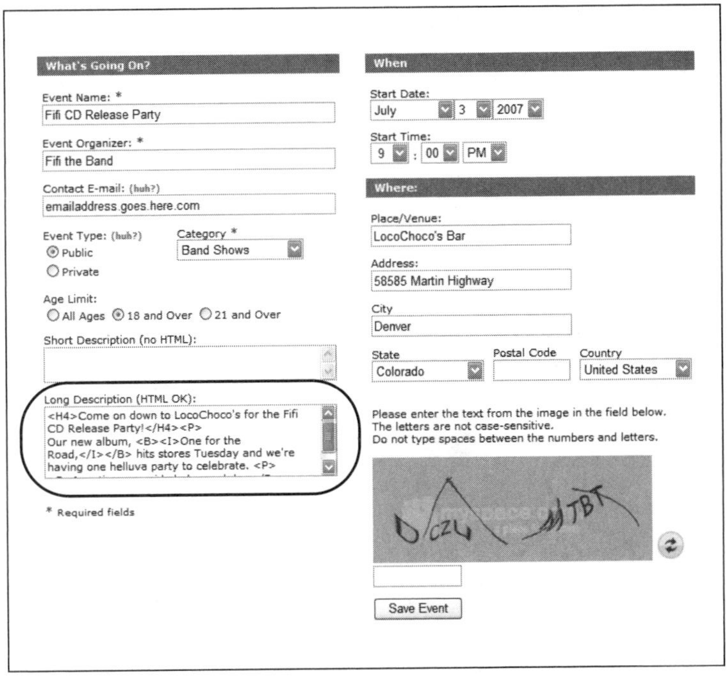

Figure 12.35
The Long Description box is the place to enter more info spiced up with HTML code. Otherwise, use the top box meant for short text descriptions.

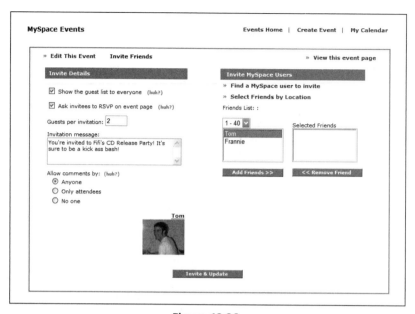

Figure 12.36
Check over this page carefully—it lets you specify whom to invite and RSVP details.

Figure 12.37
This finished invite is really enhanced by the addition of album cover art.
Try to add a photo or other artwork to your invites as well.

Your invite also keeps track of RSVPs and encourages people to post your event to their own bulletins or blogs.

When you're invited to an event, a notification will appear in the Mail section of your home control panel (see Figure 12.38). Or view your invites by clicking on the appropriate link in your MySpace Events page (see Figure 12.39). Plus, events that you post or confirm as a guest automatically appear in your MySpace calendar (see Figure 12.40)!

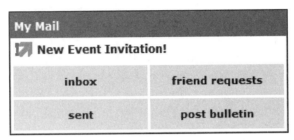

Figure 12.38
Event Invites appear in your mail area until you click on the notice.

Figure 12.39
You can also click on your Event Invites from the MySpace Events page.
The NEW icon indicates you have invitations awaiting your review.

Event invites are an excellent way to get friends to gigs, parties, and appearances. But more than that, they can be used to gain exposure within the MySpace public at large. By using public event invites, people who aren't already your friends can have a chance to see you perform.

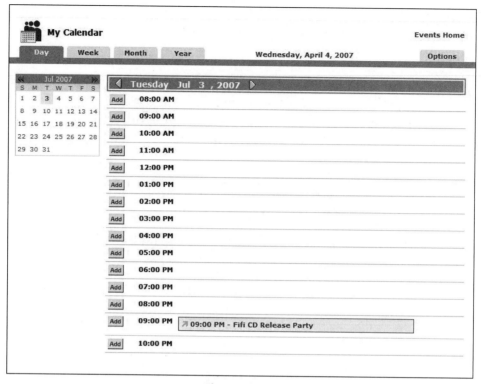

Figure 12.40
Your MySpace calendar is automatically updated with your events.
You can keep your calendar private or make it public for all to see.

13 Blogging in the MySpace World

Before MySpace, blogging became an Internet phenomenon all its own. Short for "web log," a blog is a user-generated webpage that is updated often with short news blurbs, commentary, or journal entries. Blogs typically allow comments from readers, making them an interactive format. Blogs can be standalone websites or components of a larger web presence. What started in the mid-'90s as a fledgling movement has grown today to more than 60 million blogs worldwide. Popular blogs often center around technology, politics, celebrities/entertainment, and news, but also include other genre-specific topics and even personal musings from witty individuals.

Do-it-yourself blog sites and software programs such as Blogger.com, TypePad.com, and LiveJournal.com have made it simple for anyone and everyone to have their own blog. Media moguls and grandmas into gardening alike share their thoughts with readers on blogs. And today blogging has become a cultural force as writers act as pseudo-journalists to uncover big national news items and even the latest hot bands.

MySpace offers its own blogging tools to members. Entries are posted right on the user's profile page and are searchable by other community members. Here are a few differences between blogging within MySpace and using another third-party service:

- Your MySpace blog entries remain within MySpace and accessible only by members. This can be good because you have ready access to millions in the community. It can also be a negative because non-MySpacers don't have access to your entries.

- Your MySpace blog is searchable by the community and is included in topic-specific directories.

- Your MySpace blog can be ranked within the service, giving top-ranked blogs even more exposure.

- You can limit access to your blogs by creating private lists. Each entry you make is customizable and can be open to all MySpacers, just your friends, or just the people you specify.

- The MySpace blog interface is easy to use and can embed photos; however, it's not quite as flexible or customizable design-wise as other services.

- The MySpace blog is ideal for short announcements and the latest news. It can also be set to private and used as a personal diary.

- Both MySpace and third-party blogs give you room for user-generated comments. You can decide whether you want to allow user comments in your MySpace blog entries.

The most important difference is that your MySpace blog can be categorized by you, as well as ranked and searched by members.

Why Blog?

You're probably wondering what you would use a blog for. There are many topics suitable for a blog. While it can definitely be an online journal of sorts, it doesn't have to be that deep. Here are just a few ideas for blog entries:

- Announce gigs and tours.

- Post press releases and news items.

- Use it as a brag book for positive reviews and media interviews.

- Reveal new album/record releases and where to order.

- Tell fans about personal band member tidbits, such as congrats to a member who got married.

- Boast about sales and rankings. Did your album reach the 10,000- or 1,000,000-sold mark? Are you rated best garage band on your favorite music site?

- Alert fans to new videos on your page or other music sites, such as Yahoo Music.

- Bring website and profile changes to the attention of readers. If you just added new features or redesigned your page, let people know.

- Showcase new merchandise, such as T-shirts, caps, and posters.

- Clear up any rumors or gossip. Let fans hear the truth directly from you.

- Ask fans to rate songs and review your latest records. Interactive blogs are great for bonding with fans. They love to leave comments and tell you what they think!

- Create a tour diary to give fans a sneak peek into life on the road.

Sift through blogs of MySpace artists to get even more ideas!

A blog is best used with your bulletins. When you post a new blog, announce it through a bulletin to your friends list. See Chapter 12, "Bulletins and Event Invitations," for more information. For additional tips on crafting press releases and news items, please see Chapter 18, "MySpace and Marketing."

Basics of Blogging

Let's get started on your first blog. It can be for practice only, because you can delete your blog entries at any time. I'll walk you through the steps.

Posting Your Blog

First, log on to your account. In the box where your thumbnail picture appears, you'll see links to Manage Blog and View My Blog (as shown in Figure 13.1). The latter link will allow you to view blogs you've already posted, so instead click on Manage Blog. You are presented with several options. In the main part of the resulting page, you'll see a link to view the most popular MySpace blogs. Skip over that for now and instead look to the left and notice the links above and below your picture (see Figure 13.2). This panel is where you will control most of your blogging experience.

Figure 13.1
Your home control panel contains links to access and manage your blogs.

Click on Post New Blog, as shown in Figure 13.3. The next screen is the default interface for entering your blog (see Figure 13.4). It gives you all the tools you need to create or edit your blog. Type the bulk of your blog in a text or word file *first*. This way you have it saved in a separate file in case your browser crashes, your electricity blows, or MySpace spits out an error. You won't lose all of your hard work. If you choose to type up your entry in the MySpace blog editor, at least copy and paste it frequently into a text or word file as you edit. Enter (or copy and paste) your blog text into the Body field. The default view is an HTML editor; however, you can switch to a text-only editor by clicking If You Can't Input Your Blog, Click Here. You'll see that the HTML customization options (pictured in Figure 13.5) are no longer available on the text editor page (see Figure 13.6).

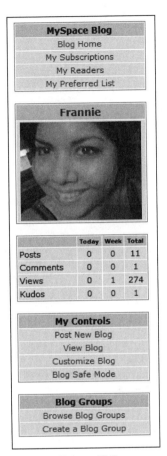

Figure 13.2
This panel in your Manage Blogs section allows you to
navigate through your blogging experience.

Let's stick with the HTML edit view and learn how to modify your text!

Figure 13.3
Post a new blog by clicking here in My Controls.

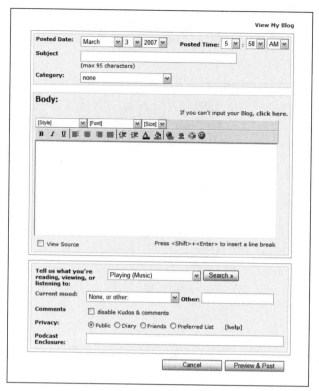

Figure 13.4
The default blog editor appears when you click Post New Blog.

Figure 13.5
These HTML controls allow you to change the look of your text
and add pictures and symbols.

Customize Your Blog Text

The HTML editing options you see probably look familiar. They are similar to those you find in popular word processing programs. Highlight the text you want to change and click on the HTML options, such as the Bold, Italic, or Underline buttons (see Figure 13.7). There are also alignment buttons for left/right/full justify and centering, as well as indent/outdent and text coloring tools. The little icon that looks like a paint bucket will actually color your text like a highlighting pen.

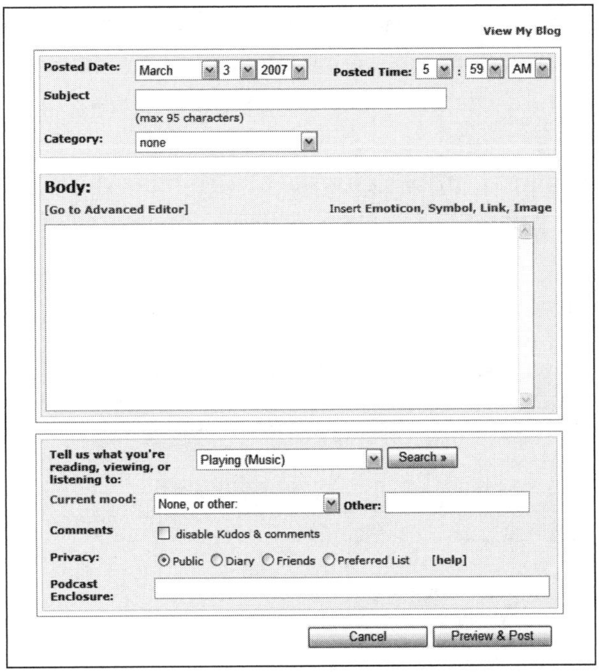

Figure 13.6
You can switch to a text-only editor at any time.
Notice that the HTML editor options are now missing.

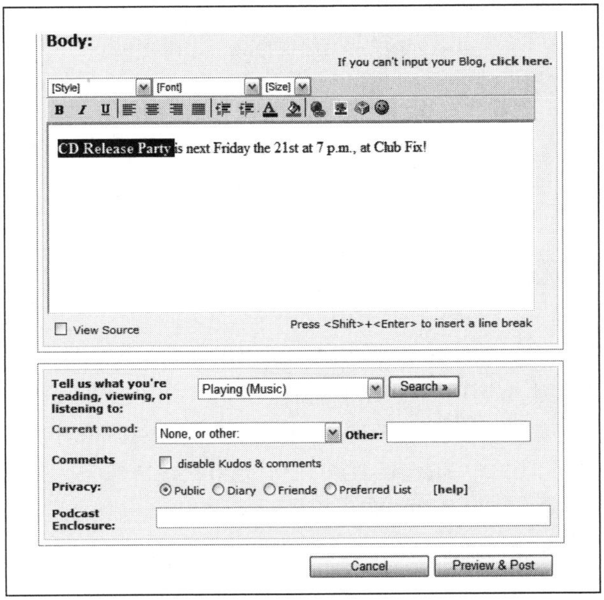

Figure 13.7
To bold this text, we highlight it and then hit the B (for bold) button.

The next four buttons allow you to add items to the blog. The first (which looks like the earth and a chain link) is the tool for adding hyperlinks to pages on the web. Highlight the text in your blog that you wish to link to another website. Then click on the hyperlink icon. A pop-up will appear, in which you can type in the address, or URL, of the link-to webpage (see Figure 13.8).

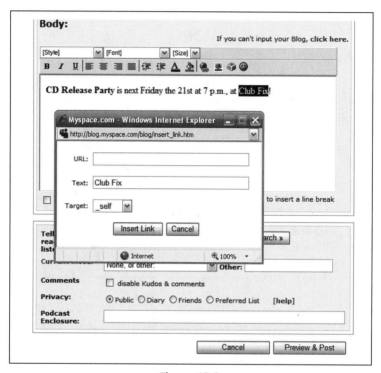

Figure 13.8
Hyperlink text within your blog by filling in the URL.

The next HTML editor icon looks like a snapshot of a tree. This is the insert image tool. Position your cursor at the point in your blog where you want to insert a photo or graphic. A pop-up will appear, in which you can enter the location of the image (see Figure 13.9). (Note that you must have already saved the image on a web server somewhere. See Chapter 8 for more details on how to do this.) The editor will insert the picture so you can see it in real time (see Figure 13.10). To center or right justify the picture, click on it and then click the appropriate HTML editor icon.

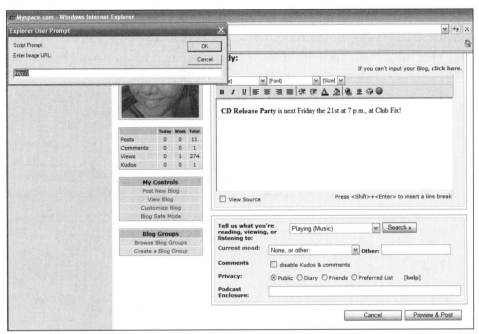

Figure 13.9
Embed a picture into your blog by providing the URL of your graphic.

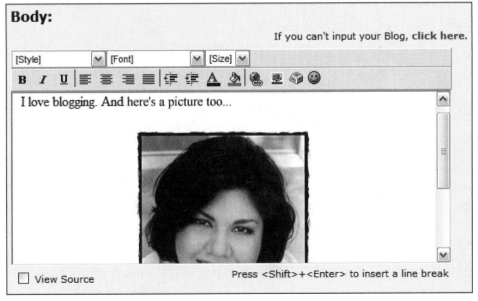

Figure 13.10
In this example, a headshot photo is inserted into the blog copy.

The next icon on the HTML editor looks like a sort of cube or paper-weight. This is the symbols button. Click here to see a list of symbols that you may want to insert into your blog, such as a copyright or registered trademark symbol, or even a heart or spade (see Figure 13.11).

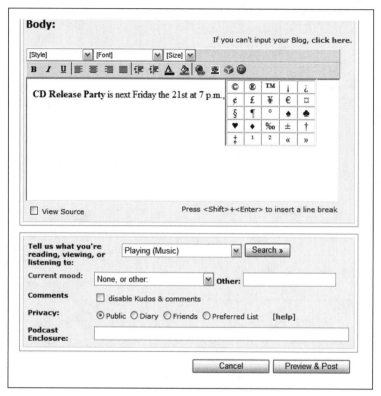

Figure 13.11
Choose from a variety of symbols to insert into your blog.

The last icon in this grouping is a smiley face. Clicking this pulls up an assortment of emoticons that you can pop into your blog. Use these to express your emotion behind a sentence or thought you typed. Some of the smileys are animated, and there are even a few unusual ones, such as a green alien face and a little red devil (see Figure 13.12).

The drop-down menus above all of these icons allow you to additionally modify the look of text. Your options are Style, Font, and Size.

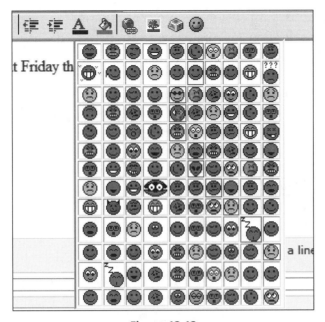

Figure 13.12
People love smileys, also known as emoticons.
Pick from this huge assortment to convey your emotions. Just don't overdo it!

Highlight the text you want to alter. Let's try Size first. Here you have size numbers 1 through 7. Seven produces the largest-sized text, and one produces the smallest (see Figure 13.13).

Figure 13.13
Font size 7 plumps up this text to huge proportions!

The Font menu simply allows you to change the default font to another. The selection is small, but some people do like to switch up their fonts now and again (see Figure 13.14).

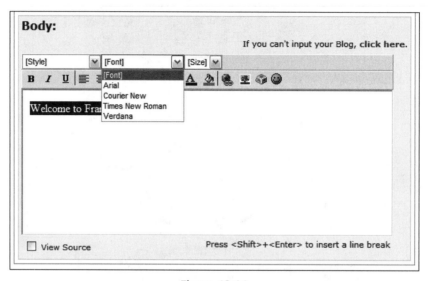

Figure 13.14
You can change up your fonts. Just try not to use more than two in one blog entry; otherwise, it's distracting to the reader.

With the Style menu you can assign various styles to your text (see Figure 13.15). Styles change your text in several ways at once. Headings 1 through 6 make your text bold and change the size. Unlike the size options, however, the largest heading number (6) actually produces the smallest text. Heading 1 makes the largest text. You can also choose Paragraph, Address, and Formatted. Each changes text in a different way. Experiment to find the style you like best. You can assign different styles to various pieces of text within a blog, but that same piece of text can only have one style at a time.

Lastly, note the View Source check box below the text field. Clicking this brings up the actual HTML tags so you can edit them by hand (see Figure 13.16). Don't edit this way unless you know enough about HTML tags to make it work without an editor. Editing the source code is useful for embedding video and other special media tags.

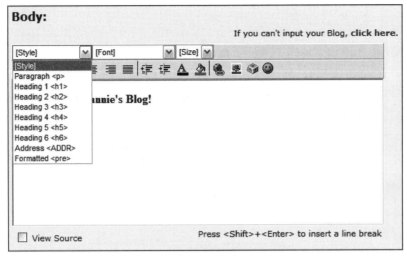

Figure 13.15
Style selections for your blog.

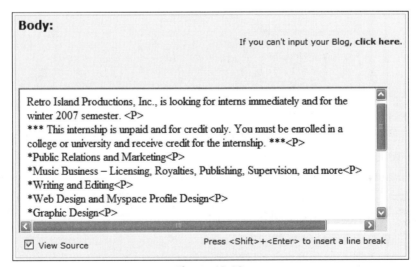

Figure 13.16
Click View Source to edit HTML tags only.

Introductions, Please

The intro fields for your blog appear at the top of the editing page (see Figure 13.17). Your date and time of blog creation are automatically entered, but you can customize them if you prefer. Your subject is the next field to fill out. Keep it to the point, but don't be afraid to be playful.

Just know when it's appropriate. Avoid misleading headlines. You may think it is clever of you to type in "Giving Away Free Tix" (or something more outrageous) so more people will click on your blog, but when they find out it was all a ploy, you will have broken that trust and alienated your audience. Who would click on any of your blogs again?

You should also choose a category for your blog. For most of you reading this book, the category will be Music. This allows readers looking for music blogs only to pull up yours in a search.

Figure 13.17
These fields introduce your blog to readers.

You're Almost Finished...

Now skip down to the bottom of the editing page. This last section contains some fun fields as well as those related to privacy and commenting. Tell Us What You're Reading, Viewing, or Listening To and Current Mood are not essential to fill out, but they make for an interesting touch (see Figures 13.18 and 13.19). You can even specify what you're listening to or watching.

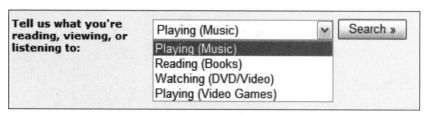

Figure 13.18
Specify what you were doing at the time you wrote your blog.

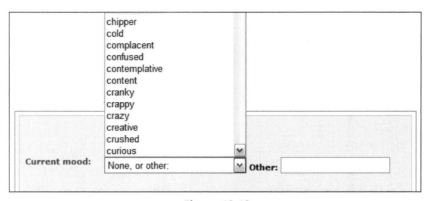

Figure 13.19
The Current Mood list contains tons of options so you can convey your
emotional state at the time you penned your blog.

The most important part of this section is the Privacy settings (see
Figure 13.20). Note the different options: Public, Diary, Friends, and
Preferred List (see Figure 13.21). As a music marketer, Public, Friends,
and Preferred List are the settings you'll stick with. Most of your posts
should be Public, meaning any MySpacer can read them. You can use
the Friends and Preferred List settings to restrict blogs about special
offers or street team info.

Figure 13.20
Privacy settings in your blog creation page.

The Preferred List, sometimes called a *Private List*, is great for inform-
ing street teamers, fan club members, and other select groups only. By
restricting access, you can create a VIP aura and use this to build a
"sign-up only" group to whom you send private messages. Have a
signup on your profile for a fan club that can gain unrestricted access
to all your blogs, special offers, and private messages. Each blog entry
can have different settings, so while one might be for public consump-
tion, another might be for select fans only. It's easy to build a Preferred
List—you simply choose the users you want to include. They appear
in a list like the one in Figure 13.22. Your blog entry will be viewable
only by these specified users.

Figure 13.21
MySpace's help pop-up describing the different blog privacy settings.

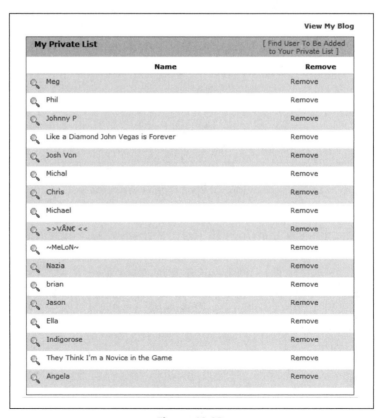

Figure 13.22
A sample preferred reader list.

Also in this section you should specify whether to allow user comments and kudos (which are like a thumbs-up). Because your goal is to be as interactive as possible with fans, allowing comments is an important component of that objective. Therefore, you'll keep that box unchecked (see Figure 13.23). Blog comments appear in a similar fashion as any other profile or image comment (see Figure 13.24).

Comments   ☐ disable Kudos & comments

Figure 13.23
In most circumstances, you'll want to allow users to post comments on your blog.

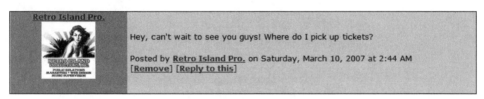

Hey, can't wait to see you guys! Where do I pick up tickets?

Posted by **Retro Island Pro.** on Saturday, March 10, 2007 at 2:44 AM
[**Remove**] [**Reply to this**]

Figure 13.24
A sample of blog comments.

Lastly, you may attach a podcast by entering its URL location in the Podcast Enclosure field (see Figure 13.25).

Podcast Enclosure:

Figure 13.25
The Podcast Enclosure field.

When you are satisfied with your blog entry, click the Preview & Post button. You'll be presented with a confirmation screen. Review your blog's text once more. Edit if necessary. Otherwise, click Post Blog to process your blog entry (see Figure 13.26).

Your posted blog will resemble something like Figure 13.27. Notice the bottom of the blog. You'll see a link for readers to add their two cents, as well as the number of comments and kudos you've received so far. You can also edit or remove your blog.

Figure 13.26
This is your confirmation page. If you're not happy with your blog text,
you can always edit before proceeding.

Figure 13.27
A sample blog in a default page design will resemble this.

Designing Your Blog Space

MySpace provides a mechanism by which you can customize the over-all look of your blog pages (see Figure 13.28). This is helpful when you want your blog to look similar to your profile. Click on the Customize Blog link in your blog control panel. Here you'll see a page that contains fields related to every aspect of your blog's design. Change the page's colors, fonts, and table alignments, or add image backgrounds and custom headers. You can even add looping music and paste in custom style sheets, similar to the way you change the look of your main profile.

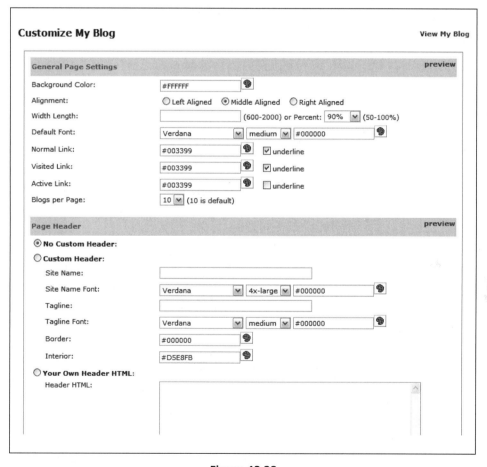

Figure 13.28
This interface helps you customize the look of your blog pages to correspond with the look of your main profile.

Click on Blog Safe Mode (see Figure 13.29) to edit your blog without pulling up all the design changes. This mode also shows your blog entries in source code (see Figure 13.30). People often find Safe Mode editing helpful when their blogs contain lots of images, colors, and custom designs, and they only want to make a few simple edits without having to reload the page each time. It's quicker and cleaner.

Figure 13.29
Find the Blog Safe Mode option in your control panel for editing at the source.

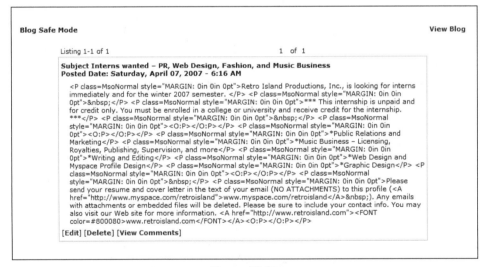

Figure 13.30
This is what the no-frills Blog Safe Mode looks like.

Blog Groups
MySpace houses hundreds of thousands of blog groups where people join to read each other's writings on a particular topic. This is different than regular discussion groups (see Chapter 15, "Contacting Your

Audience"). In your blog control panel, click Browse Blog Groups to see what's available (see Figure 13.31). Most blog groups require approval of the founder in order for you to view them. You can also start your own blog group. Click Create a Blog Group (see Figure 13.32) and fill out the information required (see Figure 13.33). Then you can start inviting others to join! This may be an option for you if there are many people out there blogging about your band or genre.

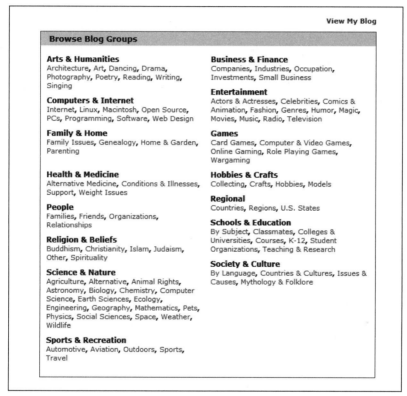

Figure 13.31
These are the many categories available for blog groups.

Figure 13.32
Click this link to start your own blog group.

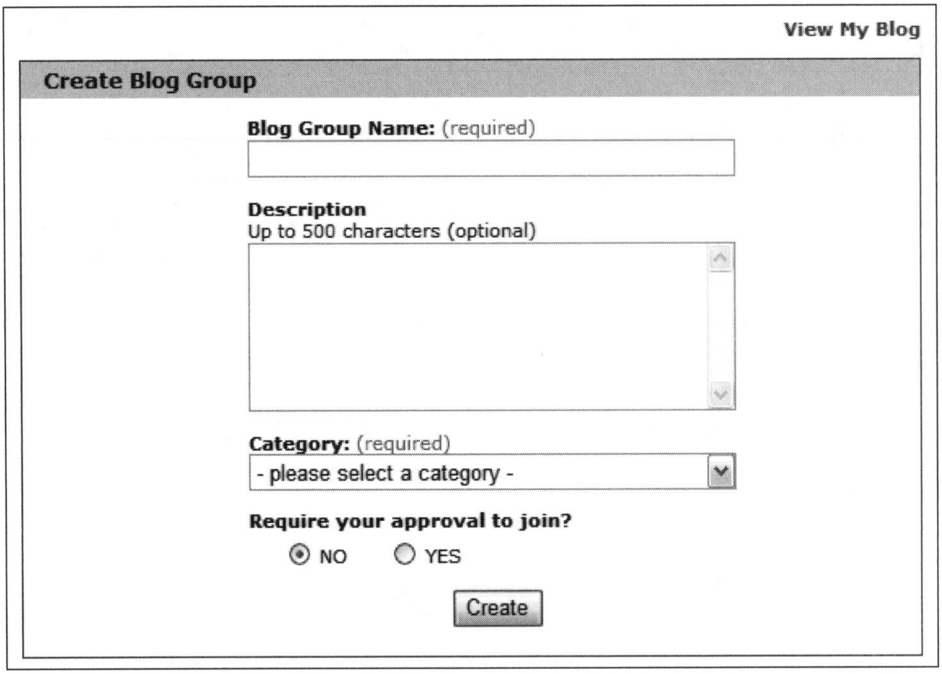

Figure 13.33
Filling in a few fields will get you your own blog group.

More Blog Features

You will also see in your blog control panel links to My Subscriptions and My Readers. If, while browsing around MySpace, you find a blog that you like and want to read again, you can click the Subscribe link next to the blog (see Figure 13.34). This will place it in your My Subscriptions section and will alert you when new entries are posted. Likewise, if a MySpacer likes your blog and wants to keep abreast of your posts, he can subscribe to yours as well. Those who are subscribed to your blog will appear under My Readers (see Figure 13.35).

The inconspicuous links in the upper-right corner of your blog entry contain a link for RSS, which is a type of web feed used to publish often-updated digital content. This link allows users to add you as an RSS feed, which means your blog content is downloaded directly into the user's computer and viewed on their RSS-capable web browser (see Figure 13.36).

Figure 13.34
Subscribe to your favorite blogs to keep on top of new entries.

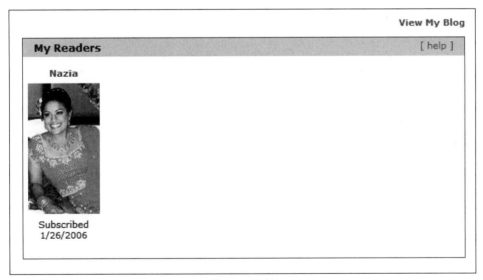

Figure 13.35
As a blogger, you can view the people who have subscribed to your blog.

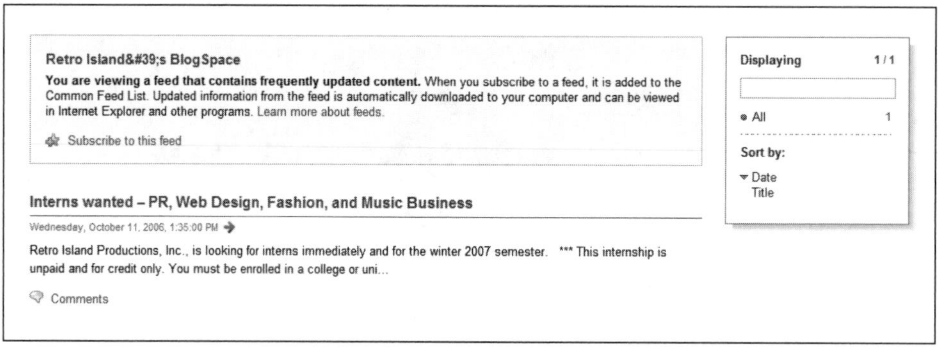

Figure 13.36
This is what your blog looks like in an RSS feed.

Figure 13.37
When you invite someone to read your blog, the person receives an email like this one.

More links allow you to forward blogs to your friends and even invite the writer to read your blog. Your invitee will receive an email message asking him to subscribe to your blog (see Figure 13.37).

Your blog's control panel tallies your blog's posts, comments, views, and kudos. You can keep track of how many hits you're getting that day, week, or all the time (see Figure 13.38).

	Today	Week	Total
Posts	0	0	11
Comments	0	0	1
Views	0	1	274
Kudos	0	0	1

Figure 13.38
Check out your blog tallies to see how much exposure you're getting.

Blogs can be an effective public relations tool for both bands and businesses to communicate with fans and customers. Today's consumers, however, demand sincerity and won't take to constant sales pitches. Be real and write clearly and concisely. And don't be afraid to speak from the heart.

Now that you know everything you need to post blogs on your profile, let's move on to learning the ins and outs of contacting your audience.

14 Using Groups and Forums

Groups and forums have been a staple of Internet interactions almost from its onset. MySpace offers both. This chapter will introduce you to groups and forums, explain how to interact when using them, and give you tips for starting your own.

Groups versus Forums

In most places on the web, the words "group" and "forum" are interchangeable and are both used to denote a place where netizens gather to hold discussions and post their thoughts on any given subject. On MySpace, however, forums and groups are distinctly separate areas. Although both allow MySpacers to generate topic discussions, individual groups are created by MySpace users, while forums are made by the MySpace powers-that-be.

Forums are currently not searchable, and the visual design cannot be altered by users (see Figure 14.1). Groups, on the other hand, *are* searchable and can be customized in a similar fashion as profiles. Forums are limited, but they are useful because they gather people on a particular topic in one place. There may be dozens of groups about hiphop and its related artists, but there is only one forum on this topic (see Figure 14.2).

MySpace forums, while buzzing with activity and discussion, contain fewer than 100 categories and subcategories total. Conversely, there are millions of MySpace groups. Music and entertainment groups alone number more than 750,000, and the Other category contains more than 2 million individual groups (see Figure 14.3). Forums are open to everyone, while groups can be deemed private and available only to a select few.

Forum Category	Rooms	Topics	Posts	Last Post
Automotive Talk about your ride. We did it for TheBoz.	Chat	46752	786828	Thu Apr 5, 2007 6:15 PM by: **I LUV MY BLUEBERRY!!!!!!** » **View Post**
Business & Entrepreneurs Need advice or a partner for your latest venture?	Chat	59114	99322	Thu Apr 5, 2007 6:14 PM by: **Mandy** » **View Post**
Campus Life Study partners, PARTIES, and alumni.	Chat	24829	213122	Thu Apr 5, 2007 6:14 PM by: **Ørganism ²¹²** » **View Post**
Career Center Career advice, discussion and opportunities.	Chat	15502	43571	Thu Apr 5, 2007 6:04 PM by: **Angel** » **View Post**
Comedy Forums for comics and lovers of comedy.	Chat	11737	302108	Thu Apr 5, 2007 6:15 PM by: **SERPY** » **View Post**
Computers & Technology From PCs to iPods; technoid congregation.	Chat	41394	262327	Thu Apr 5, 2007 6:04 PM by: **Mandy** » **View Post**
Culture, Arts & Literature The finer things in life be here.	Chat	35290	413960	Thu Apr 5, 2007 6:15 PM by: **Đrëdd Hœdèd Pòê†™** » **View Post**
Filmmakers Forum for Filmmakers	Chat	26608	101370	Thu Apr 5, 2007 6:08 PM by: **FREETHESOULS** » **View Post**
Food & Drink Best food in town is where...?	Chat	14083	129574	Thu Apr 5, 2007 6:12 PM by: **1/2 PINT** » **View Post**
Games Video games improve motor reflexes and strategy skills.	Chat	86895	702368	Thu Apr 5, 2007 6:13 PM by: **Herzog des Gottes Daevion** » **View Post**
General Discussion Whatever doesn't fit everywhere else.	Chat	9677	648297	Thu Apr 5, 2007 6:15 PM by: **soggy bread** » **View Post**

Forum Home

Figure 14.1
These are just some of the forum topics available to everyone.

Forum Home » Music

Forum Sub Category	Topics	Posts	Last Post
Acoustic	15933	133599	04/05/2007 6:14 PM by: **drawler** » **View Post**
Alternative	24380	194258	04/05/2007 6:13 PM by: **CC** » **View Post**
Electronic/Dance	27593	248835	04/05/2007 6:15 PM by: **Sweet X poison INC CO Since 1991[physical]** » **View Post**
Emo	26985	503554	04/05/2007 6:13 PM by: **wrink lay** » **View Post**
General	101922	1077704	04/05/2007 6:13 PM by: **Wang chung** » **View Post**
Hardcore	15589	147735	04/05/2007 6:15 PM by: **anytown** » **View Post**
Hip-Hop	127356	1170642	04/05/2007 6:15 PM by: **Jesus F. Baby..** » **View Post**
Metal	42850	737193	04/05/2007 6:15 PM by: **Dæmonicus** » **View Post**
Punk	31249	434722	04/05/2007 6:14 PM by: **MoMo the Pirate** » **View Post**
Rock	52297	780426	04/05/2007 6:15 PM by: **Mistress Nani** » **View Post**

Figure 14.2
The music section of forums.

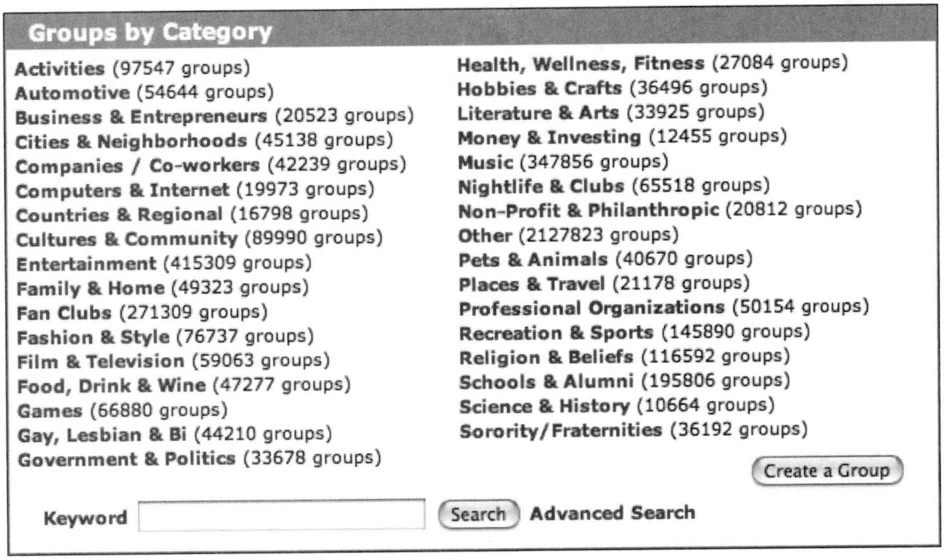

Groups by Category

Activities (97547 groups)
Automotive (54644 groups)
Business & Entrepreneurs (20523 groups)
Cities & Neighborhoods (45138 groups)
Companies / Co-workers (42239 groups)
Computers & Internet (19973 groups)
Countries & Regional (16798 groups)
Cultures & Community (89990 groups)
Entertainment (415309 groups)
Family & Home (49323 groups)
Fan Clubs (271309 groups)
Fashion & Style (76737 groups)
Film & Television (59063 groups)
Food, Drink & Wine (47277 groups)
Games (66880 groups)
Gay, Lesbian & Bi (44210 groups)
Government & Politics (33678 groups)

Health, Wellness, Fitness (27084 groups)
Hobbies & Crafts (36496 groups)
Literature & Arts (33925 groups)
Money & Investing (12455 groups)
Music (347856 groups)
Nightlife & Clubs (65518 groups)
Non-Profit & Philanthropic (20812 groups)
Other (2127823 groups)
Pets & Animals (40670 groups)
Places & Travel (21178 groups)
Professional Organizations (50154 groups)
Recreation & Sports (145890 groups)
Religion & Beliefs (116592 groups)
Schools & Alumni (195806 groups)
Science & History (10664 groups)
Sorority/Fraternities (36192 groups)

Create a Group

Keyword [_____] Search Advanced Search

Figure 14.3
The groups categories are numerous, and so are the subgroups within them.

The process of starting a discussion and replying to posts is the same in both forums and groups, so once you learn how to use one, you can try the other with no problem!

Getting into Groups

Click on Groups in the medium-blue navigation bar to access the groups directory, search function, and links to help you create and manage your groups (see Figure 14.4). Groups are organized by categories including Music, Entertainment, Pets & Animals, Money & Investing, and more than 30 other categories. While you can join groups based on any number of interests you may have, let's stick with music- and entertainment-related topics for now.

Enter the Music category and you'll see lists of groups spanning more than 33,000 pages (see Figure 14.5)... obviously too many to browse through! So let's start searching for what we want. On the right, there is a search box that allows you to find groups by keyword, name, and even proximity to your local area (see Figure 14.6). Let's start with the keywords "music in film."

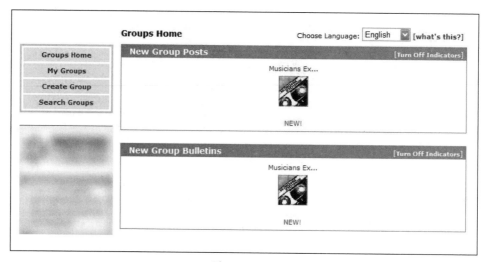

Figure 14.4
Your Groups main page helps you navigate your way through the system.

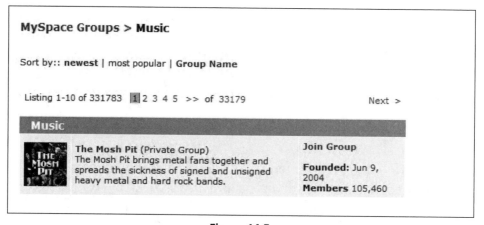

Figure 14.5
This is just a snippet of the first page of the Music groups section.
Notice how many groups and pages there are!

The resulting page gives you a variety of possible groups to join, from the Musicians Resource Center to one aptly named Music in Film. Another search for "emo music" yields about 700 groups of those who both love and hate the genre. As discussed in Chapter 9, there are also "add me" groups where you can introduce yourself and ask people to add you to their friends list.

Figure 14.6
The groups search helps you find just what you're looking for.

It usually takes some digging to find groups that really fit you. You'll find that there may be a lot of groups on any particular topic, but maybe only a few are really active and worth joining.

Try searching for groups dedicated to your favorite bands, music business, songwriting, music promotion, or even your particular genre of music. The groups will be either public or private. You can join both to receive updates and group bulletins. Some private groups require you to apply to join and be approved before you are allowed to post any messages. Other groups are by invitation only, and you cannot even view the group's content unless you are invited by a member.

Group Netiquette

You should join any and all groups or forums you like, but do resist the temptation to post your own topic thread right away. The better approach is to read through some of the threads, get familiar with the "culture" and tone of the group, and then reply to a few posts. People will get to know you that way and see what you're about. Plus, posting "Hey, I'm in a band. Add me!" right off the bat may be deemed spammy behavior (unless you're in an add me group) and get you booted out.

Posting and replying in both groups and forums is just a matter of hitting a button. Clicking on the Post a New Topic or Post Topic links/buttons starts a brand-new thread. When replying to a posted message, Quote includes the original poster's message below yours. Or hit Reply to post your message without quoting the previous poster's message. The Post a Reply button does the same thing as hitting Reply.

When you're ready to post a brand-new topic that others can respond to, click on the Post Topic button or the Post a New Topic link. Again, they do the same thing. You've probably noticed that MySpace gives you lots of ways to accomplish the same task!

Your newly posted topic now appears under the Forum/Forum Topic section toward the bottom of the group page. I know it can get confusing to see the word "forum" while in a group, but don't let the semantics throw you! Below the topic list, you may see Bulletins listed. Like regular bulletins, these are special posts that group members can send out, but others cannot reply to. It's for announcements only. Click on Post a New Bulletin in the group's bulletin section to submit your post. Whether members can post group bulletins is at the discretion of the group owner or moderator.

For those of you who are new to groups or the Internet in general, it's time to get good with netiquette, the system of online manners and socially acceptable virtual behavior. Both of these links provide great resources on the topic:

- www.albion.com/netiquette

- en.wikipedia.org/wiki/Netiquette

Some general tips to remember:

- Never type your messages in all caps, which denotes yelling and often hostility in cyberspace.

- Remember that your online text writings do not have the benefit of communicating your facial expressions, tone of voice, and other body language indicators. So write carefully to avoid misinterpretations.

- Stick to the topic of the group.

- Respect other users and forego posting large graphic files and other bandwidth-sucking media.

- Be sincere, polite, and courteous. Avoid posting advertisements and blatant commercialism.

Once you get comfortable in a group, you may start sending friend requests to other group members. It's always nice to follow up with an email introduction as well. This is another way to help you meet people and build your fan/friends list.

Starting Your Own Group

You may not have found a group that addresses your interests, so start one! In the main Groups section, click Create Group. After choosing your new group's name and category, you'll specify other details, such as whether your group will be open to the public and a short description of your group (see Figure 14.7). Once you've gone through the initial process, you can customize your profile with graphics and more.

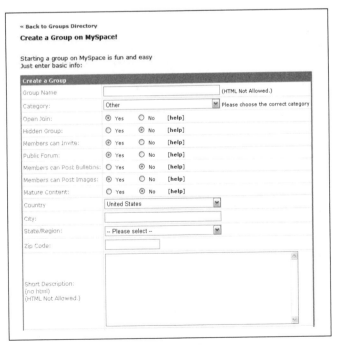

Figure 14.7
The Create Group page helps you start your very own MySpace group.

Initially, you will probably invite members of your friends list to join your group. It's best to do this in batches because sending out large numbers of invites at once may make MySpace think you are spamming people. If that happens and your account gets deleted, you'll have to start your profile all over again.

Let's move on now to learning how to contact your audience and the rules of email....

15 Contacting Your Audience

After all the planning and execution of your MySpace profile, contacting your audience is the next step in your marketing endeavors. We've already explored several ways to do this—adding friends, making comments, posting bulletins and blogs, and joining groups. This chapter will touch on the finer points of communication, such as complying with anti-spam laws and crafting a privacy policy. Although this chapter touches on some legal points, it does not constitute legal advice, so make sure to consult an attorney if these issues pertain to you.

Just Say No to Spam

U.S. anti-spam laws went into effect in 2004 and set rules for the sending of all unsolicited *and* solicited commercial email. This is called the Controlling the Assault of Non-Solicited Pornography and Marketing Act, but it is commonly referred to as the CAN-SPAM Act. Violators can be slapped with huge fines (such as $250 per message sent) and even jail time, so it's essential that every marketer know and understand these rules. These email rules apply whether you're sending messages the good old-fashioned way or distributing them via the MySpace service. Let's take a look at the major dos and don'ts of the CAN-SPAM Act.

No Fraudulent Headers

Most spam typically comes from forged email accounts, making it difficult to put spammers out of business. But it can be done. Investigators and even regular Joes can determine the origins of an email by sifting through the email's headers, which is the collection of information that notes where an email came from, where it has been, and where it's going. An email typically passes through a series of computers and servers before reaching your inbox, and normally the headers will reveal the IP addresses of those computers, making it possible to track down where an email came from. Bad guys try to conceal this information by using phony email addresses and names.

The CAN-SPAM Act bans fake, misleading, or missing information in the From portion of your email. You may not create false email accounts using made-up or inaccurate names. Missing header information, such as listing "unknown sender" in place of your return email address or intentionally trying to mask or omit the origins of an email, is a no-no (see Figure 15.1).

From: (Unknown Sender)

Figure 15.1
The From line on this spam email does not allow the
recipient to see from where the email came.

You also cannot use bogus contact information to purchase your domain names. When you purchase a domain name, say for your band's official website (www.*insertyourbandnamehere*.com), you are required to give your name, address, phone number, and a working email address. This becomes a part of the public record, and anyone can look up the owner of any domain name, thereby determining who sent emails originating from that domain. Your domain host company may offer services to mask your personal info and list your host company's info instead, but that doesn't exempt you from providing true contact info in the first place.

To stay in the clear, always use a legitimate email account to send marketing messages. It's best to obtain an account separate from your main personal or business one so you don't mix your marketing emails with other emails. You can get an email address from many providers, such as Google or Yahoo. Or, if you own a domain name, create a special email box just for your marketing activities. Your email account info must be completely accurate and traceable (see Figure 15.2). As far as domain name creation, always use up-to-date contact info and make sure it is updated yearly. Your MySpace profile also must be a real profile and not set up with fake names and pictures. There are plenty of fake profiles on MySpace touting pyramid schemes and ways to make money filling out surveys. These are typically the spammers of the community, and MySpace works to shut them down.

```
The Registry database contains ONLY .COM, .NET, .EDU domains and
Registrars.
Whois Server: whois.opensrs.net
Registrant:
 Microsoft Corporation
 One Microsoft Way
 Redmond, WA 98052
 US

 Domain name: MICROSOFT.COM

 Administrative Contact:
     Administrator, Domain  domains@microsoft.com
     One Microsoft Way
     Redmond, WA 98052
     US
     +1.4258828080
 Technical Contact:
     Hostmaster, MSN  msnhst@microsoft.com
     One Microsoft Way
     Redmond, WA 98052
     US
     +1.4258828080
```

Figure 15.2
Maintaining accurate contact information allows the public to see who owns the domain name from which your email is originating, as in this Microsoft example.

Any email address you use to send marketing messages must remain active for at least 30 days after an email message was sent. So don't close that email account or MySpace profile before that time!

Stick to the Real Subject

You've no doubt received a message in which the subject looked like it might be legit. Perhaps it said something like, "Met you at the club last night," or "Mutual friend." Hmmm... maybe it really *is* that friend of a friend who knows a record executive. Or perhaps it looks as if it might be from your bank or credit card provider. So you open the message, only to find it's an ad for pharmaceuticals, stocks, software, or porn. If you're really unlucky, it's not just an ad but something that *looks* like it's from your bank—or it might even contain spyware or a virus. At the very least, it makes you unwilling to ever open anything again.

That leads us to our next rule. The subject line in any email you send cannot be deceptive or misleading. It should clearly state the purpose of your email and indicate the content. Here are a few examples:

- Instead of "See Me This Weekend," be more specific and use "Mary Songstress appearing Saturday at the Bossa Lounge."

- Rather than "Our Album's Out Next Week," try "The Cleary Band New Album Hits Stores Tuesday."

- "Come to our party!" might be fine for friends and family, but for your marketing list a clearer subject is in order, such as "You're Invited to the JamTones' CD Release Party."

The spam email in Figure 15.3 is a prime example of what you should never, ever do if you want people to take you seriously!

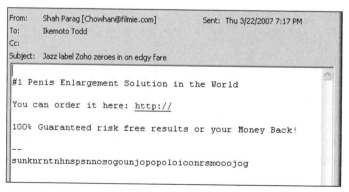

Figure 15.3
This is an actual email I received with a subject line that
mentions a "jazz label," yet the email is for penis enlargement!

Let Them Opt Out

Every time you send an email, it must contain an opt-out option. Each recipient is entitled to unsubscribe. Your opt-out mechanism can be very simple, such as a notice asking people to reply with the word "unsubscribe" or "remove" in the subject line. Or it can be a special link administered by a third-party email marketing service, such as ConstantContact.com or VerticalResponse.com. Users can click and take themselves off your list. The service will automatically remove them. Figure 15.4 shows a great example of opt-out language. Whatever you choose, your opt-out option must remain in effect for at least 30 days after the marketing email was sent.

Monster respects your online time and privacy. If you no longer wish to receive the Contract & Temporary Newsletter please click here and submit your request.

Requests for unsubscribing or for changing preferences can be made only by clicking on the link above and may take up to 10 days to take effect.

Figure 15.4
Monster.com uses plain but cordial language to describe how to opt out.

Take Them Off Your List

Fans come and go, and sometimes they decide they don't want to receive your emails after all. It's just the ebb and flow of things, and you shouldn't take it personally. You must, however, take non-interested people off your list. The law compels you to remove unsubscribers immediately. You have 10 days to take people off of your list who have requested removal. Below your opt-out mechanism, throw in some text letting people know it may take up to 10 days before they are completely removed. Then make sure you do it. Make a special effort to double-check any multiple or duplicate lists you may be maintaining.

When a person has requested removal, not only can you not send them email, you cannot use a third party (such as a friend or a company) to send emails to them for you.

No Bootleg Emails or Lists

You are probably collecting emails through a variety of methods—your website, MySpace profile, gig signups, and fan club members. These are all legitimate list sources because the recipients have chosen to be added to your list. However, randomly generated email addresses or harvested emails are strictly off limits. Spammers often use bots to comb through forums, newsgroups, and websites to find email addresses, even if those places have notices strictly prohibiting such practices. Or spammers generate random email addresses and hope they belong to actual people (see Figure 15.5). Never do this. Keep it strictly on the up and up by only using emails you've personally collected through opt-in mechanisms. You can also purchase lists from a reputable list broker or from a magazine or other website whose audience matches yours.

Figure 15.5
Randomly generated emails, including those in sequential order,
are a hallmark of spam scam artists.

Honor Thy Privacy Policy

Always post a privacy policy on your website, MySpace profile, gig sheets, and so on. It can be as short and sweet as, "We will never give, rent, sell, or lease your email address to anyone!" And *stick to it*! Under the law, you must honor your privacy policy. If you say you won't give, sell, lease, or otherwise transfer collected emails and information to others, then you must abide by your policy. On top of this, if you do sell a list of email addresses (and it's not in violation of your stated privacy policy), then you may not include anyone who previously requested removal from your list. I find that people are more willing to give their information to you (for the purposes of receiving info about your music only) if you state that you will guard their info fiercely and you will not sell it or give it away. More information on privacy policies can be found further on in this chapter.

Reveal Your Postal Address

Not only is it important to have a valid return email address in your email, it's also imperative to include your valid postal address. You can pop this into the bottom of the email, below your opt-out statement and near your copyright details. Try not to put your home address, but include a business address instead. Virtual office addresses and boxes that look like street addresses can be had for a reasonable fee. Including your valid postal address reinforces that you are indeed a legitimate entity, and not one of the many anonymous spammers plaguing the Internet (see Figure 15.6).

privacy policy | FAQ | terms & conditions

unsubscribe | cancel membership

For further information, please write us at
Borders Rewards Customer Care, P.O. Box 7002, LaVergne, TN 37086.
Or call us at 800.443.7359.

Figure 15.6
This Borders Inc. email gives the company's address below links to
unsubscribe and to the privacy policy.

Don't Use Protected Networks

Steer clear of using unprotected computers or networks without permission. This means you may not use open-relay or unauthorized computers to send multiple email messages or to conceal your identity. Spammers often do this, unbeknownst to the owners of these networks. Your very own computer may have even been commandeered by a virus to send spam (making it what is known as a *zombie computer*).

Identify Advertisements

You must clearly identify any unsolicited emails you send out as advertisements. This means that if your recipient did not specifically opt-in to your list, then you must clearly note that the recipient is receiving a solicitation from you. For instance, when emailing someone on referral from a friend or a business associate, you can introduce yourself with text such as, "Bob GuitarGuy recommended I contact you because he thought you would enjoy my music, so I hope you won't mind this solicitation! Details about my music are below, and you can even listen to clips on my website. Thanks!"

You may even note the nature of your solicitation at the bottom of the email. This is common when someone purchases a list or trades email addresses with another entity. You may have seen wording such as, "You are receiving this email advertisement because you opted into a list that indicated interest in products and services similar to the above." Always be sure to follow with unsubscribe links.

All of the preceding information assumes you are not a porn marketer —there are additional rules for the dissemination of sexual content and solicitations. For further research, visit www.spamlaws.com/federal/ can-spam.shtml or www.ftc.gov/bcp/conline/pubs/buspubs/canspam.htm.

Triggers

Most ISPs have built-in spam filters that look for a host of things in every email that passes through their gates. Filters search for missing header information, unknown senders, and even words that trigger suspicion. Each and every item is assigned a score, and if your total email score is above a certain threshold, it is deemed spam, even if it isn't.

Marketers and spammers alike often scrutinize their emails in an effort to circumvent the system and get their messages through, making filters more restrictive and less tolerant. We, as music marketers, have to be conscious of what we are putting in our emails to avoid as many of these triggers as possible. Items that comply with the U.S. CAN-SPAM law (such as complete To/From information) are a start. Your word choice is also integral, because some words and phrases common to junk mail will cause a filter to block you out (see Figure 15.7).

Figure 15.7
SpamAssassin is one of the best-known filters used by email providers around the world.

Don't drive yourself crazy about the words you're using. As a music marketer, it's unlikely you'll be including some common triggers, such as "stock tips" and "cheap software." But, there are a few that you may consider using that are red flags for filters.

- Avoid using the word "free" in the subject of your email. And never, *ever* use it in all caps.

- In the body of your email, the word "free" in conjunction with words such as "offer," "preview," and "sample" can get you banned from an ISP.

- Don't put any text in your email claiming to be in compliance with CAN-SPAM laws or any other law. Spammers do this all the time, and the filters weed them out.

- While you do have to provide an opt-out or unsubscribe mechanism in your emails, using the word "unsubscribe" seems to cause filters to spit you back into the ether. This is why marketers try to get creative when putting in opt-out language. Try something like, "Don't want to receive emails anymore?"

- Avoid using sales-y words and phrases, such as "Act now!" or "Supplies are limited!"

- "Click here" standing by itself with a link to an outside site can also raise filter eyebrows.

- Resist funky font colors, especially red, yellow, blue, and green.

- Spammers try to trick the filters by misspelling words, but the filters eventually get wise. Avoid intentionally misspelling words or using symbols instead of letters. It gives people the impression that you *are* a spammer, or at least you are really sloppy.

You're probably wondering how anybody is supposed to get an email through with all these annoying, confusing rules. Remember that filters use a point system to decide whether your email is unwanted. Too many points, and you won't get through. Being mindful of some of the triggers will help you draw less filter attention to your emails and will increase the likelihood your messages will get through to your recipients.

If you want to really go bonkers, you can take a look at a list of spam word triggers at www.wilsonweb.com/wmt8/spamfilter_phrases.htm or www.wordbiz.com/avoidspamfilters.html.

You've Been Tagged as a Spammer!

It's going to happen, so you might as well resign yourself to it. Sometimes you'll know when it does; sometimes you won't. A spam filter may add your domain name or ISP to a blacklist. Email servers consult these blacklists before deciding which messages will be allowed to pass through to their email account holders. That means that at least for a while (which could be days or could be weeks), emails from your domain name or ISP server can be actively blocked.

It happens to every marketer, whether you're sending email from your AOL or Yahoo account or from your own personal domain name and server. Perhaps you sent an email to someone who forgot they signed up for your list. Then they hit that Report Spam button, and now you're flagged. Sending out lots of emails at once to the same domain name can also get you marked as a spammer. So send out in small batches if you're using a regular email account. And try to keep your marketing emails to no more than one to two times a month at most.

But it might not even be your fault. If someone using the same web-hosting service as you is sending out emails that filters consider suspicious, the IP address of the web-hosting service will end up on a blacklist. Consequently, all emails originating from the offending IP address, including yours, can be blocked by any service that consults the blacklist.

You'll know you've been blocked if:

- The email you sent comes back to your inbox marked undeliverable. Open all undeliverable emails, and if it says the recipient's account or mailbox is "not found," you're okay (see Figure 15.8).

- If you see anything in the email that indicates your email has been deemed suspicious or has been flagged by a filter, then you may have been blocked. Look for words such as "abuse," "spam blocked," "spam cop," and so on (see Figure 15.9).

```
This message was created automatically by mail delivery software.

A message that you sent could not be delivered to one or more of its
recipients. This is a permanent error. The following address(es)
failed:

  jared@franvincent.com
    SMTP error from remote mail server after RCPT TO:
<jared@franvincent.com>
    host MAIL.musicianshotline.com [                    ]:
    550 unknown user <jared@franvincent.com>
```

Figure 15.8
Notice in this returned email that the notes indicate "unknown user."
This means the email is no longer valid and should be removed from your list.

```
This message was created automatically by mail delivery software.

A message that you sent could not be delivered to one or more of its recipients. This is a permanent
error. The following address(es) failed:

  ngpt@franvincent.com>
    SMTP error from remote mail server after MAIL FROM:<SRS0=pylKw1=
2J=franvincent.com=media@franvincent.com>
    host mail.ccsi.com [              ]: 553 5.3.0 Spam blocked see:http://spamcop.net/b1.shtml?
```

Figure 15.9
In this example, the returned email does not indicate it came back because the recipient's
address was invalid. Instead, it shows that the email has been blocked as spam.

- Many emails bounce back to you, and you can't find anything in the returned email indicating that it's due to an incorrect email address.

- The email you sent comes back to your inbox with a subject header stating plainly that you've been blocked.

Once you've determined you've been flagged as a spammer, you should contact your Internet or email service provider immediately. It is their job to get their IP addresses off of blacklists. Be patient and have a backup email account somewhere else. It sometimes takes weeks to get taken off of blacklists.

One quick tip for helping your emails get through to your recipients is to ask them to add your email address to their address book or email safe list. This identifies you to the email server as a preferred sender, and it is more likely that your messages will get through, as shown in Figure 15.10.

© 2007 Borders, Inc. and Walden Book Company, Inc. All rights reserved.
To ensure our messages are delivered properly to your inbox (not bulk or junk folders), add **borders@e.bordersstores.com** to your Address Book or Safe List.

Figure 15.10
This is a capture of a Borders Inc. email asking recipients to add the company's marketing email address to their safe list.

Crafting Your Privacy Policy

Businesses and bands alike post privacy policies (also known as *privacy statements*) to state exactly how they will use information gathered from website visitors and those who submit information to be included in mailing lists. These policies let visitors and customers know exactly what to expect, and as shown in the rundown of the CAN-SPAM law, marketers are expected to abide by their policies to the letter.

Most privacy policies you'll find on the Internet are lengthy dissertations filled with legalese. But yours doesn't have to be. A simply stated policy is fine and actually is much more user-friendly to regular, non-attorney people! For most of you solo artists or bands who only want to collect contact information in order to send notices about your music, gigs, and merchandise, the simplest of privacy policies will suffice. For example:

> The Hard Rockers may collect information that you submit on its websites, through gig signups, and through fan club memberships. We will use this information to distribute content about the band in the form of emails, newsletters, mailings, and other types of updates, at the discretion of the band. We will not share, distribute, lease, rent, give away, or sell your information to any third parties not connected with the promotion of the band or the dissemination of band updates and content.

The preceding example assumes you don't use cookies to collect raw data. A good website to consult for a primer on what to include in a privacy policy is www.hooverwebdesign.com/privacy-policy-form.html. You may decide you want a more comprehensive policy, especially if you are an entertainment business that intends to share names and contact data and collect raw info. The Direct Marketing Association has a free privacy policy creation tool that will generate the text for you. Find it at www.the-dma.org/privacy/creating.shtml.

There are many ways to write a privacy policy. Here are a few examples from major and independent record companies and artists:

- Sony Music: www.sonymusic.com/privacy

- Universal Music Group: privacypolicy.umusic.com

- Wind-Up Records: www.winduprecords.com/privacy.htm

- Virgin Records: www.virginrecords.com/home/privacy.aspx

- Blue Note Records: www.bluenote.com/privacypolicy.asp

- Alligator Records: www.alligator.com/privacy.cfm

- Astralwerks Records: www.astralwerks.com/privacy.html

- Black Eyed Peas: www.blackeyedpeas.com/about/privacy_statement

- Faith Hill: www.faithhill.com/legal-privacy

Put a link to your privacy policy at the bottom of your emails and official website. Link to it from your MySpace profile as well. On gig signup sheets, include a simple sentence at the top stating how you will or won't use fans' information, such as, "We will never sell or give away your info!"

Let's move on now to guarding your personal security when using MySpace....

16 Protecting Your Virtual and Physical Security

Myspace and other social networking sites offer almost unlimited opportunities to connect with an audience. Unfortunately, this can also bring unsavory people to your doorstep. Whether you are an artist, a businessperson, or a regular Joe, you must be extremely diligent in protecting your private information and be mindful that personal details you post on your profile should be kept to a minimum.

Regular account users who only use MySpace to keep in touch with friends and family sometimes choose to keep their profiles private and only viewable by members of their friends list (see Figure 16.1). As entertainment marketers, this defeats the purpose of having a MySpace profile. Therefore, we must be careful in how we present ourselves.

This profile is set to private. This user must add you as a friend to see his/her profile.

Figure 16.1
Visitors will see this when a profile is set to private (viewable by friends only).

Too Much Information

When you are setting up your profile and filling in the fields or creating a custom bio, have a trusted friend comb through the info to make sure you haven't revealed anything that could indicate where you live, where you or your spouse work, or where your children go to school. Along with the words you use, the pictures you display also offer the world information about you. Your audience doesn't need to know your children's names or see their pictures, nor do they need to know you live on the south side of town across from that distinctive bank building that many think of as a landmark, as in Figure 16.2. Too much information invites trouble.

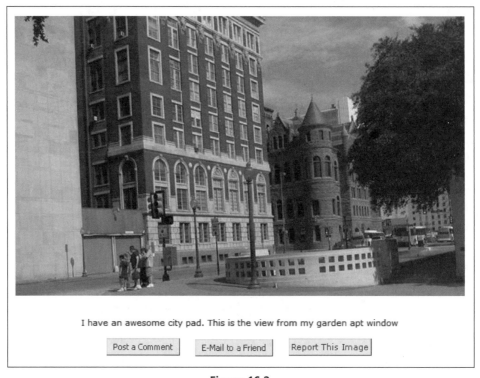

I have an awesome city pad. This is the view from my garden apt window

Post a Comment   E-Mail to a Friend   Report This Image

Figure 16.2
This photo of the view from a person's window gives away the location of a home without listing an address, making it easy for stalkers to find.

Your goal should always be to gain exposure for your product, whether it is music, comedy, films, or other business. Keep this in the forefront of your mind to help you filter through what should and shouldn't be available to the public. Consider these tips when populating your profile with pics, videos, and text:

- **Disguise your city location.** Go into profile edit mode and choose Basic Info. Here, you can specify your city, state, and zip code. Your zip code is used for search purposes (if a user is looking for bands within 50 miles of your zip, you will pop up in the results). However, you can actually make the city and state whatever you want. If you don't live in a metropolitan area, choose a major city in your area instead. For instance, if you live in Clermont, Florida, choose Orlando, Florida as your location. This is especially important if you are using your real name as your stage name and you or your family is listed in the phone book. For those of you who already live in a large city, you can keep the city/state intact if you are sure no one in your family is listed in the phone book. Or, you may want to put a general region identifier instead, such as South Florida or northern California.

- **Adopt a stage name.** Although this option may not be for everyone, for some it makes sense to keep your personal and stage identities separate.

- **Do not post your actual phone number.** You may be looking for bookings and contacts, but using actual phone numbers is not a good idea. Instead of posting your home, business, or cell phone, use a disposable phone number. PrivatePhone.com is a great free service powered by NetZero. You can get a voicemail number in your area code that will never show up in a phone book and is not traceable to your address. Anyone can leave messages for you 24/7, and those voicemails are accessible by phone, website, or email. If you must post a phone number, use this type of throwaway voicemail. If you have an agent or manager, he may prefer you list his number for booking instead.

- **Do not post your address.** Never list where you live or work. If you absolutely must put an address, use a P.O. box in a nearby city (not your own), or if you have one, use your manager's business address.

- **Create a special email address only for MySpace.** Use a unique email address to receive messages through your MySpace account and from fans. Never post your usual email address on your profile. If you must post one, use the dedicated email address instead. This way, you can maintain some separation between personal and stage messages. And, if your "performer" email account is ever compromised or a stalker type is bombarding you with hate messages, you can easily close the account and start fresh without disrupting your other personal email flow.

- **Mask your website Whois info.** Have you bought your own domain name for your personal/music website and posted the URL on your profile? You may be surprised to know that anyone can do a Whois search on your domain name to find out about the registrant (that's you), including your full name, address, phone number, and email address. US law requires that accurate information on domain registrants be kept up to date and available to the public. However, it is permissible to allow the Internet company you used to register your domain to list itself as the administrative contact, thereby taking the place of your info and protecting your identity. A domain name registration company will provide this service, called *Whois privacy*, for a nominal fee. As an alternative to Whois privacy, you may want to use a P.O. box instead of your home address, a disposable voicemail number, and a unique email address.

- **Get unlisted.** When you're out there gigging and attracting attention online, getting your name out of the white pages is the first step in keeping stalkers guessing. Although it may not be possible to wipe your information off of every directory in the world, your local white pages are the logical place to start.

- **Keep it all business.** Keep your profile clear of very personal details, such as places of work; frequent hangouts; children's names, info, pictures, and school locations; birthdates; friends and significant others' info; sexual details; drug/alcohol use; and location of where you worship, shop, and so on.

- **Pick photos carefully.** Like the text you write, the photos you display are important in protecting your personal life. Refrain from taking or displaying photos of you or your band outside your house, school, or other places you frequent. Stay away from posting family pictures, especially those that might give away where you or your family lives, works, or learns. Also, be discreet with provocative photos. Outright porn is prohibited. If you have a provocative act, simply be restrained online, keeping in mind that young people of all ages are able to see your profile. Portray yourself as a professional by using photos that are separate from your personal surroundings. It may be as simple as going to another location or using a backdrop, such as a white sheet, to mask your setting.

- **Don't be pressured.** You should never feel as if you have to give out information about yourself that has nothing to do with your product, service, or business. You are not obligated to disclose your sexual orientation, your religion, your political preferences, whether you are in a relationship, your day job, or how much money you make. Although these and many other personal information fields appear in the regular, comedian, and filmmaker MySpace accounts, you do not have to fill them out, nor do you have to volunteer this info in a musician profile.

The more exposure you get, the more wary you need to be about public access to your information. There are many other ways people can find out where you live, such as DMV and voter registrations. Check with your local authorities and department of state to find out how you might limit the information available to the public.

Employers and MySpace

There's another reason to be discreet with life details you disclose online, including nightlife habits, alcohol and drug use, provocative photos, and lifestyle choices. More and more employers are checking out their workers and potential hires online, and this includes web searches, blogs, and social networking sites such as MySpace. Because aspiring musicians usually keep day jobs, this can be cause for concern (see Figure 16.3).

> **About Death by Metal**
>
> Hey, I'm a nihilistic guitarist by night and a disgruntled legal assistant by day. I work for Dilliston and Mooney, one of the biggest marketing firms in the downtown area. I friggin' hate it. My boss is an ass-clown and my department is filled with four no-talent skanks I secretly refer to as "The Pros." They're disgusting. To make it worse, the religious zealots in production are always collecting for charity and crap. I hate every last one of them. Check out my music. It's thrashing, head splitting metal guitar. I'm all about subverting the system and if you're a part of it, you're the enemy.

Figure 16.3
Would you want to hire this person?

A 2006 CareerBuilder.com survey of hiring managers revealed that one in four use Internet search engines to research potential employees. And, one in ten say they've searched social networking sites to screen candidates. Of those managers, the majority (63 percent) did not hire the person based on what they found.

Those are pretty sobering numbers, especially since social networking sites are still relatively early in their evolution. What does this mean for you as an artist and a music marketer? It doesn't mean you shouldn't aim to build your personal brand on MySpace, but it does mean that if your intended image is a risqué or controversial one, employers may find it incompatible with their company and decide to pass on your employment.

So how do you make your artist image compatible with your work persona? First, use a stage name in your act and online. Joe Smith, mild-mannered computer programmer by day, can be Vampiro by night, channeling Marilyn Manson and Ozzy Osbourne at raucous, fake-blood-filled gigs.

Your boss or potential employer can use your name and email address to search for you on MySpace, but if you're not using your real name and they don't know your stage name, it will be awfully difficult to find you. Second, use a completely separate, dedicated email account for your MySpace activities. If you use a special email known only to you (because all you use it for is to log into MySpace), then others will not be able to do a successful email search. Get a free email account from Yahoo, Hotmail, Gmail, or the like. Under no circumstances should you use a work email for your MySpace account. Not only will that make it ridiculously easy for your boss to find you, but once found, it will make you look like a horrible moocher who uses company resources to promote his band.

In addition to your artist or business profile, you can create a completely personal profile that is "clean" and speaks only wonderful things about you as a person and a professional. No mention of your moonlighting, no off-color language, and no links to your artist profile. Instead, it will have information about you as a professional, possibly your resume (no phone or address), maybe even a work bio, some lighthearted banter, and a flattering picture of you. For this profile, use the same email address you put on your resume, and if you feel very confident that your profile supports your professional image, you can even put the URL right on your resume. Make sure to go into your Account Settings and check Approve Comments Before Posting so you don't get any friends or family members ruining your perfect façade. You may decide to hide your friends as well if you're worried about tidbits on your other life popping up on other people's profiles.

This may sound deceitful, but really it is a marketing tool to help you get a job or keep the one you have. Just as you market your music, so must you promote yourself in your chosen field. If someone wants to do a MySpace search on you, then at least let that person find something that says you are a person who takes his job seriously. When the person in question has found your personal/professional profile that supports your resume claims, hopefully he will be satisfied and end his snooping there.

Some of you may be lucky enough to work in an industry or at a company that is very footloose and fancy free and doesn't care that your act is a little out-there. Consider yourself fortunate. Or perhaps you are at a stage where you want to let it all out in the open. If you are already employed, you may find that being upfront with your boss is the best preemptive action. At least she won't be shocked when she hears about your activities around the water cooler.

As for potential employers, pay close attention to various clues that tell you this company does not approve of employees taking second jobs or moonlighting, or that they feel employees represent the firm 24/7 in everything they do.

Many employers couldn't care less what you do on your time, but there will be some who will care very much, especially if you're employed as a teacher, a childcare provider, a government employee, or a city official, or if you work for a charitable or religious organization or you are in law enforcement. Be aware that it's not always possible to reconcile who people want you to be at work with who you want to be onstage. All you can do is try to protect your stage identity, be forthright when asked or confronted about what you're doing, and be willing to accept that sometimes it simply won't be okay with the boss man and it may mean your job.

In every case, watch for colorful, racist, or sexual language and jokes, derogatory comments, lewd or revealing photos, and info about drug or alcohol use—both in what you put in your own profile and in comments you leave for others and those you allow to be left for you. All of these can be construed as an indication of your character.

Gig Notices and Stalkers

Any performer, regardless of whether he uses the Internet, should always be wary of his physical security while performing in public. However, using MySpace and/or your personal website to advertise gigs can bring so many more people to your audience. They connect with you online through the image you portray on your profile, the pictures you post, and the blogs you write. For some people, the connection is a very powerful one. And this can sometimes lead to trouble. Women and young people especially have to be very careful because they are sometimes more vulnerable when out gigging late at night. MySpace, like many corners of the Internet, has its share of sexual predators.

There have been many instances in the recent past where dangerous fans with sinister intentions have followed performers to gigs, including the shooting of Pantera's heavy metal guitarist Dimebag Darrell

Abbott at a show in Columbus, Ohio in 2004. Crazed fan Nathan Gale shot and killed Abbott while he was onstage with the band Damageplan. It's not known exactly why Gale, who was shot on scene by police, murdered Abbott, although investigators have theorized that Gale believed Abbott stole a song from him. At the end of the killing spree, not only was Dimebag Darrell Abbott dead, so were Damageplan's security guard, a club employee, and a concertgoer. In another well-publicized case of a lunatic obsessed with a celebrity, 22-year-old actress Rebecca Schaeffer was murdered in 1989 when stalker fan John Bardo, who had disguised himself as a flower delivery man, broke into her home and shot her to death.

The more you put yourself in the public eye, the more you must be on guard and aware of your safety. This doesn't mean you shouldn't go out and perform. But you should have a plan in place for protecting your personal welfare.

The first step is being careful with what you post on your profile, as discussed previously. The second step is always having a plan when going to and from performances to ensure you arrive at your gig and back home safely.

Here are a few tips to help you stay safe:

- If you are a solo artist without a manager and with no other backup musicians with whom to share the stage, try to take someone with you or at least have one friend in the audience.

- It's especially important toward the end of a gig to have someone around. If you don't have anyone in the audience or backstage looking out for you, then have someone from the venue, such as a security guard, watch out for you while you load up your vehicle. Make sure someone escorts you to your car. Going out into the parking lot alone or packing up in the alley of a bar by yourself is an invitation to thieves and other criminals.

- Always call a family member or a trusted friend when you arrive at a gig and when you are on your way home, so people know to expect you.

- Whenever possible, don't go home to an empty house. When your family or significant other can't be there, go straight to a friend's house first or have someone meet you. If you suspect you are being followed home, go straight to a police station. These tactics are important because obsessive fans who have come to your gig may try to follow you home, and you don't want to be there by yourself. It has happened before, and we don't want it to happen to you.

- Think of gigs as you would a blind date. Even if you live alone, you would certainly let people know where you'll be, who you'll be with, and when to expect you home.

- Keep your wits about you at all times. If you take public transportation home, try not to fall asleep. Those who listen to headphones on the bus or train should keep the volume low so they can hear people approaching. Since iPod thefts are on the rise, some experts advise replacing the distinctive white earbuds with plain, dark-colored headphones, which attract less attention.

- For tips on dealing with stalkers and the obsessed, visit www.antistalking.com.

Consult Chapter 17, "Managing MySpace," for details on how to handle abusive or obsessive emails received through the MySpace system.

Being diligent about discouraging access to your personal information will help you guard against identity theft and stalking. Now that you've gotten the lowdown on keeping yourself safe, let's take a look at how to more fully manage your MySpace experience....

17 Managing MySpace

By now your profile is up and running, and you're an old pro when it comes to tweaking and navigating. This chapter will give you some hints on managing your experience—a few little tidbits to make your time in the MySpace world as smooth as possible.

Converting to a Band Profile

You may need to convert to a band profile if, in your gleeful enthusiasm, you accidentally signed up for a regular account instead. Once upon a time there used to be a topic in the MySpace help pages addressing this, but as of early 2007, there is nothing that tells one how to convert an account. Tech forums around the Internet offer advice about how to accomplish this feat by entering a special URL into your browser, but the truth is it almost never works. This URL, which varies depending on the tech forum you consult, takes you to a page that looks like the Edit Profile mode for a band, but when you enter information it never "sticks"—it just fades into the ether once you log out. So until a real—and simple—fix is created by MySpace, you have one of three options:

- Contact customer service. Many users report that MySpace customer service is not always very helpful, but it's worth a try.

- Email MySpace founder Tom for assistance (www.myspace.com/tom). He probably gets thousands of emails a day, so it's a crapshoot. But some users report that he has helped them on this topic.

- Create a new account by clicking on Music > Artist Signup.

What the "Terms of Use" Mean

That inconspicuous little Terms of Use link at the bottom of the MySpace common pages explains what you are agreeing to when you visit the community. It seems like an endless, boring stream of legal jargon, but it's still important to be familiar with the greater points.

Almost since the very beginnings of this relatively young phenomenon, an urban legend has been pervading the Internet and real-world media—rumors claiming that MySpace takes over ownership of your music and graphics when you upload them to your profile. The story goes that MySpace can then license your art and photos to whomever they want, bogart all the profits, and cut you out of the deal, with no recourse or chance to get your rights back.

Although the story still persists today, it is nothing more than an urban legend stemming from a misunderstanding of the Terms of Use, which was created with unclear and confusing language. In October, 2006, MySpace revamped their posted agreement to make it more user-friendly and absolutely clear. Section 6 of the Terms of Use, entitled "Proprietary Rights in Content on MySpace.com," basically says the following:

- MySpace does not own the material you upload onto your profile, be it music, graphics, text, videos, and so on.

- By uploading copyrighted content, you agree to allow MySpace a limited, non-exclusive license to display, modify, and distribute that content within the scope of the MySpace service.

- Without granting this license, MySpace would not be allowed to permit others to view your content or license to your music because it wouldn't have the permission to do so.

- MySpace does not have the right to sell your content or distribute it outside the service.

- You claim that you own the copyright in the content you are uploading and you have the right to license it to MySpace, royalty-free. You are also verifying that posting this content doesn't violate anyone else's rights.

- You are solely responsible for the content you post.

- The license ends when you remove your profile and content from MySpace.

Like any non-exclusive license, you still own the copyright, are allowing someone else to use it on a limited basis, and can license your content to anyone else at the same time (for example, another social networking site).

The section further notes that the only copyright MySpace owns is in the proprietary content and coding they provide, as well as the *collection* of user-provided content as a whole, in a similar way that a record label producing a compilation album of oldies owns the copyright in that collection of music as presented, but not in the individual songs or recordings (or user-posted content, in this case).

Here's a quick rundown of some of the finer points of the rest of the agreement. Be sure to peruse the actual agreement for yourself to learn about all the other nuances that may not be mentioned here. And if you still are concerned and you need additional guidance, please contact a qualified attorney.

- Your profile is technically not supposed to include any phone numbers; physical addresses; last names; or nude, obscene, lewd, excessively violent, or sexually explicit photos. (If you must include a phone number or a mailing address for business purposes, refer to Chapter 16 for tips on minimizing your stalker appeal.)

- No content is allowed promoting racism, hatred, or physical harm against a group or individual, nor any content promoting harassment of anyone or exploitation of people in a sexual or violent manner.

- You may not be younger than 14 years old.

- MySpace is only for personal use, not for commercial use. (Although the terms state this, there is no shortage of businesspeople and their profiles on the service!) They are specifically prickly about using MySpace to place ad links and sponsored ads.

- You cannot gather usernames and email addresses for the purpose of spamming people.

- No posting of pirated content, such as unauthorized music or computer programs.

- You may not post photos of people without their consent.

- Bands, filmmakers, and the like may not use misleading or sexually aggressive imagery just to draw people to their profile.

- Criminal activity, including child porn, fraud, spamming, and phishing, and many other activities, are prohibited.

- You may not send more than a certain number of email messages within a 24-hour period (although that number is unspecified and is at MySpace's sole discretion). If you are deemed to be a spammer, you agree to pay MySpace $50 for each unsolicited email/communication sent through the service.

- You are not allowed to use automated scripts and the like (bots) to send messages, add friends, or make comments. (People do use these, but MySpace explicitly states that it is forbidden. You risk losing your account every time you use a bot.)

- MySpace can suspend or boot you out at any time for violating any terms of the agreement.

Spammers, Phishers, Hackers, and Scammers

One of the first things that happens to all MySpacers, usually within two weeks of signing up, is that they receive their first spam email. It's usually a lonely girl named Cami or Jenny who wants you to call her 1-900 number, or some irksome mortgage loan offer. There are only two ways the MySpace Powers That Be will know that the spammers are out there harassing the community: 1) Cami and her friends exceed the number of emails they are allowed to send in any given day, and 2) recipients hit the Flag as Spam link that appears above every email message (see Figure 17.1). So, when you get emails that are clearly unsolicited and questionable, that aim to get you to fork over personal info, or that try to entice you to click on another profile or outside web link, click on that Flag as Spam link. This lets MySpace know who is being naughty (in a bad way) in the MySpace community. Enough reports, and those spammers, scammers, and phishers will be kicked off the service.

Flag as **Spam** or Report **Abuse** [?]

Figure 17.1
Don't be afraid to let MySpace know that spammers and scammers are lurking about.

As a marketer, you want to avoid being flagged a spammer yourself. Refer to Chapter 15 for guidelines on contacting your audience.

You also have to be on the lookout for account hackers and virus spreaders. Once your account has been hacked and the password has been stolen, criminals will use it to post fake bulletins selling things such as ringtones and porn, or to send spammy or virus-infested messages to all your friends. Your friends may alert you that many identical bulletins are appearing under your name (because criminals often post multiple bulletins) or that they're getting weird emails from you. However you discover it, as soon as you find that your account has been compromised, *immediately* change your password. Go to Account Settings within your profile control panel to do this. Report the incident to MySpace by clicking on Help. Then, delete any offending bulletins sent out by the imposters. (Click on Bulletin Posts to do this.) You should also post a bulletin alerting friends that your account was compromised and that they should delete any spammy emails sent by the hackers from you.

So how does this happen in the first place? Here are some ways that your account can be compromised:

- You received a friend request from someone who is already your friend. You approve the request, and *voilà*—your account is now in the hands of criminals.

- You received a friend request from someone you don't know and you approved it. This is why many MySpacers have a policy of not approving friend requests from strangers and people who don't make an effort to send a proper email message introducing themselves.

- You received an email from someone and clicked on an outside website that ran a script to steal your password.

- You clicked on a profile that contained some type of script that scammed your password or otherwise hacked into your account.

- You logged into MySpace, but then were redirected to a page that asked you to log in again. This turned out to be a spoof page that just stole your login information.

How can you protect yourself and what can you do if you are compromised?

- If you receive a friend request from someone you believe is already on your friend list, check your list first to verify that the person is indeed already a friend. If so, report the incident to MySpace and your friend. If not, send an email to your friend first to see whether he or she really did send you a request. It's possible your friend accidentally deleted you.

- Although it's not practical for bands and entertainers to require everyone to send an email before requesting an add, it is doable and advisable if you are using a personal profile. In either case, be suspicious of profiles with no photos and those that look odd.

- Be wary of fake login pages. Always look at the web address of login pages. It should be a myspace.com page and will look like http://[subdomain].myspace.com/....

- If you click on a "profile" that doesn't look like a profile at all (but more like an advertisement) or one that unexpectedly takes you to a webpage outside the community, immediately close your web browser and run a virus scan.

- Never click on unsolicited or suspicious-looking links sent to you by friends or non-friends, especially those for ringtones, porn, real estate offers, money schemes, bank loans, pharmaceuticals, or software.

- Never click on a profile whose thumbnail doesn't jive with what you're looking for. For instance, if you're doing a search on a popular male jazz musician, and a random profile with a picture of a naked girl turns up in the search, it's a sign that the profile is a fake one used to entice curious users into a trap.

- Never disclose any personal or password information to anyone who contacts you through MySpace, including Social Security numbers and driver's license numbers.

- Always report an incident to MySpace (see Figure 17.2). You may be surprised to know that much of the junk email generated in the US originates from a handful of prominent spammers. In January, 2007, MySpace filed suit against a notorious alleged spam king. MySpace claimed email marketer Scott Richter used technology to phish for passwords and post fake bulletins through the accounts of unsuspecting MySpacers.

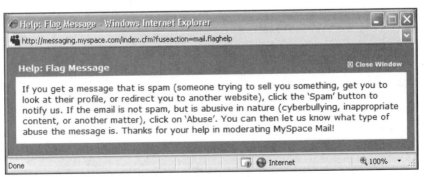

Figure 17.2
If everyone pitches in and reports spammers and abusers, hopefully MySpace will be able to better monitor, delete, and prosecute them.

- If you think you've been compromised, change your password. Run a virus scan on your computer. Empty your Internet cache and clear out all cookies, which can be done within the Internet Options of your web browser.

When spammers, phishers, scammers, and the like are kicked off of MySpace, the thumbnails beside emails they sent you (and in your friend lists, if you approved them) will appear as grey boxes with big, red X's through them. The email subject will say something like, "This profile no longer exists." Clicking on these will give you a notice that this person's account is invalid.

You may also notice new friend request alerts, but when you click to see who has sent you a friend request, either there's no one there or the profile thumbnail has an X through it (see Figure 17.3). This means that these MySpace baddies were discovered and removed from the service.

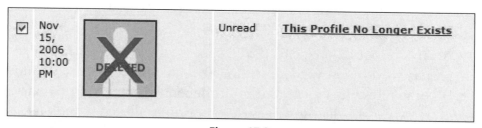

Figure 17.3
Busted! This spammer was kicked off before you ever got a chance to open the email.

Dealing with Abusers

In Chapter 16 we discussed how to protect your physical security. When someone is sending you abusive or harassing messages, MySpace suggests that you report those abusive messages by clicking the Report Abuse link, and then ignore further communications from the abuser. If this person is on your friends list, delete him from your list and remove any comments he has left for you. You can keep that person from viewing your profile by setting it to private, making it viewable by friends only. This is a good option for personal users. You can also block anyone from contacting you by clicking on the Block User link in their profile's contact table (see Figure 17.4). A dialog box will appear, asking you to confirm (see Figure 17.5).

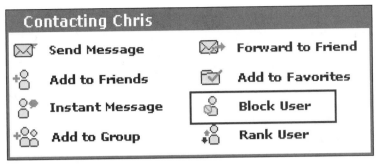

Figure 17.4
The Block User button appears on a user's contact table.

Figure 17.5
Confirm that you want to block a user, and he will be prohibited from contacting you.

MySpace does not like it when people insert profile code to remove the Block User button from their contact tables. You can get around this, however, and still block someone by trying one of the following tactics:

Paste this link into your web browser, and in place of the X's, paste in the abuser's friend ID. (Review Chapter 8 for details on locating the friend ID.)

www.myspace.com/index.cfm?fuseaction=block.blockUser&
userID=XXXXX

The resulting webpage will give you the option of blocking the user.

Because MySpace may have changed its blocking mechanism and web URL since the printing of this book, you can also try to locate the hidden Block User button on the user's contact table. Even though a user can create his own contact table graphic (see Chapter 8), the links remain in the same position. You can remove the words "Block User" from the table or change them to something else, but the link to the Block User function remains fixed in the MySpace environment. The link is still the third down on the right side of the contact table, even if there is no text there at all. Try clicking in the contact table to find it.

Lost Passwords and Defunct Email

Recovering a lost password is easy. The process is the same as it is for almost every registration-driven website—enter the email address you used to sign up, and the password will be emailed to you, as shown in Figure 17.6. Things can get sticky, however, if you have since cancelled that email account. Obviously, MySpace won't be able to email your password, and you are pretty much out of luck in accessing your account ever again unless you remember the password on your own.

> ### Forgot Your Password? No Worries...
>
> Just enter the email account you signed-up with, and we'll mail you your password
>
> -Sign Up!-   -Log In-
>
> **Please enter your email address:**
>
> Email [   ]
>
>   [Find]

Figure 17.6
To find your password, you must know what email account you
used to sign up for, or previously log into, MySpace.

In Chapter 16, I recommended that you always use an email account separate from your primary personal or work email. Keep this account especially for MySpace and other social networking activities and guard your MySpace password. Never close this email account before starting a new one and changing the email in your MySpace account.

Changing your email address in MySpace is a multi-step process. In your Account Settings, the email address field is at the top (see Figure 17.7). Type your new email address in this field and press the Change button at the bottom of the page. MySpace will send an email to your *old* address containing a confirmation code. You must enter that code into your Account Settings before the new email change will take effect (see Figure 17.8). This is why it is so important to not close your old email account before you have fully implemented the change in MySpace. Change your preferred email in MySpace *first*.

Change Account Settings

NOTE: Changing your default email or name can make it hard for your friends
to find or recognize you on MySpace

[View My Profile] [Edit My Profile] [Cancel Account]

My Account Settings	
Email Address:	cathleen@snydereditorial.com
Change Password:	- Change Password: -
Notifications:	☐ Do not send me notification emails -help-
Newsletters:	☐ Do not send me MySpace newsletters

Figure 17.7
Type your new email address into the field within Account Settings.

Email Change

You have requested to change your account email address. This requires that you respond to a confirmation email that we have sent to the current email address You can respond by either clicking the link in the email, or by entering the confirm code from the email below

New Email:	newemail@your.domain.com
Confirmation Code:	
	Submit Code
Resend Confirmation Email	Cancel Email Change

Figure 17.8
MySpace will send you a confirmation email code, which you must enter into Account Settings to complete the process.

Away Messages

You can set an email away message in MySpace so that when anyone tries to send you a message, that person is presented with a personal message from you. Your Away Message options can be accessed through Account Settings. While away messages are of course useful if you will be away from MySpace for a while, some musicians and performers use away messages to inform users how to contact them outside of MySpace. This is most commonly used by the artist who has a manager or agent who fields all questions, especially those concerning career issues, such as touring and publicity (see Figure 17.9). It is also used to inform fans that the artist does not accept emails through MySpace. Many fans find this off-putting, and I don't recommend it. If you feel you are bombarded by fan emails and you really don't have the time or the resources to answer them all, it's better to put a note on your profile that you try to read all messages and you thank the fans for contacting you, but you may not be able to respond to all emails personally.

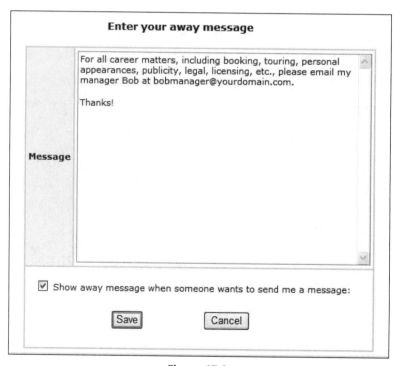

Figure 17.9
You can direct MySpacers who try to email you to your manager for business matters.

Music Settings

In Chapter 7, we looked at the artist profile's sound player capabilities. Regular accounts, often used by music business people, such as bookers, publicists, and promoters, also have music settings located in the Account Settings (see Figure 17.10). You can disable songs from playing automatically when you visit a band site, and you can disable your player from automatically launching when someone visits your profile. If you've added a band's song to your profile, you may want to disable it from automatically playing. It can be extremely annoying for visitors to be bombarded with sound when visiting other people's profiles, especially if the sound tramples over the music they're already listening to in the privacy of their home or office.

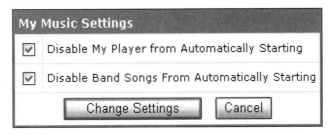

Figure 17.10
Music settings can keep songs from automatically playing.

Hiding Online Now

Hiding the Online Now icon that appears near your thumbnail is a must for many MySpacers who like to travel incognito (see Figure 17.11). Your Privacy Settings in your Account Settings give you the option to conceal the Online Now icon. This is useful if you don't want to field quickie emails from friends or fans or alert your real-life crew that you are home sitting in front of the computer.

Figure 17.11
Your Online Now icon.

Mobile Alerts

For MySpacers who like to keep on top of all their communications, Mobile Alerts can be customized to send you a cell phone text message whenever you receive a MySpace email, friend request, comment, or event invite (see Figure 17.12). Entertainers and suits who do a lot of networking through MySpace and get lots of leads will love this. They'll never have to miss an opportunity. Although this service is provided free by MySpace, your mobile carrier may charge you for text messages received.

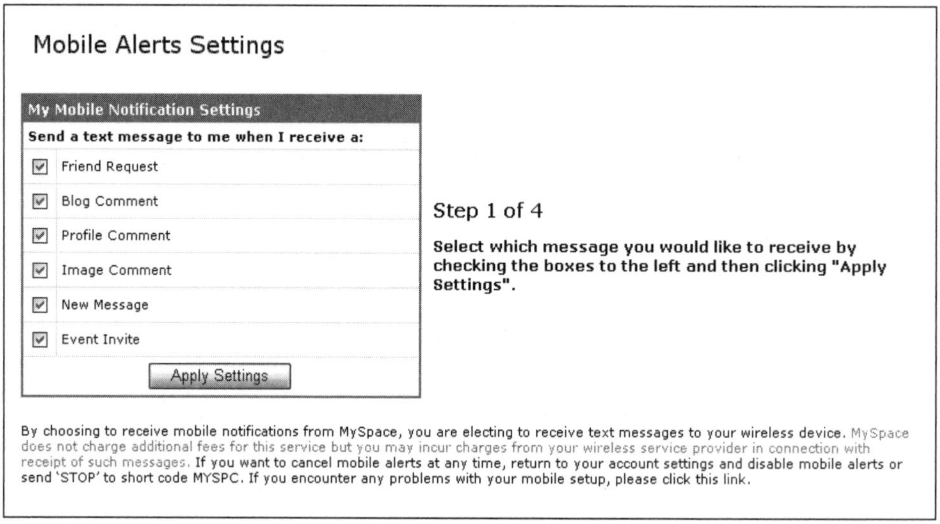

Figure 17.12
Set Mobile Alerts so you'll never miss a beat.

Groups Settings

Along with the spam emails you are sure to receive in your MySpace account, you will also encounter Group Invites. Yes, lonely 1-900 operators and get-rich-quick schemers start their own MySpace groups, but you can keep these invites out of your inbox in your Privacy Settings. Within this area you can disable all group invites or keep out those not sent by "friends," as shown in Figure 17.13.

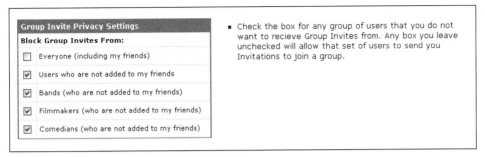

Figure 17.13
Group settings prohibiting non-friends from sending you invites can
keep spam-vites out of your mailbox.

Instant Messaging

MySpace offers instant messaging, called MySpaceIM, which is a downloadable program that is similar to other types of Internet messaging software (see Figure 17.14). MySpace used to offer a web-based IM service, but it has been phased out in favor of the downloaded IM software. At this time, your MySpace account still has settings for the web-based IM, but these are actually obsolete. To keep others from sending you instant messages through the new MySpaceIM, you must download the program, install it, and alter your preferences by going to File > Preferences > Privacy. Bands sometimes find it helpful to restrict IM access to a select group of friends, instead of opening it up to the public or their entire friends list.

This chapter explored many of the most important customization options available to you as an entertainment marketer. Consult your account settings page for additional choices not covered here.

Now that you've customized your experience and privacy settings, let's move on to more ways to market yourself.

Figure 17.14
MySpaceIM is handy for chatting with MySpacers. It also opens a separate
window so you can easily access your MySpace account, mail, pics, and blogs.

18 MySpace and Marketing

Having a MySpace profile is truly a necessity right now. It's considered by the industry to be a marketing must because of its ability to present a quick snapshot of the artist, all within a large, diverse community. This chapter will offer a few tips to help you best utilize your MySpace membership for its marketing potential.

Consider some of these ways you can promote and use your profile:

- Keep your profile fresh. Add new content regularly, such as blog entries, announcements, banners, photos, videos, and novelty toys such as cell phone alerts.

- Put your MySpace URL on everything, including CDs, stickers, your official website, tees and other merchandise, posters, fliers, advertisements, press releases, and press kits. Be sure to mention your MySpace page to writers and editors, reviewers, venue owners/managers, and other people with whom you are conducting business.

- In some cases, it makes sense for individual band members to also have their own MySpace accounts. There they can not only promote the band's profile, but they can also discuss solo projects and even topics more personal to them. Put members in the band's Top Friends and vice versa.

- Insert a link on your profile to your band's press kit, which should be available on your official website. This way, if a journalist is perusing your profile, she doesn't have to try to track down your press kit on your official site.

- Use MySpace to recruit a street team or build a fan club. You need a big enough following to accomplish this, of course, but when you do, these are natural additions to your promotional activities. Offer street teamers free tix for promoting your shows in their area. Fan club members could have access to early ticket sales, discounts, and special merchandise not available to the general public.

- Target local media with news about your MySpace profile. Small newspapers and publications in your area love to cover local artists. Got a new profile? Offering streaming music on your page? Or did you add downloadable ringtones or music for purchase? Are you launching a new album? Even bigger news qualifies, such as tour announcements and promotional partnerships. Send press release announcements to local newspapers. For tips on press releases, do a web search on "how to write a press release." Make sure to include your contact information at the top of every page, and keep the writing clear and concise. Always include a headline, and double-check to be sure your release is free of any spelling or grammatical errors. Call each media outlet and ask who handles news about local artists and the music scene. Post your press releases on your profile as well.

- MySpace profiles can act like virtual demos, but you have to include other elements as well. Artsy photos, a great bio, and video clips show club owners and record label execs how polished you are.

How to Target Musicians

Industry service and product providers use MySpace to target musicians. Recording studios, software and gear manufacturers, managers, stylists, lawyers, designers, photographers, and marketers go through the same process in figuring out which artists could use their services. However, simply adding friends isn't usually enough. Providers must carefully target their artists and interact with them directly. Email or chat with musicians to see what their needs are and how you can help them. And, since many businesses serve local markets only, getting a face-to-face meeting is often essential in closing a deal.

Audacity Recording in Hollywood, Florida, uses MySpace to find local musicians who could use their recording studios, video production, and DVD-authoring services. Owner Linda Thornberg monitors the company's profile at www.myspace.com/audacitystudios and uses it as part of their strategic marketing plan. She tasked freelance producer Jack Beasley to seek out bands who would benefit from their premier facilities.

Beasley notes that to target local clientele, businesses should use the MySpace music search function to target specific genres in a suitable radius around their business.

"In any given week, I would focus on one genre. One week I would concentrate on bluegrass bands within a five-mile radius only," said Beasley. He would then listen to their music and offer suggestions on how the studio could help the artists. Sometimes he would go to gigs and approach bands personally, inviting them to the studio for a tour. Even a 10-percent return, he said, is a good investment of time.

Beasley suggests the real key to success for providers is "to develop a relationship and show [musicians] you care about their project.... MySpace has really helped us develop relationships."

Now for some final thoughts on *MySpace for Musicians*....

19 Last Words

While writing this book, my research and discussions with artists and other marketers kept bringing me back to the same conclusion. The key to using MySpace successfully to build your band's or company's exposure isn't about how many glittery, sparkly bangles you can add to your profile or how well you can demonstrate your programming prowess. It's about staying consistent and constantly looking for ways to market yourself on the service. The profile that sits dormant for months on end isn't the one that draws the most interest. But the artist who takes the profile and works it, scouring the community for friends, business associates, and other collaborators, is the one who gets results. What if you met and bonded with another artist and got to tour with that artist? Wouldn't it all have been worth it?

The only way to even get close to that point is to get out there, network, introduce yourself, find fans that fit your target, and keep applying what you know. It's that consistency that brings results. Spend an hour every day focused on improving your profile, adding new content, announcing it to friends, sourcing new friends, and getting people to listen to your music and review it. For some artists, one day a week works best. But they do it every week and work it like a day job, or they focus that one hour a day on the task at hand.

It's not any different than the small-business person who must network regularly to bring in customers. She goes to chamber of commerce functions, attends community events, calls on referrals, hands out business cards. At first she wonders whether anything will ever come of it. Soon, however, she sees that continually getting her name out there, having people hear her name from various sources, produces results.

Opportunities come her way. That big account she called twice finally agrees to meet with her to hear what she has to say. They heard good things from an associate and decided to give her a chance.

MySpace isn't any different really, except you're doing your networking in a virtual world. Gigging musicians and clubgoers especially see that translated into real life. They're always being asked for their MySpace address. Now they can build relationships inside and outside of the service.

Hopefully, this book has at least given you the tools you need to feel comfortable getting onto MySpace. My greater hope is that you are inspired to take it further than just establishing a profile. Treat the "working" of MySpace as an essential part of your music marketing plan because it is. Fans, managers, and labels alike expect you to have it. Major-label artists do, so why shouldn't you? Leave any apprehension behind and dive in. You have all the tools you need to build a plan, create an awesome profile, showcase and sell your music, and maximize the time you spend on MySpace. For all the new tech developments that are sure to come your way, you have the foundation. You can make your way through, learn as you go, and tackle the ever-changing Internet landscape.

So will I see you on MySpace? I hope so! You'll find me at www.myspace.com/retroisland. Send me your stories, tips, and of course a friend request. After Tom, I'll be your second friend!

A | Marketing and Merchandise Resources

This appendix lists providers who can help you with marketing, web design, music services, promotion, and merchandise.

A&R and Artist Development

Find opportunities, get discovered, and be developed by the following companies.

- **Cordless.com.** A Warner Music Group company, Cordless Recordings is an artist development firm that helps break new artists.

- **SonicBids.com.** Members create online press kits and can submit themselves for various promotional, festival/event, and A&R opportunities. Pricing is about $50 per year plus submission fees for some festival opportunities.

- **Taxi.com.** This A&R company gives members exclusive opportunities to pitch their music to record executives. The full one-year membership is about $300. Song critiques are also available.

Blog Hosting

The following blog hosting sites and management platforms offer free and premium services.

- Blog.com

- Blogger.com

- NewBlog.com

- OpenDiary.com
- TravelPod.com
- TypePad.com
- WordPress.com
- Vox.com

CD/DVD Manufacturing

Why wait for a record deal? Get your CD or DVD replicated and sell them on your own!

- **DiscMakers.com.** A well-known leader in CD/DVD manufacturing, Disc Makers also prints up CD inserts, posters, and more.

- **OasisCD.com.** Another respected CD/DVD manufacturer also offering many premium packaging and insert products.

- **TheDubHouse.net.** A popular CD/DVD manufacturer with no minimums and no setup fees.

Contests

American Idol isn't the only contest to recognize new talent. Below are just a few of the many contests available to performers and songwriters.

- **Famecast.com.** American online talent competition, awarding the top winner $10,000.

- **John Lennon Songwriting Contest (www.jlsc.com).** Songwriters could win an EMI Publishing contract, studio equipment, and more.

- **Turner Classic Movies Young Film Composers Competition (www.turnerclassicmovies-yfcc.com).** This contest gives composers a chance to win $15,000 and a chance to give a silent film new life by creating the score and debuting it on the Turner Classic Movie network.

Email Providers

- **AardvarkMailingList.com.** This free web tool lets you add an email signup list to your website.

- **Campaigner.com.** This tool sets up email campaigns based on various schedules and criteria you specify, allowing you to really customize your contacts with fans. Monthly fees start at $25 and are based on volume.

- **ConstantContact.com.** A very popular web program that allows you to create email campaigns and manage lists. Your monthly fee is based on the number of email addresses on your list.

- **EliteEmail.com.** Build lists and newsletters, as well as track your email campaign to see how it's doing. Instead of monthly fees, you pay for "credits" and use them as needed.

- **Everyone.net.** An email provider for businesses and small groups alike. You can even offer free email accounts to your fans using your own domain name.

- **VerticalResponse.com.** Specializing in web-based marketing and printed postcards, VerticalResponse helps you collect email addresses and create snazzy email and printed postcards to send out to your list. They charge based on the number of emails you send per project.

- **YourMailingListProvider.com.** A web-based application that helps you gather and manage email addresses and send out newsletters and e-zines. The fee you pay depends on how many emails you send in any given month.

Merchandising

Musicians can make a lot of money by selling merch at shows and online. These vendors offer tees and more, ready for printing your band logo.

- **CafePress.com.** Create your own merchandise store by uploading band logos, photos, and designs and putting them on CafePress-provided merchandise, such as T-shirts, hats, mugs, mousepads, and more. Basic stores are free. Premium stores are $4.99 to $6.95 per month.

- **CustomInk.com.** Design your tees and hats online, with lots of funky merchandise colors to choose from.

- **Disc Makers Merch (DiscMakers.com/merch).** Get custom merchandise with low minimums at really reasonable prices.

- **Oasis Wearables (OasisCD.com/Products/Wearables.asp).** Printable band tees, hoodies, and hats with no setup fees and low minimums.

- **WeNeedMerch.com.** Merchandise printers whose owners are full-time musicians. They say they'll beat anyone's prices and offer quickie turnarounds.

Mobile Music

The following sites offer mobile content delivery and management for such items as ringtones, text messages, and videos. Many of them allow you to create modules to sell your ringtones on your MySpace page.

- **Bango.com.** Offers programs for entry-level mobile content providers all the way up to leading brands.

- **GroupieTunes.com.** Specializes in helping bands and unsigned artists offer their music as ringtones.

- **JivJiv.com.** You can create a free or premium store. The latter costs $4.99 a month, but you earn a higher percentage of every item a fan purchases.

- **Laiwa.com.** Fans can get your music by text messaging for their favorite ringtones.

- **MediaPlazza.com.** Publish your songs, videos, and pictures for fans from around the globe to download from your site.

- **Mozes.com.** Fans can sign up for your mobile mob and leave messages for each other and you. Artists can communicate with all their fans with just one text message to the "mob."

- **mPush.com.** Another site to help you sell your mobile content to a worldwide audience.

- **MyNumo.com.** Sell content on your website or through text messaging. Even create voice ringtones with a phone call.

- **Myxertones.com.** Earn 30 percent of every item you sell. You won't have to sign a contract or pay setup fees, either.

- **PhoneSherpa.com.** This site helps you create mobile content. Use Phone Sherpa to make ringtones of your songs and wallpapers of your band, then create a web store to sell to fans.

- **Saynow.com.** Fans subscribe to your broadcasts and can leave messages for you or others on your list.

- **Upoc.com.** Create interest groups and interact with members via text messaging.

Music Downloading

These are just a few of the dozens of downloading sites available. Some deal directly with artists; others deal with labels and distributors only.

- **BandSpace.com.** Artists make 70 cents per song they sell through BandSpace, and can also offer merchandise to fans through an online store.

- **BandWagon.co.uk.** Sell vids, ringtones, and songs on your webpage and MySpace pages.

- **CDBaby.com.** An online record store where indie musicians can sell their CDs direct to consumers.

- **DiscRevolt.com.** Artists upload music for sale, then order printed cards to sell to fans at shows. Fans get credits toward the purchase of the artist's music.

- **EMusic.com.** eMusic is the largest retailer of indie music, and consumers can find new and upcoming bands in all genres. However, eMusic works in labels online, and not directly with unsigned artists.

- **Indiestore.com.** Based in the UK, IndieStore allows indie artists to create and manage their own digital download stores.

- **iTunes.com.** Now an icon in digital downloads, Apple's iTunes offers singles, albums, and even TV shows for download for a per-item fee.

- **Musicane.com.** Musicians and labels can upload their music, videos, and ringtones to Musicane and create a portable store for their website or MySpace profile. Fans can drag and drop their favorite artist's store onto their own website. Fees start at $19.99 per month plus a 20-percent transaction fee per sale.

- **Mysongstore.com.** They'll host your store, which can integrate your graphics and band look. Fees are membership-based depending on how much song storage you need.

- **Napster.com.** After shedding its former life as a file swapping service for unlicensed music, Napster has reinvented itself as a completely legit download service.

- **Passalong.com.** Users legally share music from indie and major labels and earn points toward free music for referring their friends.

- **Rhapsody.com.** A membership-based downloading service that also offers a free program where you can listen to dozens of preprogrammed radio stations or create your own.

- **Sony Connect (MusicStore.Connect.com).** Works directly with labels that have 200+ tracks to offer for download. Sony Connect also partners with other distributors who take artists and labels with less than 200 tracks available.

- **Soundation.com.** Sell your songs online by creating your own web store. You keep all of your profits and pay only an annual store fee.

- **TuneCore.com.** A service that brings your music to major online distributors, including iTunes, Rhapsody, Napster, and others.

- **TuneTribe.com.** Offering music downloads from artists and labels, plus music news and editorial.

- **Walmart Music Downloads (MusicDownloads.Walmart.com).** Is it any surprise that one of the biggest discount retailers in the world also sells digital music? Their music downloads are also discounted at less than the usual $1 per track.

Press Release Distribution Services (Wires)

These sites will take your press release, such as an album release announcement, and distribute it to media outlets in categories you specify. Some also go direct to consumers and are also sent to online aggregators and search engines, such as Google! News.

- **BillboardPublicityWire.com.** Specializes in music and entertainment media targets. Also sends to opt-in consumers.

- **BlackPR.com.** Get your music news out to almost 900 black media outlets, including print, TV, and radio.

- **BusinessWire.com.** A favorite of PR professionals, Business Wire is a well-known distribution service that sends direct to journalists.

- **Collegiate Presswire (www.cpwire.com).** Send your press release to college print and broadcast media nationwide.

- **HispanicPRWire.com.** This Miami-based company sends releases to key Hispanic media.

- **PRWeb.com.** A well-known service used by large and small businesses alike.

- **PRNewswire.com.** A staple of the PR pro's toolbox, PR Newswire has a stellar media reputation.

- **Send2Press.com.** Frequently used by entrepreneurs, Send2Press has many circuits from which to choose, including music and entertainment.

- **TheOpenPress.com.** Offering free and paid Internet distribution in a variety of topical areas.

- **uWire.com.** Send news items to more than 700 college media outlets in the U.S., Canada, Europe, Asia, and South America.

- **WDCMedia.com.** Specializing in Christian content, WDC Media is especially valuable for the contemporary Christian or gospel artist.

Promotion Sites

Promote yourself to your audience through these music and general interest sites.

- **Eventful.com.** Create and promote gigs and events online, or locate them in your area.

- **GarageBand.com.** An artist promotion site where bands create profiles, and fans review and rate music and can listen to and download favorite songs.

- **LocateBands.com.** Build a profile, offer music samples, and promote gigs in your local area.

- **PureVolume.com.** Create an artist profile and upload your music for others to view and purchase. PureVolume offers free and premium memberships.

- **TopsinAmerica.com.** Promote yourself as the tops in your area or category, and see others who are tops in various categories.

Radio

Whether you want to just listen or actively broadcast, check out these radio providers and research sites.

- **Radio@AOL (Music.aol.com/radioguide/bb.adp).** Features XM content and more than 200 free, preset stations.

- **Last.fm.** Makes music recommendations and creates custom radio stations based on your artist preferences.

- **Live365.com.** Listen to one of the hundreds of Live365 radio stations or broadcast your own.

- **Pandora.com.** A creation of the Music Genome Project, Pandora helps users discover new music based on what they already like to listen to.

- **Radio-Locator.com.** Search for terrestrial radio stations nationwide. Great for deciding which stations to target in a promotion.

- **Rhapsody.com Radio.** Listen to dozens of free radio stations or create your own. Songs played are accompanied by album artwork, song info, and artist bio blurbs.

- **ShoutCast.com.** Free Internet radio stations compiled by DJs and broadcasters around the globe. Even you could be the next DJ.

- **Vh1.com Radio.** Programmed by industry DJs and execs, VH1 has bunches of hip stations to explore.

- **MTV.com Radio.** MTV's radio station selection comes mostly from celebrity playlists and themes inspired by the network's own shows.

- **Yahoo! Music Radio (Music.Yahoo.com).** Take advantage of free and premium stations or create your own. Plus, you can watch streaming video stations.

Web Hosting

The following providers offer server space with email accounts, plus many webpage tools at competitive prices.

- FatCow.com

- HostBaby.com

- PowWeb.com

- SmallBusiness.Yahoo.com/webhosting

Web Templates

Use ready-made templates to help you create your official website.

- **Bandzoogle.com.** Build your very own band site.

- **MusicMogulDesign.com.** Download customizable templates for your official band website.

Miscellaneous

These goodies didn't fit into the other categories, but are still worth a look!

- **Dizzler.com.** Free downloadable application to help you search for music and play media on your computer or mobile device.
- **SoundFlavor.com.** This application creates playlists for you based on the music you already listen to and have in your library.

B MySpace Resources

This appendix lists sites that offer layout codes, generators, tweaks, tutorials, and other MySpace toys. Plus, it details hosting sites for photos, video, slideshows, podcasting, as well as news sites and blogs that focus on social networking. Note that some of the sites may contain advertising, pop-ups, and possibly adware, so proceed with caution and run your adware scans after visiting.

MySpace Code Sites

These sites offer free layouts, code generators, and tweaks.

- Coshed.com/Generators
- FreeFlashToys.com
- FreeWebLayouts.net
- HotFreeLayouts.com
- HTMLHelpSite.com
- KawaiiSpace.com
- KazSpace.com
- MSJoint.com
- MyBannerMaker.com
- MyFlashFetish.com
- MyGen.co.uk
- MySpace.NuclearCentury.com
- MySpaceCore.com

- MySpaceGens.com
- MySpaceGraphicHelp.com
- MySpace-Images.com
- MySpaceLayoutSupport.com
- MySpaceProDesigns.com
- MySpaceScripts.com
- MySpaceSupport.com
- MyTheme.com
- New.ModMyProfile.com
- PimpItOut.net
- PimpMaSpace.com
- PimpMyArea.com
- PimpMyCom.com
- ProfilePimp.com
- ProfileTweaks.com
- RapidCodes.com
- Skize.com
- XGenerators.com
- Zoodu.com/top-banner

Layout Editors

Use a layout editor to custom-create your profile.

- Pimp-My-Profile.com/generators/myspace.php
- PimpWebPage.com/band.php
- www.Pulseware.com.au/site_pi.asp?p=wpa-167088
- RealEditor.com

Free Div Overlays and Generators

The div overlay will completely change the way your profile is structured.

- DivOverlay.com
- Groups.MySpace.com/Freedivs
- LayoutMySpaceCodes.com/div-layouts-overlay/divgenerator.php
- MSMods.com/myspace-generators/div-overlay
- Squidoo.com/MySpace_Div_Overlay

More MySpace Profile Toys

Add more fun widgets to your page.

- Snapvine.com
- Quizilla.com
- Frazy.com
- MyFlashFetish.com

HTML and Bulletin Editors

Edit HTML for your profile, bulletins, or comments with these tools.

- BulletinPimper.com
- Pimp-My-Profile.com/htmledit
- Zoodu.com/html-editor

Web Design Resources and Tutorials

Brush up on HTML and CSS with the following sites.

- **Basic HTML Tutorial:**
  www.chasebadkids.net/reborn/index.php?x=basic
- **How to Create Special Characters in HTML:**
  www.chasebadkids.net/reborn/index.php?x=specialcharacters
- **Extensive CSS Tutorial:** W3Schools.com/CSS/default.asp
- **Extensive HTML Tutorial:** W3Schools.com/html/default.asp

Media Hosting Sites

This list is a compilation of photo, video, and slideshow hosting sites. Some, in fact, offer all three services.

- Box.net
- CastPost.com
- DailyMotion.com
- Flickr.com
- Grouper.com
- iFilm.com
- ImageShack.us
- JumpCut.com
- MediaWart.com
- MetaCafe.com
- OneTrueMedia.com
- Pbase.com
- PhotoBucket.com
- PicLynk.com
- www.Pixagogo.com
- Pixilive.com
- PutFile.com
- Revver.com
- Ripway.com
- RockYou.com
- Slide.com
- Stickam.com
- Streamload.com
- UncutVideo.AOL.com

- VideoEgg.com

- VideoShoutOut.com

- Vimeo.com

- VMix.com

- VSocial.com

- YouTube.com

- Zorpia.com

Social Networking Blogs and Updates

Stay abreast of current topics in social networking.

- Bloggersblog.com/socialnetworks

- DMWMedia.com

- Mashable.com

- SocialNetworkingNews.com

- SocialNetworking-Weblog.com

Podcasting

The following sites offer podcast hosting, tools, and directories.

- 75minutes.com/podcast

- Apple.com/itunes/podcasts

- GCast.com

- MusicOnlyPodcasts.com

- MyPodcast.com

- PodcastAlley.com

- PodcastDirectory.com

- PodcastingNews.com

- Podcasts.Yahoo.com

- PodcastSpots.com

- Poderator.com

- PodHoster.com

- PodShow.com

Favorite MySpace Profiles

Here are just a few favorite band sites that really seem to reflect the personality and image of the artist (at least at the time of this writing).

- MySpace.com/ChantellePaige

- MySpace.com/Daughtry

- MySpace.com/Diddy

- MySpace.com/HawthorneHeights

- MySpace.com/IndiaArie

- MySpace.com/JeffreeStar

- Myspace.com/JenniferEdison

- MySpace.com/Lumidee

- MySpace.com/NellyFurtado

- MySpace.com/PanicAtTheDisco

- MySpace.com/PattyGriffin

- MySpace.com/PinksPage

- MySpace.com/PrettyRicky

- Myspace.com/SelfAgainstCity

- MySpace.com/Sugarcult

- MySpace.com/TilaTequila

C Music Business Resources

This appendix lists music industry organizations, companies, and other resources.

Performing Rights Organizations

Songwriters should join a performing rights organization, which helps protect performance rights through collecting and disbursing performance royalties to artists and publishers.

American Society of Composers, Authors and Publishers:
ASCAP.com

Broadcast Music:
BMI.com

SESAC (originally known as Society of European Stage Authors & Composers; represents U.S. artists as well):
SESAC.com

Mechanical Copyright Protection Society (UK):
www.mcps-prs-alliance.co.uk

Canadian Musical Reproduction Rights Agency:
www.CMRRA.ca

Conventions

The following conventions are some of the most popular in the U.S. for musicians.

Audio Engineering Society Convention:
AES.org

Billboard Events (for more Billboard conferences and seminars):
billboardevents.com/billboardevents/index.jsp

Billboard/Hollywood Reporter Film & TV Music Conference:
billboardevents.com/billboardevents/filmtv/index.jsp

Billboard Latin Music Conference:
billboardevents.com/billboardevents/latin/index.jsp

International Music Productions Association Convention:
NAMM.com

Millennium Music Conference:
musicconference.net/mmc11

National Association of Recording Merchandisers Convention:
NARM.com

South by Southwest:
SXSW.com

Vegas Music Conference:
lvmc.us

Winter Music Conference:
wintermusicconference.com

Music Licensing and Supervision

The following providers can help you secure licenses for using others' songs, or find music for your project.

Harry Fox Agency:
HarryFox.com

Mobile Business Information Group:
MBIG.com

Musync Music Licensing:
www.musync.com

The Music Bridge Music Clearance:
themusicbridge.com

Ricall Music Licensing and Clearance:
www.ricall.com/ricall/pre/index.jsp

Organizations

The following organizations serve as support and resources for various sectors of the music industry. Some are also trade groups and unions.

American Federation of Television & Radio Artists:
AFTRA.org

American Association of Independent Music:
A2IM.org

American Composers Forum:
composersforum.org

American Federation of Musicians:
AFM.org

American Music Conference:
AMC-Music.com

Audio Engineering Society:
AES.org

International Alliance for Women in Music:
IAWM.org

International Association for Jazz Education:
IAJE.org

International Computer Music Association:
ComputerMusic.org

International Musical Products Association (NAMM):
NAMM.org

Latin Recording Academy:
Grammy.com/Latin

Music Publishers' Association of the United States:
MPA.org

Music Teachers National Association:
www.MTNA.org

MusicUnited:
musicunited.org

National Association of Black Female Executives in Music & Entertainment:
Womenet.org

National Association of Record Industry Professionals:
NARIP.com

National Association of Recording Arts and Sciences (aka The Recording Academy):
Grammy.com

National Association of Teachers of Singing:
NATS.org

National Music Publishers' Association:
NMPA.org

Percussive Arts Society:
PAS.org

Recording Industry Association of America:
RIAA.com

Society for Electro-Acoustic Music in the United States:
SEAMUSonline.org

The National Association for Music Education (MENC):
MENC.org

The Society of Composers & Lyricists:
TheSCL.com

Index

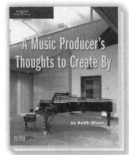

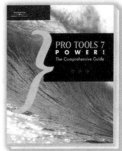
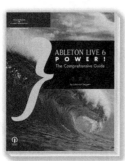